THE TECHNOLOGICAL RESPONSE TO IMPORT LIBERALIZATION IN SUBSAHARAN AFRICA

Also by Sanjaya Lall

FOREIGN INVESTMENT, TRANSNATIONALS AND DEVELOPING COUNTRIES (*with P. P. Streeten*)

THE GROWTH OF THE PHARMACEUTICAL INDUSTRY IN DEVELOPING COUNTRIES

THE MULTINATIONAL CORPORATION: Nine Essays

DEVELOPING COUNTRIES IN THE INTERNATIONAL ECONOMY

DEVELOPING COUNTRIES AS EXPORTERS OF TECHNOLOGY
The Indian Experience

THE NEW MULTINATIONALS: The Spread of Third World Enterprises

MULTINATIONALS, TECHNOLOGY AND EXPORTS

THEORY AND REALITY IN DEVELOPMENT: Essays in Honour of Paul Streeten

LEARNING TO INDUSTRIALIZE: The Acquisition of Technological Capability by India

BUILDING INDUSTRIAL COMPETITIVENESS IN DEVELOPING COUNTRIES

CURRENT ISSUES IN DEVELOPMENT ECONOMICS (*editor with V. N. Balasubramanyam*)

ALTERNATIVE DEVELOPMENT STRATEGIES IN SUB-SAHARAN AFRICA (*editor with Frances Stewart and S. Wangwe*)

TRANSNATIONAL CORPORATIONS AND ECONOMIC DEVELOPMENT (*editor*)

TECHNOLOGY AND ENTERPRISE DEVELOPMENT: Ghana under Structural Adjustment (*with G. B. Navaretti, S. Teitel and G. Wignaraja*)

SCIENCE AND TECHNOLOGY IN THE NEW GLOBAL ENVIRONMENT: Implications for Developing Countries

LEARNING FROM THE ASIAN TIGERS: Studies in Technology and Industrial Policy

The Technological Response to Import Liberalization in SubSaharan Africa

Edited by

Sanjaya Lall
University Lecturer in Development Economics
and Fellow of Green College
University of Oxford

The United Nations University
INTECH

First published in Great Britain 1999 by
MACMILLAN PRESS LTD
Houndmills, Basingstoke, Hampshire RG21 6XS and London
Companies and representatives throughout the world

A catalogue record for this book is available from the British Library.

ISBN 0–333–73526–9

First published in the United States of America 1999 by
ST. MARTIN'S PRESS, INC.,
Scholarly and Reference Division,
175 Fifth Avenue, New York, N.Y. 10010

ISBN 0–312–21800–1

Library of Congress Cataloging-in-Publication Data
The technological response to import liberalization in SubSaharan Africa / edited by Sanjaya Lall.
p. cm.
Includes bibliographical references and index.
ISBN 0–312–21800–1 (hardcover)
1. Free trade—Africa, Sub-Saharan. 2. Imports—Government policy—Africa, Sub-Saharan. 3. Technology and state—Africa, Sub -Saharan. 4. Clothing trade—Africa, Sub-Saharan—Case studies. 5. Manufacturing industries—Africa, Sub-Saharan—Case studies.
I. Lall, Sanjaya.
HF2416.T43 1998
382'.71'0967—DC21 98–25288
CIP

---

10 9 8 7 6 5 4 3 2 1
08 07 06 05 04 03 02 01 00 99

Printed and bound in Great Britain by
Antony Rowe Ltd, Chippenham, Wiltshire

Contents

Preface and Acknowledgements

It is now widely accepted that the response of manufacturing industry to recent adjustment and liberalization programmes in SubSaharan Africa (henceforth 'Africa') has been disappointing. Manufacturing growth has been low and, in several cases, negative. The new, more liberal, trade regime has not generally sparked off a rise in manufactured exports; where growth has occurred, most of it has been in traditional products. With some exceptions, labour-intensive exports, where falling wages should have created a competitive edge for Africa, have not emerged to any significant extent. Nor has there been a rise in skill or technology-intensive exports. Foreign direct investment in manufacturing has continued to bypass Africa, despite a more welcoming environment. In a world of accelerating technical change and intensifying competition, Africa is not only failing to improve its international economic position – it is falling behind. Thus despite the optimistic prognoses by the institutions promoting liberalization and structural adjustment, there is cause for grave concern regarding the effects of these policies.

Most African governments undertook liberalization and adjustment in the expectation that this would lead to a revival of growth in manufacturing output, exports and employment. They largely accepted that past industrial policies, protectionist and state-dominated, had failed to create a competitive industrial base. The dominant model of policy reform was that proposed by the IMF and World Bank – stabilization and structural adjustment – applied uniformly across countries regardless of the level of industrial development. Adjustment policies intended to improve the capacity of the productive sectors mainly by the removal of inefficient interventions and exposure to international competition, in the belief that such exposure would, by itself, lead to increased efficiency and technological dynamism. Almost the entire burden of policy reform was laid on 'getting prices right' – liberalization was considered not just *necessary* but also *sufficient* for better performance. There was, at least in the early days of adjustment policies, even the expectation that liberalization would lead Africa to emulate the success of export-oriented countries of East and South-East Asia.

This view may have been naive. It was based on a particular, and oversimplified, view of how technological processes occur in developing countries. Numerous studies show that technology development in developing countries is complex and variable, and faces many hurdles where markets do not function efficiently. Since many markets are in fact deficient in developing economies, there may be a positive role for government interventions to remedy market failures in technological development (though these interventions have to be very different from those mounted earlier). The 'common-sense' economics view that competition promotes technological dynamism and efficiency may require closer examination and qualification.

This study, financed by the United Nations University's Institute for New Technologies (INTECH), investigates the technological responses to import liberalization in three countries: Kenya, Tanzania and Zimbabwe. It is based on firm-level research in two common (and basic entry-level) industrial activities, garments and engineering. The three countries represent different stages of adjustment at differing levels of industrial development. At one end is Zimbabwe, with the most advanced industrial structure in SubSaharan Africa (apart from South Africa) and a relatively recent experience of liberalization. At the other is Tanzania, with a small and less-developed industrial base and considerable liberalization of the industrial sector. In between lies Kenya, with a sizeable industrial base by regional standards and a mixed and patchy record of opening up to import competition. This diversity of countries and sectors should produce findings of interest to Africa in general.

The fieldwork for the study was undertaken in early 1995. The team was directed by Sanjaya Lall, and consisted of three researchers at Queen Elizabeth House, Oxford, and counterpart researchers from each of the three countries. The primary material consists of interviews with a total of 135 manufacturing enterprises in the two industries, in which some teams were assisted by other local researchers. Much of the data processing and analysis took place at Oxford, with each of the African researchers spending some time there working with their colleagues.

The team accumulated many debts in the course of this study and it is a pleasure to acknowledge them. The first is to INTECH for financing the bulk of the study, and to the International Development Research Centre of Canada for providing a substantial proportion of the funds through INTECH. We would also like to thank the Gatsby Charitable Foundation for financing part of the study at QEH and the stay of the African researchers at Oxford. This study would not have been possible without their generosity.

The Director of INTECH, Professor Charles Cooper, gave us his constant support and guidance, and showed exemplary patience with the (inevitable) delays in the final stages of preparation. Professor Frances Stewart, Director of Queen Elizabeth House, originally conceived of the study and supported it throughout with vigour and enthusiasm. The team greatly appreciates her advice and comments on earlier drafts. A number of other people at Queen Elizabeth House helped to administer the study and host the scholars based here or who visited us from Africa. We would like to thank, in particular, Julia Knight for handling all the financial and administrative matters.

We are grateful to Professor Samuel Wangwe, Director of the Economic and Social Research Foundation, Tanzania, who identified the local researchers in the three countries studied, hosted an initial meeting of the team in Dar-es-Salaam, and gave the team the benefit of his experience of enterprise research in Africa.

The preliminary findings of the project were reviewed at a workshop at Queen Elizabeth House. We wish to thank Dr Martin Bell and Dr John Enos for participating in that workshop and giving us their comments.

Finally, our thanks to all the people who cannot be named individually, but who were critical to the research: the managers, entrepreneurs, employees and officials in the three countries who agreed to be interviewed and gave generously of their time and information.

We hope that this study will be useful to these people on the front line of liberalization, and to policy makers in the three countries and elsewhere who constantly have to make difficult decisions to promote development in their economies. It is to them that our study is dedicated.

SANJAYA LALL

Notes on the Contributors

Sonali Deraniyagala has a doctorate in economics from Oxford and is Lecturer in Economics at the School of Oriental and African Studies, University of London.

Gerrishon Ikiara is Senior Lecturer at the Institute of Diplomacy and International Studies, College of Humanities and Social Sciences, University of Nairobi, Kenya.

Sanjaya Lall is University Lecturer in Development Economics at Oxford University and a Fellow of Green College, Oxford.

Wolfram W. Latsch is Lecturer in Economics at Trinity College, Oxford, and is studying for a doctorate at Wolfson College, Oxford.

Peter Robinson is a graduate of Oxford University and has a doctorate in economics and engineering from Stanford University. He runs an economic consultancy, Zimconsult, in Harare, Zimbabwe.

Haji Semboja is Senior Research Fellow at the Economic and Social Research Foundation in Dar-es-Salaam, Tanzania.

Ganeshan Wignaraja has a doctorate in economics from Oxford and is Senior Economics Officer at the Commonwealth Secretariat in London.

1 Introduction and Setting

Sanjaya Lall

1.1 OBJECTIVES

This is a study of the impact of import liberalization on manufacturing technology in three countries of SubSaharan Africa: Kenya, Tanzania and Zimbabwe. These countries are opening up their economies to import competition as part of a broader strategy of policy reform and structural adjustment. Each is at a different stage of the liberalization process, and each starts with different bases of industrial and technological development. Each is 'adjusting' in the hope that exposure to market forces and the removal of the legacy of inefficient interventions will stimulate rapid industrial development and export growth. In each, as in much of Africa (the term is used here to refer to SubSaharan Africa), the response to liberalization has been weak, faltering and disappointing.

Clearly the raising of efficiency in existing activities, their diversification into more complex and higher value segments, and the entry of new investors, foreign and local, are crucial to successful adjustment. Each of these requires an underlying *technological response*, in improving existing technological processes, mastering more difficult ones and developing the wherewithal to allow new technologies to work at competitive levels. The adjustment process must therefore take direct account of the nature of this technological response at the micro level: it cannot simply assume that enterprises will mount the technological effort and investment needed in response to the new incentive environment. Yet much of adjustment and liberalization, at least as implemented in Africa, seems to make just this assumption. This suggests that the theory on which adjustment is based is deficient; it does not really look at the way in which enterprises grow technologically and respond to changing market and policy signals. The present study aims to add to our knowledge and understanding of this phenomenon by using case studies in each of the three countries to see how enterprises behave technologically, the levels they have achieved and what differentiates them in technological performance. As such, it hopes to improve the basis of policy reform (for it is evident that such reform is needed) and promote sounder industrial development in Africa.

The 'technology' under study here is not technological innovation – new products and processes at the frontiers of manufacturing knowledge, based primarily on research and development. If it were, there would be little to analyse in much of Africa, since none of these countries innovates in the normal sense and there is practically no formal R&D activity in industry. 'Technology' is used here in a wider sense to refer to the entire gamut of capabilities involved in importing, absorbing, adapting and improving upon manufacturing technologies. While innovation in the normal sense is one end of the spectrum of technological activity, the bulk consists of different kinds of production and engineering-related activities dealing with technologies that are already in existence. The nature of technological capabilities is analysed in detail in the next chapter; here we need only note that technological activity in this broad sense exists in African countries as it does anywhere else. Indeed, given the low level of industrial development in Africa, the need to raise technological capabilities there is probably more urgent than elsewhere.

This study takes for granted that industrialization is a desirable and feasible objective for Africa. The poor record of industrial progress in the region, especially in its participation in export growth and foreign direct investment flows, has led some analysts to think that in a market-oriented world, Africa may do better to focus on resource-based activities and ignore manufacturing development, as apparently dictated by its current endowments of capital and skills. This may be too pessimistic. 'Endowments' can be changed and new comparative advantages created – the story of the most successful industrializing countries in East Asia (Lall, 1996). Moreover it is still the case that most countries will only undergo the structural transformation that economic development involves by going through a phase of industrial development (Chenery *et al.*, 1986). Manufacturing continues to provide the most powerful general engine of growth, diversification, skill creation and social modernization available to the developing world, and few African governments would accept that they persist with the present patterns of heavy dependence on a few primary activities.

While some research on technological activity in Africa has been undertaken recently,[1] the coverage remains limited in comparison with other regions. We still lack a full understanding of how African enterprises absorb technology, move up the technological ladder or compare with similar enterprises in other industrializing countries. The institutions needed to accelerate the technological development process in Africa have not been properly investigated.[2] But most important of all is the scant base of information and understanding of the impact of the recent 'opening up' on manufacturing technology. This study intends to add to this base.

This chapter provides some background to the study. It starts by describing briefly the choice of industries and countries, and goes on to the progress of liberalization in these countries. It reviews the recent industrial experience of SubSaharan Africa in response to adjustment and liberalization. It then provides general data on manufacturing growth, structure and export performance in the sample countries. It reviews the human resources available for industrial development, as measured by educational enrolment figures. Finally, it describes the structure of the study.

1.2 INDUSTRIES AND COUNTRIES STUDIED

The study focuses on two industries – garments and engineering – that are common to all developing countries. These are basic 'entry level' manufacturing activities, important in different ways for launching a successful industrial drive. The garment and clothing industry, in its modern organized form, is important because processes remain very labour-intensive, skill requirements are generally low and exporting garments is still one of the best ways to enter world markets and create industrial employment. All three countries have garments production and exports, and their privileged access to the European market (under the Lomé convention) can make the industry a special attraction to foreign investors.

Engineering is a broad-based industry, ranging from the simplest metal products to highly sophisticated equipment, consumer durables and components. Simple, traditional metal-working activities exist everywhere; however industrial development requires the ability to provide more complex engineering goods, directly as a producer of capital goods and durables and indirectly as a supplier of components and services. The capital goods sector is regarded as the 'hub' of technological development, and much of recent technical advance is based on advances in electronics engineering. Thus the technological status and progress of engineering is an important indicator of the response to import liberalization and of the potential for future development.

The present evaluation of technological capabilities and dynamism is essentially qualitative (though we quantify and econometrically 'explain' some aspects of this diffuse activity). This approach is deliberate. A more thoroughly quantitative approach to technological activity, measuring total factor productivity (TFP) change, was thought unsuitable for present purposes. The measurement of TFP change is fraught with conceptual and empirical problems, and it is difficult to compare firms (even in ostensibly similar industries) making different products, operating different technologies or at different scales and rates of capacity utilization. The data requirements are high, and many of the smaller firms interviewed would have been unable to provide the required information over time. In any case, TFP analysis does not reveal much about the specific nature of technological activity within the firm, the different forms that it can take and the differing constraints that it may face, all of which are worth investigating.

The three countries studied have been selected to capture different levels of industrial development (and differing degrees of liberalization, see below). With the exception of South Africa, Zimbabwe is the most highly industrialized economy in SubSaharan Africa, with per capita manufacturing value added (MVA) of US$129 in 1992[3] and a long-established industrial sector with a tradition of exporting. This sector underwent considerable diversification and deepening during a period of relative isolation from the world economy (South Africa was its major trading partner) just before independence, further increasing certain kinds of capabilities. At the other end is Tanzania, with a low level of industrialization (per capita MVA of $4) that is narrowly based and of recent origin. Tanzanian industry, moreover, went through a very difficult period of shortages and decline during the decade prior to liberalization. Kenya lies in the middle, with per capita MVA of $30, a relatively diversified base and some experience of industrial export activity, mainly to its neighbours.

The broad level of technological capabilities in any country is likely to be reflected in its stage of industrial development: *ceteris paribus*, the larger the industrial base and the longer the experience of industrialization, the more proficient a country is likely to be in using and adapting technologies. This suggests that Zimbabwe would have the most advanced level of capabilities and the best capacity to respond to the challenges of import liberalization, Tanzania the least. The extent to which this is true is investigated in this study, but we are able to go further. We examine differences in capabilities between firms in selected industries, and try to explain these differences with reference to various factors that are expected to affect the technology learning process. The fact that the three countries are at very different levels of manufacturing development is in fact an advantage.

It serves to illustrate the capability development process in industrial structures of differing depth and complexity, with different historical backgrounds and resource bases. It also illustrates differences due to varying availability of human resources, the efficacy of supporting institutions and the nature and intensity of the liberalization process itself.

1.3 IMPORT LIBERALIZATION

1.3.1 Evaluating Liberalization and its Impact

Import liberalization, the 'opening up' of an economy to international competition, may comprise a range of measures: removing or reducing quantitative restrictions (QRs), lowering tariffs, reducing the dispersion of tariffs, reducing sales and other taxes affecting imports, simplifying trade procedures, and moving to a market-determined system of foreign exchange allocation. There is generally considerable variation between developing countries in the number and intensity of the measures undertaken during liberalization and in the order in which they are launched. Some opt for sweeping liberalization across the board, others for gradual liberalization, and others for a trial-and-error process in which some elements of opening up are tried while others are reversed. The extent of liberalization also tends to vary within each country by industry. The impact on enterprise behaviour depends not only on the nominal measures undertaken but also on the firmness, clarity and credibility of the policy and the extent to which the industrial sector is informed about current and future changes.

For these reasons, analysing the degree, spread, effectiveness and credibility of import liberalization is often very difficult in practice.[4] The ways in which particular policy changes are implemented in different countries, or even in the same country over time, can differ, and are often not 'transparent', certainly to an outsider. Different agencies of the government may differ in their practice, and some measures may conflict with and offset each other. The impact of some reforms on the trade regime can only be evaluated by direct price comparisons for each product between domestic and international markets, which is difficult in the best of circumstances and impossible in the context of this study, except for a few specific items that the interviewed firms knew about. In some cases (in these countries, the most important being second-hand clothing) imports are semi-legal and data on their incidence is not officially collected. All these problems make a detailed quantification of the extent of liberalization almost impossible.

In addition, the issues raised by the credibility of the liberalization process, which determines its impact on industrial firms, are even more complex to handle empirically. Much depends on the political and economic beliefs of the government itself, its bargaining position *vis-à-vis* the proponents of liberalization (primarily the Washington-based multilateral institutions and aid donors) and its ability to devise effective alternative strategies (Mosley *et al.*, 1991). The degree of import liberalization in Kenya, Tanzania and Zimbabwe *has* varied considerably (see below), as has the governments' commitment to the adjustment process. It would have been ideal to have precise indicators of how far each has proceeded, in general and in the clothing and engineering industries, to assess the impact on technological activity. As this was not possible, our studies had to use published and firm-level information to judge roughly how much liberalization had taken place.

There are also serious methodological problems involved in separating the effects of liberalization (even assuming that this could be measured) from other factors that affect economic performance (Mosley *et al.*, 1995; Toye, 1995). None of the usual methods used to compare countries 'before and after' liberalization or different countries 'with and without' liberalization are fully satisfactory. Many evaluations of the impact of liberalization across countries end up comparing apples and oranges, failing clearly to separate the exogenous events that may affect economic performance and controlling for them between countries or between different periods within the same country. The analysis of firm level case studies overcomes some of these problems, since it is easier to trace more clearly the impact of particular events such as exposure to import competition – but not entirely, since firms also often respond to multiple stimuli from the environment and may themselves be unclear about which stimulus caused which response. Much depends, in the final analysis, on the skills and perceptions of the researcher; but this is inevitable in all such studies.

1.3.2 The 'Ideal' Liberalization

While it is difficult to assess with any precision the impact of import liberalization across countries, it is important at the start to understand what *liberalization as a strategy* is trying to achieve. It is not the intention here to enter into methodological issues of analysing liberalization. For our purposes, a fairly general idea of the extent and nature of liberalization, supported by the perceptions of industrial firms on how import competition is affecting them, has to serve. However it is certainly relevant to the analysis to look at the underlying principles of import liberalization. Some idea of what constitutes an 'ideal' liberalization strategy and how it is supposed to work, as seen by its main protagonists, could be useful in assessing the theoretical strength of the argument and weighing it against the evidence, qualified as it may be with all the problems just noted.

The most important institution supporting liberalization is the World Bank, which embeds it in its structural adjustment programmes (SAPs). Given the close relationship between the two, we may use SAPs as a proxy for import liberalization in the present discussion. There is, however, no strict, universally accepted definition of 'structural adjustment'. What is often referred to as structural adjustment really has two different components. One is macroeconomic reform or 'stabilization', policy changes to achieve internal and external balances in the short to medium term, and generally considered the province of the IMF. The other is 'adjustment' proper, or what Toye (1995) calls 'structural adjustment in the narrow sense': reforms to free up market forces and so promote long-term growth, the province of the World Bank. SAPs can take many forms, but they share a common set of premises. Essentially they involve 'unleashing markets so that competition can help improve the allocation of resources ... getting price signals right and creating a climate that allows businesses to respond to those signals in ways that increase the returns to investment'.[5]

It is important to distinguish between *stabilization* and *structural adjustment*, even if the dividing line between the two is blurred in practice (Mosley *et al*., 1995; Lall, 1995). Macroeconomic stabilization generally precedes adjustment, but many stabilization measures are also important features of adjustment: exchange rate adjustment, for instance, can be an important stabilization as well as adjustment measure. However it is generally agreed that adjustment as practised by the World Bank involves longer-term policy changes than involved in correcting macroeconomic imbalances. For this reason it is important to look separately at adjustment 'in the narrow sense', to assess the long-term effects of reforming the structure of the economy.

There is another reason. There is little debate about the *need* for good macroeconomic management – no one argues that poor macro policies and instability are conducive to growth. Thus stabilization is generally accepted as a policy goal, even though it may be very difficult to achieve in practice and there may be serious disagreements over the form and speed of stabilization. In contrast the premises of adjustment are themselves the subject of debate. Let us take the need for stabilization as given, and focus on the principles of adjustment.

The principles underlying structural adjustment are based on simple neoclassical models whose precepts are generally taken to be so self-evident that they are rarely spelled out explicitly (see the following chapter). These are based on assumptions that ensure that free markets are efficient, leading to an optimal allocation of resources, with a further assumption that such static optimisation leads to dynamic long-term growth. Given efficient markets, government interventions in resource allocation are essentially distorting and inefficient. The only exceptions allowed are for market failures in the provision of infrastructure and education, where functional or 'market friendly' interventions that do not discriminate between activities are recommended.[6] Selective interventions, on the other hand, are considered 'market unfriendly' because they distort efficient resource allocation as given by free markets. The same approach forms the basis of SAPs. Existing trade and other restrictions that affect resource allocation are distortionary (by assumption), and the ideal policy reform should remove these distortions, with minimal government intervention in the process of opening up.

The analytical basis of this argument is taken up at length in the next chapter. All we need note here is that it is a premise of standard structural adjustment programmes that *immediate and sweeping liberalization* is the most efficient means of economic reform. No activity that is efficient will by definition die out, and none that is inefficient will survive. The demise of inefficient activities will release productive resources for others that are efficient and that will spring up in response to the new prices signals. Resources will move with little lag and no constraints, since there are few or no missing or defective markets. Comparative advantage in industry, given by resource endowments, will be fully realised, and new advantages will emerge as resources are accumulated with no need for policy support. There can be no difference in response between countries apart from that given by different factor endowments, and so no need to design different adjustment programmes according to differing levels of development.

To summarize, then, the 'ideal' adjustment/liberalization strategy is:

- Remove all forms of selective intervention and restore free-market-driven allocation, exposing all activities equally to international competition.
- Apply this to all economies regardless of the level of development, since by definition all markets are 'efficient' (or more efficient than governments).
- Carry out the reforms quickly and across the board since there is no economic justification for continuing to select activities for more gradual liberalization. No 'strategy' is needed to guide the restructuring or upgrading process at the level of industry or firms since markets will give the correct signals.
- Do not link the pace of reforms to the incentive structure to market friendly measures to improve human capital or infrastructure, since factor markets will also respond better if the overall set of signals is correct.
- Finally, having got rid of the legacy of inefficient interventions, do not retain any further scope for selective interventions to promote industrial growth.

While the SAPs undertaken in many African countries may not correspond to this ideal, the 'best' performing countries according to the World Bank (for example Ghana) have indeed implemented rapid, sweeping and non-discriminating liberalization. What then is the evidence on the effects of adjustment on African industry? Let us briefly consider the available data, bearing in mind all the difficulties noted above on trying to isolate the effects of SAPs.

1.3.3 Adjustment and Manufacturing Performance in Africa

Industrial performance has been abysmal in much of SubSaharan Africa. The growth of manufacturing value-added (MVA) in the region was only 1 per cent per annum in real terms from 1980–94, and the rate of growth declined over time, from 2.2 per cent the 1980s to negative figures in the 1990s (Table 1.1, with details in Appendix 1.1).[7] The table divides the countries into three categories based on the World Bank's 1994 study of adjustment. The first two groups include countries that underwent structural adjustment in the 1980s; they are differentiated according to whether or not their policies improved or deteriorated during adjustment. The third comprises the rest, that is, African countries that did not undergo adjustment.

Most liberalization in Africa started in the late 1980s, and a comparison of the periods 1990–94 and 1980–90 should show the effects of adjustment. The data give conflicting impressions. On the one hand, adjusting countries as a whole have done better than non-adjusting ones, and within the adjusting group, countries with improved policies did better in the later period than countries with deteriorating policies. This supports the World Bank's (1994) contention that 'adjustment is working' in Africa. On the other hand, growth rates deteriorated in all countries in the second period compared with the first, pointing to a worsening environment for manufacturing in the region as a whole. However, why this should have been so in African countries when the rest of the developing world was enjoying healthy manufacturing growth is not clear. In any case, adjustment as such seems to have been unable to dynamize industrial performance.

The fact that the deterioration in growth performance is less in the policy-improving than in the policy-deteriorating countries does suggest that 'good' adjustment, measured by improved policies, did lead to better manufacturing performance. This impression is strengthened if we look at the countries that account for the weakening of growth in the policy-improving countries. Two large countries dominate the 15 countries in this group: Nigeria and Zimbabwe account for nearly three quarters of total MVA for the group, and both have suffered a

Table 1.1 Growth of manufacturing value added, 1980–94 ($ million and per cent)

	MVA values (constant 1985 $ m)			*MVA growth p.a. (%)*		
	1980	*1990*	*1994*	*1980–90*	*1990–94*	*1980–94*
Total SSA	16 830	20 815	19 846	2.2	−1.2	1.2
Total adjusting	16 764	20 407	19 674	1.9	−0.9	1.2
Policy improvement	11 250	13 436	13 180	1.8	−0.5	1.1
Policy deterioration	3 534	4 981	4 500	3.5	−2.5	1.7
Non-adjusting	2 046	2 398	2 166	1.6	−2.5	0.4

Source: African Development Bank, *African Development Report, 1995*.

deterioration in growth over time. If they are excluded, the average growth rate for the group in the 1990s rises to 1.7 per cent per annum instead of being negative.

However, other data cast doubt on this interpretation. In Nigeria and Zimbabwe, for instance, adjustment seems to have affected industry negatively, or else has coincided with other damaging factors. Moreover, only five countries in the policy-improving group had higher growth in the 1990s compared with the 1980s, while ten did worse. In the policy deteriorating group there are many more cases of falling MVA in the 1990s. Over half the group (eight countries out of 14) suffered falling MVA; of these, seven had positive growth rates in the 1980s (the exception is Mozambique). This seems to suggest that adjustment with worsening macro policies is worse than no adjustment at all. Or it could simply mean that other factors than adjustment are at work in influencing manufacturing growth, and that these also accounted for the inability of countries to improve their management of the economy. The data do not allow a clear answer to be given.

In the 15 countries without adjustment, five had negative manufacturing growth in the 1990s compared with four in the 1980s, and ten countries saw a worsening of their growth rates. It is not clear from the available information whether these countries had improving or worsening policies, and whether or not they needed to undergo adjustment. However their conformance to the general pattern of deteriorating industrial performance suggests that there was a generally worsening environment in the region, and that adjustment did not have much effect on growth one way or the other.

Such comparisons of group averages can in any case be misleading in statistical terms. In the absence of data, particularly on country-specific measures of liberalization, we cannot conduct proper econometric tests. However we can at least check if variations within these groups are statistically meaningful. If they are, groupings by policy reform are not significant: differences in group averages are due to other factors than the ones used to construct groupings (in this case, adjustment and the quality of policy response). Comparing specific groups in the two periods, F-tests show no statistically significant differences between the policy-improving and policy-deteriorating groups in either the 1980s or the 1990s. The same applies to comparisons between the adjusting and non-adjusting groups. Thus there is no reason to attribute differences in growth performance between the groups to differences in approaches to adjustment. There are clearly other factors, not explored, that are causing the observed intercountry differences in industrial performance. Taking all the countries together, we do find a statistically significant fall in MVA growth rates over the two periods – the only meaningful result obtained in this exercise. This only serves to reinforce that there is a region-wide deterioration in manufacturing growth: whatever the reason for the general fall, this deterioration seems to override participation in SAPs and the quality of policy changes.

In any case the distinction between 'good' and 'bad' adjusters, as drawn by the World Bank, is based entirely on *macro-economic management and has little to do with import liberalization or, indeed, any other form of long-term structural adjustment*. Even if 'good' adjustment in this sense had been found to improve performance significantly, all it would have shown is that good macro policy is conducive to growth. The existing data do not even establish this (Mosley *et al*., 1995), but the point is that the need for sound macro management is not really in dispute. No analyst or government argues that poor macro management is actually desirable, even though there may be debate on the best way to improve such management. This is not the case with adjustment and liberalization. Here there *does* exist genuine debate, and the World Bank has evidently been biased: it has jumped too readily to conclusions that support its own ideology and policy stance.

This does not establish the reverse, that adjustment actually harmed industry. The existing data simply do not allow one to draw a clear conclusion one way or the other: all this exercise does is to caution against strong conclusions. There is, nevertheless, a crucial methodological point to be noted for the present study. The 'ideal' adjustment package is based on certain simplifying assumptions about how firms behave in technological terms (this is taken up at greater length in the next chapter). The reactions to adjustment in the 'ideal' scenario depend strongly on a technological process that has few if any risks, costs or externalities. Once these features of technological effort are included, it would appear that simply opening up to market forces cannot be sufficient to spark off industrial upgrading and growth in a setting where existing capabilities are weak and support systems practically non-existent. A consideration of how to help firms to upgrade their capabilities, then, has to be an essential part of the design of policy reform.

The multilateral institutions that have designed and supported past adjustment efforts in Africa have tended to shy away from these implications of poor industrial performance, instead blaming the pace and extent of reform, lack of credibility or other factors. However it is interesting to note that a World Bank study of technological capabilities in Africa, using a very similar methodology to the one adopted here, has this to say in its opening paragraph:

> The supply response of the industrial sector to structural adjustment programmes has been more sluggish than expected in Africa. This is causing concern in African governments as well as in the development community at large, and is stimulating an examination of factors beyond price distortions that may underlie the inadequate rates of growth. In addition to issues such as policy uncertainty and financial constraints, a critical area of concern in this context is the problem of technological capability. For firms to respond effectively to changes in incentives and to grow over time, entrepreneurs and workers must have the requisite technological capabilities – the skills and information required to establish and operate modern machinery, and the learning ability to upgrade these skills when needed (Biggs *et al.*, 1995, p. 1).

The reading here is clearly less sanguine than in the World Bank's own authoritative study, *Adjustment in Africa*, published a year earlier, which ignored problems of technological capabilities in industry and, as noted, skated over the empirical problems in interpreting the data. For this reason its policy recommendations – essentially to persist with liberalization – are at odds with those reached in the other study, and even more so with those of our own study (see Chapter 7 below).

1.3.4 Manufactured Exports and Liberalization

The value of manufactured exports in SubSaharan Africa as a whole came to $2209 million in 1992. Of this, the policy-improving countries accounted for $1180 million, the policy-deteriorating countries for $983 million and the non-adjusters for $46 million. The rates of growth for these exports in 1980–92 and 1988–92 (Table 1.2) suggest that the countries that did not undergo any form of adjustment performed worse than all the others, and much worse in the later period. While the best performers in the later period were the policy-deteriorating countries, neither the improving nor the deteriorating adjusting countries improved their manufactured export performance. Statistical tests show that the only significant differences between the groups are between the non-adjusting countries and both groups of adjusting countries in the 1990s. However the non-adjusting group is so small in export activity that we cannot draw any conclusions about the impact

Table 1.2 Manufactured export growth rates

	1980–92	*1988–92*
Policy improvement	2.75	9.35
Policy deterioration	4.66	10.03
Non-adjusters	−8.25	−15.77

Source: World Bank, *World Development Report, 1994.*

of adjustment. The fact that policy-deteriorating countries did better that improving countries suggests again that other factors were at work.

In general, while the growth rates for manufactured exports in Africa are better than for MVA, the share of manufactures in total exports remains low and the long-term growth rates are far lower than for other developing regions. The total value of manufactured exports for the region in 1992 was less than 10 per cent of that of Malaysia, or around 3 per cent of Korea's. The bulk of manufactures that are exported are slightly processed primary products rather than 'value-added' items where technical efficiency is important. Even low-wage items such as garments have not made much progress in Africa, with the sole exception of Mauritius.

1.4 BACKGROUND TO KENYA, TANZANIA AND ZIMBABWE

1.4.1 Manufacturing Performance

Table 1.3 shows the MVA values and growth rates for the three countries; the country studies deal with their performance in more detail. Kenya had the highest MVA growth rate in 1980–94 and Tanzania the lowest, with Zimbabwe in between. Kenya had the most consistent performance over the period, while Zimbabwe suffered the largest fluctuations, with a large decline in the early 1990s caused by a severe drought and a stringent stabilization programme. Tanzania started the 1980s with declining MVA and reversed this in the latter part of the decade (though not sufficiently to give a positive growth rate for the 1980s). MVA growth accelerated in the 1990s to an average of 3.7 per cent per annum, due largely to a spurt in 1990–91 (11.4 per cent),

Table 1.3 MVA growth in Kenya, Tanzania and Zimbabwe

	Kenya	*Tanzania*	*Zimbabwe*
MVA values (1985 $m)			
1980	523	493	820
1985	631	382	922
1990	834	430	1143
1991	865	479	1175
1992	876	490	1064
1993	892	500	975
1994	910	515	1034
Growth rates (per cent)			
1980–85	3.83	−4.97	2.37
1985–90	5.74	2.40	4.39
1990–94	2.20	4.61	−2.47
1980–94	4.04	0.31	1.67
1990–91	3.72	11.39	2.80
1991–92	1.27	2.30	−9.45
1992–93	1.83	2.04	−8.36
1993–94	2.02	3.00	6.05

Source: African Development Bank, *African Development Report, 1995.*

after which growth fell back to around 2 per cent. The fluctuations in growth appear to dominate the performance of all three countries in this period; no clear trends seem to emerge.

1.4.2 Manufactured Exports

Different sources give different estimates for manufactured exports from the three countries. Table 1.4 shows the best combination of available data on a comparable basis. The national sources used in the country chapters below may give somewhat different figures, but the general trends are similar. Zimbabwe's manufactured exports are much larger than the others (Zimbabwe accounts for around one quarter of manufactured exports from SubSaharan Africa, excluding Mauritius and South Africa), and since 1980 it has been the only country in the group to show significant growth.

Both Kenya and Tanzania suffered declining manufactured exports over the period as a whole, but with improved performance in the 1990s compared with the 1980s. Tanzania in particular showed an impressive

Table 1.4 Export performance of manufactured goods, 1980–93

	Values ($ million, current)						*Growth rate (% p.a.)*		
	1980	*1989*	*1990*	*1991*	*1992*	*1993*	*1980–89*	*1989–93*	*1980–93*
Kenya	181.9	144.3	113.6	146.5	175.4	178.6	−2.5	5.5	−0.1
Tanzania	86.4	31.2	33.0	43.3	60.0	63.0	−10.7	19.2	−2.4
Zimbabwe	184.0	559.0	N/A	569.3	395.2	542.8	13.1	−0.7	8.7

Sources: Calculated from World Bank, *World Development Report*, various; UN, *International Trade Statistics Yearbook*, various.

increase during 1990–92, when manufactured exports rose by 92 per cent over the two years (if from a small base). But this was a one-off surge. Growth slowed to 5 per cent in the following year; by 1993, manufactured exports were still 27 per cent lower in nominal dollar terms than in 1980. Kenya also had a large 54 per cent increase in manufactured exports during 1990–92, but suffered a relapse to 2 per cent growth in 1993, with values in the final year somewhat lower than in 1980. Zimbabwe's manufactured exports declined in the early 1990s, but since 1993 (as discussed in the country chapter but not shown in Table 1.4) they have revived strongly. While this suggests that there has been a positive response of manufactured exports to adjustment and liberalization in all three countries, the evidence adduced below suggests that this has been due more to an improved export climate, domestic recession and the greater availability of imported inputs rather than to industrial restructuring and resource reallocation consequent upon import competition *per se*.

1.4.3 Import Liberalization

Let us compare the status of liberalization in the three countries, bearing in mind the problems in quantifying and assessing the real extent of policy change. According to the information available, each had arrived at a different stage of liberalization by mid 1995, when our fieldwork was conducted. Tanzania was the most advanced in terms of opening up manufacturing to world competition, and had moved from nearly total government control over imports to the complete removal of quantitative restrictions and moderate tariff-based protection (Mans, 1994). More importantly, it was by all indicators continuing to liberalize. Kenya had been the first to start liberalization, but its efforts were marked by hesitation, reversals and exceptions (Swamy, 1994). In the early 1990s it reversed some of its earlier reforms and was moving back to heavier use of trade barriers, though by 1995 donor pressure was forcing a more serious attempt to 'open up'. Some import controls were still in place, and the effective protection levels were still substantial; however the signs were that the government would move towards greater liberalization. Zimbabwe did not start to liberalize until 1991. However in a brief period it substantially reduced many of its trade barriers and by 1995 was reaching the stage of moderate tariff-based protection. The latest available study of effective protection, for 1992, showed high rates, but this had probably declined significantly by the time of the study. Further details are given in the country chapters. Figure 1.1 reproduces a graphic evaluation by the World Bank of the progress of trade policy reform in the three countries.

The extent of import liberalization at the industry level varies between the two activities studied here: engineering and garments. The engineering sector was relatively less exposed to direct import competition in all three cases because of the 'natural' protection arising from high transport costs and the specific nature of the products made – generally simple implements or machinery, or customised metal products for local users, with whom there were often long-standing linkages – and, in the case of Kenya and Zimbabwe, because of remaining tariffs. The garment sector was hit in each country by strong competition from the legal, semi-legal or illegal imports of very cheap 'second hand' clothing (a mixture of end-of-run or rejected new clothes and used clothes). By the time of the study this competition had grown to capture a significant proportion of the local market for low-quality clothing, with devastating effects on the local garment producers that specialized in this segment.

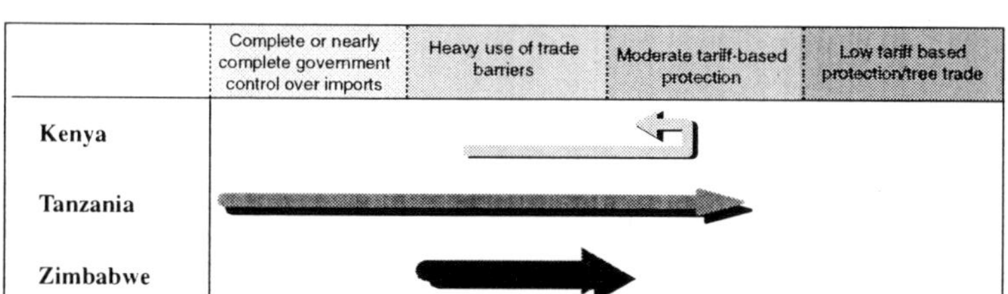

Figure 1.1 Progress of import liberalization until 1994
Source: World Bank (1994), Figure 3.1.

1.4.4 Skill Levels

The success of adjustment depends not just on the strength and clarity of the signals emerging from the incentive regime, but also on the factors that affect the 'supply response': physical infrastructure, the quality and relevance of available skills, in-house technological capabilities, technological support systems, supplier networks and so on. Here it would be useful to look at one crucial factor: skills.

Table 1.5 shows educational enrolments in the three countries, Sub-Saharan Africa as a whole, and, for comparison, four Asian newly industrializing countries (Korea, Malaysia, Thailand and Taiwan).

Table 1.5 Educational enrolments

Country	*Numbers enrolled as percentage of age groups*						*Tertiary level students per 100 000 inhabitants (year)*	*Adult illiteracy rate (% 1992)*
	Primary		*Secondary*		*Tertiary*			
	1970	*1992*	*1970*	*1992*	*1980*	*1992*		
Kenya	58	95	9	29	1	2.0	187 (1990)	25.5
Tanzania	34	68	3	5	0	0.2[1]	21 (1989)	35.6
Zimbabwe	74	119	7	48	1	6.0	582 (1992)	16.6
SubSaharan Africa[2]	50	67	7	18	1	4.0		
Selected Asian countries								
Korea	103	105	42	90	16	42	4208 (1992)	2.6
Malaysia	87	93	34	58	4	7	679 (1990)	18.5
Thailand	83	97	17	33	13	19	1763 (1989)	6.5
Taiwan	98[3]	100[4]	66[3]	94[4]	18	31[4]	2919 (1993)	6.0[5]

Notes:
[1] 1989.
[2] Includes South Africa.
[3] 1976–77.
[4] 1989–90.
[5] 1990.
Sources: UNESCO, *Statistical Yearbook 1994*; World Bank, *World Development Report*, various; UNDP, *Human Development Report 1995*; Government of Taiwan, *Educational Statistics of the Republic of China*, Ministry of Education, 1991.

Zimbabwe is one of the best endowed countries in the region; it also has the highest enrolments at all levels among the three sample countries. Tanzania lags at all levels, particularly at the secondary and tertiary levels, where it has among the lowest enrolment rates in the world (a result of a deliberate policy of deemphasizing post-primary education to increase basic literacy). Kenya's secondary enrolment levels are above the regional average, but at the tertiary level these fall below the average. This may be because of the relatively high level of tertiary enrolments for South Africa (14 per cent); most other SubSaharan African countries have tertiary enrolments of around 2 per cent.

In general, the African group lags well behind the levels reached by the Asian countries, but there are exceptions. Zimbabwe has a higher secondary enrolment rate than Thailand and almost the same tertiary enrolment rate as Malaysia. The more advanced 'Tiger' economies such as Korea and Taiwan, however, are well in advance of the others and their enrolment rates are at the levels of advanced OECD countries. At the other extreme, Tanzania appears very deficient in providing the base of formal skills that industrial development may require, and Kenya seems very weak at the higher levels. The shortage of human capital of SubSaharan Africa and its effects on industrial development have been analysed by the present author (Lall, 1992a).

These comparisons should also take into account two facts: first, the accumulated stock of trained manpower in Asia is far larger because of higher enrolment rates over time; second, the quality and relevance of the training imparted by the education system seems to be far better in Asia than in Africa. To quote the World Bank:

> The main educational issues in Africa today are the stagnation of enrolments and the erosion of quality. Although total enrolments in sub-Saharan Africa grew at an average annual rate of 6.5 per cent during 1960–70 and 8.9 per cent during 1970–80, the rate of increase plummeted to 4.2 per cent in the first three years of the 1980s. ... Complicating the problems of stagnating enrolments are the low levels and recent erosions of educational quality. Cognitive achievements among African students are low by world standards, and there is some suggestion of further decline recently ... in the few studies that have been conducted, academic achievement in Africa has been sufficiently poor to be a cause for serious concern (World Bank, 1988, p. 2).

Let us now consider enrolment data of particular relevance to technology development: technical education at the tertiary level (Table 1.6) and vocational training (Table 1.7). As far as tertiary level technical training is concerned, the differences between the three sample countries are evident, with Zimbabwe far in advance of the others and Tanzania lagging badly. So is the vast gap between all the African countries, including Zimbabwe, and the Asian comparators. The whole of SubSaharan Africa's enrolments in industry-related technical subjects is less than half that of Taiwan (5 per cent of its population).[8] In terms of engineering enrolments, the three countries together have less than 2 per cent of Korean enrolment, though they have a combined population that is 45 per cent larger than Korea's. The industrial development of Malaysia and Thailand, despite much higher levels of technical education, are strongly constrained by skill shortages.

These comparisons should be treated with care since the respective industrial structures are very different (though the differences may themselves reflect the disparities in skill levels). However the vast gap in high level technical skills does suggest that the African countries may face serious problems with the upgrading of industrial efficiency, as their existing technologies have to cope with open competition.

Coming now to the vocational training data (with very out-of-date information for the African countries), it is Zimbabwe that seems to lag while Tanzania does relatively well. However all three countries provide very little training relative to the Asian countries, where once more the extent of investment by Taiwan is worth noting. Studies of the quality of vocational training in Africa suggest that it is poor and out-of-date, and has little direct connection with industrial needs (Middleton and Demsky, 1989). This contrasts with Asia, where this problem exists but is being overcome by strong efforts to involve industry and revise curricula to meet industrial requirements. These trends in education led McMahon (1987, p. 19) to conclude that 'The educational structure of SubSaharan Africa is unsuitable for industrialization'.

It is useful to bear these broad comparisons in mind when we come to the country chapters. The analysis of individual firm studies may not clearly capture skill deficiencies, since it is difficult to evaluate competence by international standards at the micro level and economic researchers are often dependent on information given by firms. Firms themselves are often not aware of their own deficiencies compared with 'best practice' levels, unless they are operating in export markets and are able to keep up with technological trends and regularly

Table 1.6 Tertiary enrolments in technical fields

Country	Year	Natural science (No.)	Natural science (% pop.)	Maths/computing (No.)	Maths/computing (% pop.)	Engineering (No.)	Engineering (% pop.)	Total technical (No.)	Total technical (% pop.)	Pop. (m) 1993
Sample countries										
Kenya	1990	3593	0.01	N/A	N/A	1 046	0.00	7168	0.03	25.3
Tanzania	1987	180	0.00	13	0.00	664	0.00	857	0.01	28.0
Zimbabwe	1992	1799	0.02	399	0.00	4 718	0.04	9331	0.09	10.7
Total above	–	5577	0.01	N/A	N/A	6 428	0.01	17 356	0.03	64.0
SS Africa[2]	1985	48 000[3]			0.01	48 100	0.01	96 100	0.02	418.0
Selected Asian countries										
Korea	1992	75 778	0.17	145 948	0.33	367 846	0.83	730 346	1.66	44.1
Malaysia	1990	8776	0.05	4557	0.03	12 693	0.07	32 222	0.18	19.0
Thailand	1992	77 098	0.13	1292	0.00	105 149	0.19	249 952	0.44	58.1
Taiwan	1993	16 823	0.08	32 757	0.16	179 094	0.86	303 964	1.45	21.0

Sources: UNESCO, *Statistical Yearbook 1994*; Taiwan, *Statistical Data Book, 1994*; World Bank, *World Development Report 1995*.

Notes:

[1] Apart from the three fields shown, this also includes medicine, architecture, trade and crafts, transport and communications.

[2] Excluding South Africa.

[3] This figure for SSA includes natural science, mathematics and computing.

Table 1.7 Enrolments in vocational training

Country	*Year*	*Enrolments*	*% pop.*
Kenya, Tanzania and Zimbabwe			
Kenya	1988	8880	0.04
Tanzania	1986	12 750	0.05
Zimbabwe	1985	292	0.00
Selected Asian countries			
Korea	1994	851 495	1.90
Malaysia	1993	40 944	0.21
Thailand	1992	448 174	0.77
Taiwan	1990–91	449 111	2.18

Sources: As for Table 1.6; Enos (1995).

visit foreign plants. They may also attribute competitive lags to other causes rather than factors that reflect unfavourably on their own management, training and engineering. While the validity of their responses are difficult to decipher, the above comparisons provide a useful backdrop.

We should remember, however, that data on educational enrolments are only crude and preliminary indicators of industry-related skills. Apart from differences in educational quality and the differing industrial structures, skills can be substitutable. Thus different firms in the same industry may be equally efficient with very different skill profiles, especially in technologies where formal education is not necessary for operational competence. Education enrolment data cannot not capture such major sources of skill formation as on-the-job learning or formal training given to employees. We do not have cross-country data on employee training (though the country studies do have indicators of training provided by individual firms), so we cannot account for this.

1.5 STRUCTURE OF THE STUDY

The remainder of this study is structured as follows. Chapter 2 provides a review of the theoretical and empirical literature on import liberalization, technology and industrial growth, analysing the concepts involved and the way in which the traditional literature has arrived at some widely held beliefs on the benefits of liberalization. It goes on to analyse, from a different (evolutionary) perspective, what technological activity consists of in developing countries, what determines it and how import liberalization may be expected to affect it. It concludes with some methodological considerations on the case studies. Chapters 3 to 5 present the case studies of Kenya, Tanzania and Zimbabwe respectively. Each analyses the nature of the technological capabilities of the sample firms and seeks to 'explain' this both intuitively and by econometric analysis. Chapter 6 uses econometric techniques to examine the cross-country patterns of technological behaviour. Chapter 7 closes with a synthesis and policy conclusions.

Notes

1. Biggs *et al.* (1995); Lall *et al.* (1994); Stein (1995); Stewart *et al.* (1992); Teitel (1993); Wangwe (1995).
2. An exception is Enos (1995) on the impact of liberalization on science and technology policies in Africa.
3. Data on manufacturing value added and population from World Bank, *World Development Report, 1995.*
4. World Bank (1994), pp. 64–5.
5. World Bank (1994), p. 61. Also see the article by Husain (1994), the main author of the World Bank's *Adjustment in Africa* study (1994), for a discussion of what SAPs involve and how they differ from stabilization programmes.
6. See, for instance, World Bank (1991, 1993a).
7. The data are from the African Development Bank, *African Development Report 1995*. This analysis updates the one in Lall (1995).
8. The gap is more startling if South Korea is taken as a comparator: in 1987 Korea had 227.6 thousand students enrolled in engineering, 4.7 times more than the whole of SubSaharan Africa (excluding South Africa), with a population only 10 per cent of that of the region.

APPENDIX 1.1 MANUFACTURING VALUE ADDED IN SUBSAHARAN AFRICA, 1980–94

	Values (1985 $ million)			*Annual growth rates (%)*		
Country	*1980*	*1990*	*1994*	*1980–90*	*1990–94*	*1980–94*
Adjusting countries with improved policies						
Burkina-Faso	55	86	75	4.57	−3.36	2.24
Burundi	137	176	186	2.54	1.39	2.21
Gambia	10	17	19	5.45	2.82	4.69
Ghana	649	709	764	0.89	1.89	1.17
Kenya	523	834	910	4.78	2.20	4.04
Madagascar	396	313	313	−2.32	0.00	−1.67
Malawi	135	202	204	4.11	0.25	2.99
Mali	65	94	106	3.76	3.05	3.55
Mauritania	48	74	93	4.42	5.88	4.84
Niger	67	114	121	5.46	1.50	4.31
Nigeria	7520	8703	8245	1.47	−1.34	0.66
Senegal	258	423	423	5.07	0.00	3.59
Tanzania	493	430	515	−1.36	4.61	0.31
Uganda	74	118	172	4.78	9.88	6.21
Zimbabwe	820	1143	1034	3.38	−2.47	1.67
All improving	11 250	13 436	13 180	1.79	−0.48	1.14
Adjusting countries with deteriorating policies						
Benin	89	98	117	0.97	4.53	1.97
Cameroon	492	1270	1054	9.95	−4.55	5.59
CAR	67	95	77	3.55	−5.12	1.00
Chad	76	150	131	7.04	−3.33	3.97
Congo	61	133	128	8.11	−0.95	5.44
Côte d'Ivoire	698	1110	848	4.75	−6.51	1.40
Gabon	143	331	340	8.75	0.67	6.38
Guinea	131	116	146	−1.21	5.92	0.78
Guinea Bissau	24	18	19	−2.84	1.36	−1.65
Mozambique	977	551	544	−5.57	−0.32	−4.10
Rwanda	209	261	264	2.25	0.29	1.68
Sierra Leone	44	56	53	2.44	−1.37	1.34
Togo	55	75	61	3.15	−5.03	0.74
Zambia	468	717	718	4.36	0.03	3.10
All deteriorating	3534	4981	4500	3.49	−2.51	1.74
All adjusters	16 764	20 407	19 674	1.94	−0.91	1.15

APPENDIX 1.1 (*Continued*)

	Values (1985 $ million)			*Annual growth rates (%)*		
Country	*1980*	*1990*	*1994*	*1980–90*	*1990–94*	*1980–94*
Non-adjusting countries						
Angola	336	273	159	−2.05	−12.64	−5.20
Botswana	45	118	137	10.12	3.80	8.28
Cape Verde	5	9	11	6.05	5.14	5.79
Comoro	3	5	5	5.24	0.00	3.72
E. Guinea	1	1	2	0.00	18.92	5.08
Ethiopia	422	407	397	−0.36	−0.62	−0.44
Lesotho	13	42	53	12.44	5.99	10.56
Liberia	67	72	71	0.72	−0.35	0.42
Namibia	56	79	107	3.50	7.88	4.73
Sao Tome	4	3	4	−2.84	7.46	0.00
Seychelles	15	28	38	6.44	7.93	6.86
Somalia	50	36	30	−3.23	−4.46	−3.58
Sudan	384	534	671	3.35	5.88	4.07
Swaziland	41	184	219	16.20	4.45	12.71
Zaire	604	607	262	0.05	−18.95	−5.79
All non-adjusters	2046	2398	2166	1.60	−2.51	0.41
All SSA	16 830	20 815	19 846	2.15	−1.18	1.18

Source: Calculated from African Development Bank, *African Development Report, 1995*.

2 Import Liberalization and Industrial Performance: Theory and Evidence

Sanjaya Lall and Wolfram W. Latsch

2.1 INTRODUCTION

There appears to be at least implicit agreement among neoclassical development economists on certain propositions: free trade (at least as a benchmark ideal) optimizes global resource allocation; increased import competition leads to greater industrial efficiency, increases welfare in developing countries and allows specialization in accordance with natural comparative advantage; trade interventions are justifiable only under particular restrictive conditions, and even then are nearly always a second-best measure; and developing countries that pursue liberal trade policies industrialize faster and more efficiently than those that intervene in trade. According to this view, the role of government in promoting industrialization should be restricted to alleviating rather narrowly defined market failures. The concomitant and largely neoliberal policy prescription is that, where trade interventions exist, their rapid removal is likely to be the best policy. This is particularly the view of the Bretton Woods institutions, constituting what John Williamson has called the 'Washington consensus'. The government, in this view, can at best act as a mild corrective force in enabling a natural and largely given development path.

We argue that such neoliberal policy positions, and the largely negative view of government they embody, can no longer be justified with reference to any canonical economic theory. This is due to the fact that, over the last ten years, advances in the tools and techniques of economic theorizing appear to have outpaced thinking about development histories, paths and policies. A limited or even neutral government role and the greatest possible freedom of trade may still be the best policy prescriptions, but such a prescriptions are no longer based upon a widely accepted standard economic model: instead it is one of many possible positions, all of which may be formulated in a theoretically rigorous way. As Krugman aptly summarizes,

> free trade is not passé, but it is an idea that has irretrievably lost its innocence. Its status has shifted from optimum to reasonable rule of thumb. There is still a case for free trade as a good policy, and as a useful target in the practical world of politics, but it can never again be asserted as the policy that economic theory tells us is always right (Krugman, 1987, p. 132).

Over time, and despite widespread criticism, neoliberal propositions have acquired almost axiomatic status. They continue to inform thinking about development policy in institutions such as the IMF and the World Bank, although more recently there has appeared to be some reconsideration of old orthodoxies in the context of the so-called 'East Asian miracle'. This chapter reviews the literature on trade liberalization and industrialization, focusing on the assumptions underlying various approaches. In particular, we look at assumptions concerning technological processes (such as innovation, diffusion and the accumulation of technological capabilities) that are crucial to the achievement of efficiency in industrial production and to the attainment of a higher level of economic development. We argue that the debate on the links between liberalization and industrial development is, importantly, a *conceptual* one, and not merely a question of variously interpreting empirical evidence within a given and unchanging theoretical framework.

The neoliberal approach is based on certain assumptions that are brought, often implicitly and without question, to the policy debate.[1] These assumptions are the ones underlying the standard neoclassical conception of economic processes and behaviour, a conception that has undergone considerable modification in the past two decades (not least due to the theoretical efforts of many neoclassical economists dissatisfied with textbook theory). Yet these radical theoretical developments seem to have largely bypassed the Washington institutions: to use a scientific metaphor, they appear to be prescribing Newtonian policies for an relativistic world. We will look at those aspects of industrial development that are largely neglected in the literature, even in recent neoclassical contributions that have otherwise introduced a useful new vocabulary into economic analysis. These neglected aspects concern the micro-level processes by which enterprises become technologically efficient.

In the standard neoclassical formulation it is often assumed that such processes are costless and automatic: in the simplest case, firms choose technologies under conditions of perfect information. Under these conditions there is no need to delve into what goes on within firms, since market prices *by definition* give the correct signals for investments in capital, labour and technology. This formulation is based on the metaphor of an economy as an equilibrium system: Stiglitz (1996b, p. 154) correctly points out that such a metaphor 'provides little insight into the dramatic changes that occur in [developing] societies'.

A different conceptualization of firm-level processes yields very different conclusions: in the presence of market failures markets will not by themselves give the correct signals to guide the allocation of resources in accordance with a more dynamic view of comparative advantage. This is true, for example, in the case of widespread information imperfections. In such cases, free trade and import liberalization may not be the best policy for developing countries undergoing structural change and adjustment. This is not to deny that increased competition through trade may still be beneficial in highly protected and technologically backward economies; the point is that free markets will not by themselves result in a more desirable outcome. The design of liberalization has to take account of the extent and type of market failure. In the simplest neoclassical models, market failures are narrowly circumscribed and it is possible to correct them with a minimum of intervention. However, recent advances in information economics suggest that under conditions of widespread informational failures (and with realistic assumptions regarding the distribution, acquisition and processing of information), free market outcomes may not even be *constrained* Pareto-efficient. It can be shown that there generally exists a set of Pareto-improving government interventions, *even if the government faces the same informational constraints as private agents.*[2] Information economics stresses the ubiquity of market failure, and the pervasiveness of imperfect information: for a recent exposition of the information-economic critique see Stiglitz (1994).

Since import liberalization is one of the cornerstones of neoliberal policy recommendations to developing countries, it is important to clarify the conceptual underpinnings of the neoliberal argument.

2.2 WHAT ECONOMIC THEORY SAYS ABOUT 'OPENING UP'

The literature on import liberalization is not clearly divided into theoretical and empirical analysis. Moreover, most of the literature treats openness and liberalization in general, rather than import liberalization in particular. This section outlines the main approaches to the role of openness in economic development.

2.2.1 International Trade: The Standard Model and its Variations

The canonical version of trade theory (the neoclassical Heckscher–Ohlin model) is not concerned with the richness and variety of economic and technological processes as these occur in the real world. Aspects of technological change that are widely believed to be important (such as strong uncertainty and the often tacit nature of knowledge) simply cannot be accommodated within such simple neoclassical models. The Heckscher–Ohlin model assumes that technology and knowledge are exogenously given, identical across firms and countries, and freely available, with constant returns to scale, perfect competition in all markets, perfect intracountry (but no intercountry) factor mobility; and identical consumption patterns across countries. It is essentially an open-economy general equilibrium model, with all the restrictiveness this implies.[3] It is designed to explain static allocation rather than the dynamic change associated with processes of technological change. Its application to development and structural adjustment in developing countries is problematic since the Heckscher–Ohlin model takes endowments as given. It does not address the question where these endowments come from in the first place. This is particularly problematic in the case of endowments that are not natural resources: are skills and knowledge really 'endowments' in any meaningful sense? In other words, the canonical model of international trade has little to say about the different *initial conditions* from which growth and industrialization started in different countries.

The assumptions of the Heckscher–Ohlin model make it easy to conclude that free trade is optimal, and that, for countries with trade interventions, optimal resource allocation can be restored only by a rapid and across-the-board move to free trade. While in theory this should apply only where its assumptions hold good, in practice its proponents seem to take for granted that these assumptions are reasonable representations (or 'good first approximations') of reality. Policy analysis and advice in the developing world relies to a surprising extent on this presumption. An amended Heckscher–Ohlin (or 'neofactor proportions') model which includes human capital, makes the original model somewhat more realistic while leaving policy conclusions essentially unchanged. Even this expanded version does not ask how the relevant factors come into existence, or what roles markets, history and institutions play in determining endowments.

Other formulations have made more progress in moving towards an understanding of intercountry differences in technological capabilities.

Neotechnology theories claim that differences in technologies and tastes between countries are important determinants of trade. Production functions are assumed to differ across countries: some countries innovate, others imitate and others passively absorb technology as it matures. This results in technology gaps that are a basis for trade,[4] the pattern of trade depending on relative rates of innovation and imitation. Neotechnology theories are grounded in models of imperfect competition, where information and skill markets 'fail' compared with a notional and perfectly competitive optimum.

The focus of neotechnology theories is on 'major' innovations (discrete jumps in product or process technology) based on research and development. Technological differences arising from 'minor' innovations (that is, small improvements or continuous learning) and differences in the extent to which particular technologies have been effectively mastered are largely ignored. It is assumed that trade leads to the diffusion of knowledge, allowing technology gaps to be closed over time (in product cycle models direct investment is combined with trade as an agent of diffusion). The technology recipient instantly absorbs the technology and automatically uses it efficiently. As technologies mature, factor costs reassert themselves as the primary determinant of comparative advantage. Despite the origins of the theories in models of imperfect competition, market failure plays no role in these approaches. Since trade is the main channel of technology flows, trade restrictions deprive 'follower' countries of the benefits of technology diffusion (and can cause 'leader' countries to slow down innovation).[5] Where direct investment is included as an agent, similar conclusions follow about interventions in FDI flows. Thus full and rapid liberalization in developing countries is likely to be the best policy prescription.

In models incorporating increasing returns, economies of scale are important determinants of specialization and trade patterns. By marrying this idea to models used in industrial organization and game theory, the so-called 'new trade theory' emerges. Economies of scale lead to increasing returns and 'first mover' advantages, causing indeterminacy in trade patterns (or at least a strong sensitivity to initial conditions that are themselves unexplained) and 'a level of arbitrariness or randomness in the pattern of trade' (Krugman, 1989, p. 349). This is linked to intra-industry trade by the argument that *inter*-industry trade may be more traditionally comparative-advantage based, whereas *intra*-industry trade is more appropriately explained by economies of scale.[6]

In these cases trade policy may be used 'strategically' when countries are not 'small' (that is, price takers in the international market). The term 'strategic' refers to cases where, in the presence of foreign and domestic monopolies, trade policy can be used to extract rents from foreign monopolists. Subsequent formulations elaborate on the idea that government policy can play the same role in international competition that strategic moves play in domestic competition. Krugman (1984) notes that import protection can be a strategic instrument of export promotion, a variant of the infant industry argument: protection could enable industries to exploit economies of scale and learning before competitors. This also holds true in the case of import liberalization: with imperfect competition and economies of scale, reducing protection for particular industries may not be desirable where liberalizing too early could harm the competitive position. The implications of the new trade theory have been subsequently criticized (and weakened) by highlighting potential conflicts between national and global welfare, noting their inapplicability to developing countries, and bringing in political economy arguments in favour of liberal regimes (see below) and against theoretical models being abused by economic populists.

While strategic trade models are highly stylized and sensitive to particular assumptions, they underline an important fact: no *general* proposition can be derived regarding the optimality of free trade (Rodrik, 1992b). In these models, as in earlier ones, the question of where national advantages come from is not directly addressed, even though strategic approaches point to important ways in which differential learning capabilities at the firm level may have determined trade patterns, and where history and policy may have been critical in the development of such capabilities.

Since there are no longer any simple or general presumptions in favour of neoliberal policy prescriptions, political economy arguments are used to strengthen the neoliberal case. The so-called 'new political economy' approach (based on broadly libertarian rational choice or public choice approaches)[7] addresses the role of government and its relationship with individual political and economic liberty. It backs its arguments for liberal trade regimes with the assertion that government interventions in developing countries have been mostly harmful, and that the withdrawal of the state has been responsible for the most spectacular successes in the developing world (for example in the newly industrializing economies of East Asia). The principles of neoliberalism denigrate what Hayek called 'rational constructivism' in favour of the 'spontaneous order' brought about by the workings of the market process. Government interventions are assumed to have invariably high costs (bureaucratic waste and widespread infractions of individual liberties), which are likely to outweigh any possible benefits.[8] Thus even if economic theory does not prove that free market processes are the most efficient, the free market outcome is still to be preferred *a priori* over government interventionism on philosophical grounds. As Helleiner (1995, p. 4) writes in a recent study of trade policy and industrialisation, 'there is now widespread agreement that the strongest case for liberalised and neutral policies rests less on economic theory than on political economy grounds'.

Some neoliberal theorists argue that the details of empirical or theoretical analysis do not ultimately count; what counts is a *commitment to freedom* or, as Lal and Rajapatirana phrase it, 'making a stand for markets versus mandarins'. They write that 'if we accept the need for restraints on the natural and often irrational *dirigisme* of mandarins in most developing countries, then the adoption of a liberal trade regime (*irrespective of the ensuing gains from trade, static or dynamic*) becomes an important means to this end' (Lal and Rajapatirana, 1987, p. 209, emphasis added). Bhagwati (1989, p. 41) suggests that, where economic theory fails to provide secure foundations for a commitment to free trade, 'common sense and wisdom should prevail in favour of free trade'. This statement is interesting in that it appears to indicate a contrast between economic theory on the one hand, and common sense or wisdom on the other!

Helleiner summarizes his recent overview of the issues involved in studying trade and industrialization as follows:

> There [are] both theoretical and empirical reasons for doubt, however, as to the universal validity of these [neo-liberal] general assessments, recommendations, and policies. Allowing for learning effects, scale economies, externalities, and less-than-perfectly competitive markets, it is easy, on the basis of standard economic theory, to posit alternative 'optimal' trade policies for development (each dependent on specific alternative assumptions regarding these matters.... Moreover, the historical record seems to offer remarkably few cases of rapid industrialisation or development that can be associated with the generally recommended trade policies (Helleiner, 1995, p. 2).

From a purely theoretical point of view, the possibility of non-decreasing returns (that is, the more realistic incorporation of history into economic models) means that comparative advantage, future development potential and policy are all underdetermined by those factors normally assumed to be the 'fundamentals' of the economy. In the case of neoclassical economic theory, the tendency towards increasing technical sophistication appears to have outpaced the capacity to understand and interpret the implications of these new mathematical tools. The case for any particular policy prescription is theoretically justifiable, and can be formulated rigorously. While this weakens the *a priori* neoliberal case, which is based on a standard model that has been superseded by more complex approaches, it also weakens the *a priori* case for a strong government role in coordinating economic decisions and processes. This means that, in analysing the economic effects of trade policy, industrial policy, and the role of government, we have to move from the general to the specific, from formalist theorizing to a more historical and institutional analysis.

2.2.2 Alternative Approaches: Evolutionary and Informational Theories

As an alternative to standard neoclassical theories one could use an approach based on evolutionary, or 'neo-Schumpeterian' theory.[9] It was argued above that the canonical Heckscher–Ohlin model is by itself unable to explain observed trade flows, and that relaxing its least realistic assumptions leads to indeterminate outcomes, in terms of specializations and trade patterns. Evolutionary theorists suggest that new trade theory has implications that could be fruitfully employed in an alternative framework.[10] This alternative framework attempts to be more structuralist and dynamic, emphasizing the effects of trade on the overall level of economic activity, and looking explicitly at processes of technological change and factor creation.

Recent contributions from the periphery of neoclassical theory have begun to incorporate many of the factors that have long been emphasised by evolutionary theorists.[11] Krugman (1991), and Rodrik (1996), for example, emphasize the role of coordination failures, imperfect information, path dependency, and self-fulfilling expectations in models of development and trade. In their models there is a strong theoretical argument for government intervention owing to the presence of multiple potential equilibria. Rodrik (1996, p. 2) writes that 'when multiple equilibria exist, the role of government is to move the economy out of the bad equilibrium into the good one. We can think of many ways in which this could be accomplished in theory'.

Many evolutionary contributions are not explicitly microeconomic in perspective. However their focus on differences in productive capabilities clearly points to the need for a more microeconomic focus (or as Stiglitz, 1987, put it, a 'micro-microeconomic approach') that can help us study issues of knowledge, information and learning. The emphasis in evolutionary models is not on the static optimization of resource allocation, but on international differences in innovative and productive capabilities and the dynamics of evolving comparative advantage. These dynamics are related to historical processes of institutional development, increasing returns, learning and the accumulation of technology in the broadest sense (to include equipment, specialised skills and knowledge).

Evolutionary approaches, as well as recent contributions to information economics, suggest that the informational structure of the real world economy is complex if one takes into account the pervasiveness of market failure. Information-economic analysis suggests that the price signals transmitted by 'opening up' the economy can result in a variety of possible of adjustment mechanisms, and a concomitant variety of outcomes. Stiglitz (1987) shows that myopic decision making on the basis of presently available price-based information may reflect long-term growth and development potential. Localized and technology-specific learning processes (including that of 'learning to learn') need to be taken into account. Hence there is no guarantee that static allocative efficiency and what could be called 'Schumpeterian efficiency' (that is, dynamic, long-run innovative potential and flexibility) will coincide. There is therefore a rationale for government intervention in this model, given the assumptions built into it.[12]

Stiglitz emphasizes how far his essentially evolutionary ideas are from the traditional Heckscher–Ohlin formulation (which to a large extent, still informs the policy analysis and advice of the Washington institutions) when he states that:

> in this perspective, there is a certain serendipity in the determination of long-run comparative advantage.... In ascertaining static comparative advantage we need look only at current resources and capabilities relative to those of other countries. In ascertaining dynamic comparative advantage we need to look at future resources and capabilities relative to those of other countries. And these are at best conjectural (Stiglitz, 1987, pp. 142–3).

From an evolutionary perspective, an analysis of an economy's responsive capacity requires a theory of the *responsive capabilities* of the firm, and of how *firm-level responses are coordinated*, via the market and prices, or through other channels involving non-price signals. As Helleiner (1995, p. 31) puts it, ' "getting prices right", through trade and other policies, however important, can achieve little in the absence of responsive capacity'. This is important where externalities, increasing returns and 'collective learning' by groups of firms are significant. The organization of informational externalities can be achieved in a variety of structures, with competition and cooperation balanced in different ways. Which structures actually emerge is a function partly of history and partly of the ability of the economy to mobilize resources in accordance with expectations or strategies.[13] Strategy formation itself becomes a function of the ability to organize and coordinate activities. The market can then be seen as a historical, local and institutionally embedded form of organization.[14]

New trade theory and the more complex and specific models used provide the theoretical basis for a more evolutionary approach to trade, industrialization and development. They indicate the necessity of a move from the general to the specific, from the global to the local, and (according to Stiglitz) from the microeconomic to the 'micro-microeconomic'. Firm-level processes of learning and capability acquisition are part of this 'micro-microeconomic' domain and need to be studied within an appropriate framework. We argue that the so-called technological capabilities approach provides the foundations for such a framework.

2.3 THE EMPIRICAL STUDY OF LIBERALIZATION: SOME CONCEPTUAL ISSUES

The debate on trade policy and its role in development is too large to discuss here in full.[15] We provide only a brief review of the relevant features here.

During the period often referred to as the 'neoclassical resurgence' in development economics, analytical contributions often had the explicit goal of influencing policy.[16] In early works, such as Little *et al.* (1970), the debate was posed in simple terms (inward versus outward-looking trade strategies, representing intervention and free markets respectively); it was not based on exploring the actual links between trade policy and development. The basic argument was that, although selective measures may be justified in theory, interventions in the real world trade result in the excessive regulation of markets, inefficiency and slow growth. Protection in developing countries leads to a proliferation of infant industries that never mature, and to a neglect of their comparative advantage in labour-intensive industries. In contrast, export-oriented economies have grown more rapidly by following their comparative advantage in such industries and then moving up the 'ladder' of comparative advantage.

Since this is just what the canonical Heckscher–Ohlin model would predict, it seems to follow that the basic neoclassical prescription (of free trade) is also correct. In the absence of learning processes, inefficiency can only result from government interventions such as import protection. Thus wholesale and rapid liberalization is necessary and sufficient to lead these countries to growth by putting them back on the path of their 'natural' comparative advantage. Exposure to import competition causes three kinds of beneficial resource reallocation: within firms (from inefficient to efficient activities), between firms (from 'bad' to 'good' performers) and between industries (from less to more productive activities). Since market failures are, by assumption, not important, the adjustment process is expected to be smooth, rapid and efficient.[17]

Such static resource reallocation (suitably dynamized by the inclusion of an optimal growth model) is assumed to translate automatically into long-term efficiency and productivity improvements.[18] The link from liberalization to optimization of resource allocation does not need to be demonstrated, it is a syllogistic argument. The link between static optimization and growth is simply assumed, since theory gives little account of productivity development. Productivity improvements are taken to be exogenous and automatic, and in the absence of a theory of firm-level technological development, the interactions between static and dynamic efficiency remain conjectural (see Rodrik, 1992a). Even Lal and Rajapatirana (1987, p. 211), noting that trade policy reform 'would help to create an economic framework that provides the necessary incentives for entrepreneurship, productivity, and thrift', point out that 'these qualities are only dimly understood by economists'.

A World Bank-sponsored survey in 1987 concluded that '[t]rade liberalization results in the contraction of inefficient sectors and the expansion of new, efficient ones. Over time, a new and more efficient production structure develops that will be better suited to the international environment' (Michalopoulos, 1987, p. 24). However, no theoretical tools are available to model this process, except in a way where the results are built into the assumptions. As Rodrik (1992, pp. 156–7) notes, 'the theory of trade policy is generally silent on the effects of liberalization on the rate of growth of output of productivity. Different but equally plausible models can produce diametrically opposite conclusions on this score.'

Krueger's (1978) arguments against government intervention, drawing upon the East Asian experience, are good examples of the generalizations that emerge from the literature. Later works in this tradition are characterized by a combination of optimality statements derived from axiomatic theories and strong neoliberal political economy arguments in the same spirit. The best known is perhaps the World Bank's *1987 World Development Report (WDR)*, prepared at the height of the neoclassical resurgence and representing the core of its views on trade policy and the role of government. The *WDR* contrasts 'inward-oriented' and 'outward-oriented' regimes, grouped into 'strongly' and 'moderately' outward oriented: in this simplified classification, outward orientation is associated with liberal trade policies and is shown to perform distinctly better. The transition from outward-oriented trade strategy to a neoliberal government is made smoothly, glossing over issues of whether or not outward-oriented Asian countries are really 'liberal' in their resource allocation policies.[19] The policy conclusion is undiluted trade liberalization, and the advice to 'get prices right'.

Stiglitz is critical of such generalised policy prescriptions, which in his view are similar to religious beliefs:

> Undermining this particular religion was the disturbing observation that countries that seemed to get the prices right – to follow the visiting preachers of the free market – too often failed to grow. To be sure, like medieval medicine, there was always the allegation that the patient had not followed the doctor's orders precisely, and it was this that accounted for the failure of the remedy (Stiglitz, 1996, p. 155).

Korea, in the 1987 *WDR*, is classified as 'strongly outward oriented'. Although the report acknowledges that 'considerable intervention' took place in Korea, this is taken to coexist with neutral trade policies and the idealized role assigned to governments. The evidence 'that rapid economic growth and efficient industrialization are usually associated with outward-oriented policies on trade' (World Bank, 1987a, p. 92), which is by and large valid, is made to yield the conclusion that 'an economy that imposes few barriers to trade and encourages domestic competition is likely to develop an industrial sector that is more efficient in its use of resources and more competitive in international markets' (ibid., p. 131), which is not.

Recent trade liberalization experiences are analysed by World Bank-sponsored studies such as Thomas and Nash (1991a and b) and Michaely *et al.* (1991). These are not primarily theoretical works, nor are they intended to be. However both contain discussions of the theory of structural adjustment, of which trade liberalization is an important part.[20] In line with previous arguments, Thomas and Nash (1991b, p. 9) suggest that trade liberalization removes the economic 'distortions' that impede economic efficiency, and 'resources previously devoted to relatively inefficient or unproductive uses move to more efficient production'.[21] On the role of policy, they conclude that 'successful approaches [involve a] *somewhat interventionist* but *relatively neutral* policy to reforms entailing substantial liberalization' (ibid., p. 5). But this is not a justification of industrial policy: the need for a 'relatively neutral' policy with some form of intervention is not derived from theoretical arguments based on the need to remedy particular kinds of market failure. Instead it is asserted that some interventions are good or bad on apparently arbitrary grounds: thus selective trade interventions to promote or support infant industries are deemed undesirable, without any investigation of the conditions under which they might be justified.

A similar argument is made in the World Bank's 1993 study of the Asian 'miracle', which, while going beyond previous publications in recounting the extent of interventions by many Asian NIEs, concludes that selectivity in interventions contributed little or nothing to their success. At this time, the argument on the role of government draws the line of legitimacy around so-called 'functional' interventions while ruling out selectivity, where the government affects resource allocation: these arguments are discussed further below. In the context of import liberalization, the implication of the argument is again that trade restrictions (which are selective) should be removed but the government may mount policies to improve factor markets such as skills and capital, and remove any elements of selectivity that may exist in them. The admission of market failure thus does not create a case for trade intervention.

However this approach suffers from methodological problems: the analysis strays too far from established theory, or at least from those areas where theory yields unambiguous conclusions. In Rodrik's words, 'too often, the preferred method of proof is a casual appeal to common sense. In particular, no distinctions are typically made between policies for which received theory is silent ... (or has ambiguous implications), and those for which a definite theoretical presumption exists' (Rodrik, 1995b, p. 2933).

There is a further theoretical problem that the literature on trade policy and liberalization does not address. Conventional neoclassical theory does not establish that the resource reallocation benefits of trade liberalization lead to sustained higher rates of growth, as asserted for East Asia. On standard growth theory assumptions, given declining marginal returns to investment, a once-and-for-all move to remove price 'distortions' have *level* rather than growth *rate* benefits for national income.[22] Even the level effects estimated in the literature have been quite small (one-off gains of 2–5 per cent of GDP), far below the evident difference in growth rates between the NIEs and other economies. The proponents of trade liberalization argue, however, that there are strong growth rate effects from liberalization. This argument is apparently based on self-evident propositions that do not need empirical demonstration, *viz.* the general benefits of 'openness' and a 'reformed' incentive environment, the reduction of government-induced 'distortions' and the greater reliance on (essentially efficient) markets.

According to Thomas and Nash (1991b, p. 9) for instance, 'once-and-for-all gains show up in a higher *rate* of GDP growth' (emphasis added), the precise magnitude of which 'depends on how the economy adjusts to price changes'. And later, 'More difficult to demonstrate, but of great practical importance, are the dynamic effects of reorienting the trade regime. There is an empirically established correlation between outward-oriented trade policies and the growth of total factor productivity in industry' (ibid.) Similarly, in modelling the beneficial effect on long-run productivity performance, Edwards (1991, p. 3) simply assumes that 'more open economies are more efficient in absorbing exogenously generated innovations'.

The processes by which increased dynamic efficiency is achieved in response to trade liberalization are not modelled explicitly. Thomas and Nash (1991, pp. 9, 34, 42) resort to generalizations on 'the ability to take advantage of a wide range of innovations', 'greater efficiency in resource absorption' and an 'increased growth rate of technology'. Whatever a 'growth rate of technology' may be cannot be established without a theory of what 'technology' is, how it could be measured or affected, and what causes it to 'grow' in different environments. In essence these arguments presume the efficiency of markets in stimulating technological efficiency and productivity – they are apparently commonsensical conclusions that do not require further proof.

In view of the evidently disappointing effects of structural adjustment on industry in, for instance, SubSaharan Africa, these propositions need to be analysed and substantiated. In an apparent acknowledgment of such problems, Thomas and Nash (ibid., p. 44) admit that the stimulating effects of liberalization only manifest themselves 'if these policy reforms lead to supply responses'. In other words, the change in the incentive regime is theoretically justified but there is something lacking in the ability of enterprises to produce efficiently in response. This reveals two interesting assumptions in the underlying approach:

- There may exist failures in factor markets, but not in the product markets that give signals for resource allocation. The reasons for drawing such a distinction on the nature and incidence of market failures are not apparent and are not spelled out, though logically the relaxation of the assumption on market efficiency applies to all markets.
- Even if it is accepted that product markets are efficient while factor markets are not, accepting the presence of market failures in the latter requires that liberalization should not be a rapid, sweeping and uniform opening up to free trade (which is the neoclassical 'ideal'), but gradual and selective in order to allow factor markets to be improved. Moreover selectivity is entailed in having to allocate scarce intervention resources among competing uses, and the pace of incentive reform should be integrated with the pace of factor market development.

The logic of both implications points to a more evolutionary and structuralist approach to liberalization, that is, gradual, geared to market failures and allowing a significant role for selective government intervention. If product markets are prone to failure, they need corrective intervention rather than the freedom to give suboptimal signals. Where factor markets are deficient, a more graduated and selective approach may be called for. Interventions in both sets of markets have to be coordinated with each other, and both may have elements of selectivity. Thus the basic presumption of the neoliberal approach, that 'getting prices right' is necessary and sufficient for stimulating sustained and efficient industrial growth, can no longer be sustained.

It should be reiterated that this is not an argument against all forms of liberalization or increased competition in protected economies. Most analysts accept that inefficient interventions should by removed and that greater competition is beneficial for efficiency. What they question is sweeping arguments against *all* forms of selective intervention; they suggest that liberalization (in some form) was one of several conditions for improved performance, and one highly contingent on others. As Rodrik (1992b, p. 103) notes, 'At its best, trade policy provides an enabling environment for development. *It does not guarantee that entrepreneurs will take advantage of this environment, nor that private investment will be stimulated*. As the recent literature on trade and growth underscores, it certainly does not guarantee adequate levels of growth in the long run' (emphasis added).

2.4 THE TECHNOLOGICAL CAPABILITY APPROACH

2.4.1 The Nature of Technological Capabilities

A large amount of empirical evidence on firm-level processes of technical change in developing countries has been collected in recent years. The analysis has drawn inspiration from the evolutionary approach to economic change, and by locating this process in markets that are prone to imperfections and failure, it has tried to arrive at policy implications from the analysis of the firm-level experience. The approach is different from the conventional (neoclassical) one, which mostly assumes particular behavioural patterns, based on an optimising equilibrium framework, without really looking in detail at micro-level processes. The firm-level perspective offers a different interpretation of the role of interventions in promoting successful industrial development, since the analyst has directly to confront the issue of how imperfect markets are remedied or bypassed. In short the new approach is explicitly behavioural and institutional, attempting to open up the 'black boxes' of firms and markets.

This literature may broadly be referred to as the technological capability (TC) approach.[23] Technological capabilities in industry are the skills (technical, managerial or organisational) that allow firms to utilize equipment and information efficiently.[24] Such capabilities are firm-specific, a form of institutional knowledge that is composed of individual skills accumulated over time that are not merely 'linearly added', but contain a synergetic element.[25] Technological effort in developing countries, therefore, should not be thought of as investment at the global frontier of technology, although innovative capabilities are one (particularly advanced) form of TC.[26] It comprises a much broader range of efforts that every enterprise must undertake in order to access, implement, absorb and build upon the knowledge required in production. The successful transfer of technology to a developing country has to include important elements of capability building: simply providing equipment and operating instructions, patents, designs or blueprints does not ensure that the technology will be effectively utilized.

The 'market' for technology, or technological capability, is thus different from a product market. Unlike the sale of a good, where the transaction is completed when the physical delivery has taken place, the transfer of skills and information is a prolonged (or even open-ended) process. It involves local learning to complete the transaction, and recipients of the technology have to invest in their ability to absorb the new knowledge. It falls outside standard economic analysis, since it is not clearly definable as a 'good' at all. Embodied elements of technology need to be accompanied by a number of tacit elements that require further investment in the collection of knowledge, and the development of skills and institutional routines. TCs are therefore not entirely describable in terms of physical equipment, blueprints or patents purchased by an enterprise, nor in terms of formal skills, although all these are important as the receptive base for the acquisition of capabilities. Capabilities are the way in which an institution such as a firm combines all the above to function as an organization.

Any enterprise using technology acquires some capabilities as an automatic result of the production process: this is best described as passive learning-by-doing. In simple industries (say, garment manufacture or the assembly of imported kits for the domestic market) this may be entirely sufficient, especially when the activity does not involve prolonged supply or informational linkages with other manufacturing activities. The skills involved are generally easily acquired on the job in a relatively short time. However, such passive learning-by-doing is insufficient for more complex technologies, especially where interfirm and interindustry linkages are more varied and intense. In these cases, even reaching static 'best practice' technical levels involves a longer period of more demanding learning in various ways.

Where the technology is new to the firm, it has to search for and hire new skills from the market. Even if these are readily available and adequate, a number of tasks are required to make the technology operational: 'debugging', adapting the technology to local circumstances, mastering product design, improving the engineering aspects of production, and developing procurement and marketing skills. Where the technology is new to the country, these skills may not be available locally and the supply and institutional structure outside the firm may not be adequate to its needs. This makes the process of learning more difficult, unpredictable and costly, with considerable externalities and interfirm interaction involved, even when static technological mastery is concerned. The process becomes even more difficult and costly when dynamic factors are introduced. When market conditions, tastes, technologies and relative prices change, and new competitors emerge, maintaining competitiveness requires continuous, and more demanding, investment and effort.

The most important features of technological capabilities are as follows:

- Investments in technological capabilities have to be conscious and purposeful. Only very basic capabilities can be developed costlessly and automatically; it is common to find enterprises that have produced for years without developing the capabilities to operate efficiently by international standards.
- Investments in technological capabilities are sensitive to the overall economic environment and the incentive regime governing industrial operations: the stability of macroeconomic policies, the competitive environment, the availability of crucial skills and the information 'system'.
- There is no predictable learning curve along which all firms move. In any environment, some firms will invest in TCs more than others, depending on their size, product, market or business strategy. Within any country there may be wide and persistent differences in firm-level efficiency, due to different investments in capabilities. Entrepreneurial differences apart, the extent to which individual firms invest in TCs depends on the efficiency of markets and the realization by the entrepreneur that TC investments are important. Often the learning process itself has to learnt (see Stiglitz, 1987).
- The growth of TCs can take place anywhere in the production process: shop floor, engineering, design, procurement or formal R&D (Katz, 1984). Formal R&D is only one possible source of technological learning. The relative importance of investing in different capabilities depends on the nature of the technology and the level of TC development already reached by the firm. Many 'routine' functions in developed countries (quality control, maintenance, process optimization, inventory control and the like) are not routine in developing ones, and learning them is in fact an important source of cumulative productivity gains. R&D does, however, become more important as technological development advances; the absorption and adaptation of complex technologies requires a formal R&D base.
- The complexity, cost and risk of TC investments rise with the sophistication of the technology and the level of technological development reached. The cost of accumulating a viable level of TCs in automobile manufacturing, for instance, is higher than in the making of simple machine tools, which in turn is higher than

in hand tools. The process of industrial development and the dynamic evolution of comparative advantage in manufacturing involves the deepening of TCs in given technologies, and diversification into more complex technologies.

- Manufacturing enterprises do not develop capabilities in isolation. Firms operate within a network of continuous, often intense, formal and informal relationships with suppliers, customers, competitors, consultants, as well as technology and educational institutions. These networks take the form of (often intricate) contractual and non-contractual relations. Institutions and rules evolve that regulate these networks and linkages, which share and spread scarce resources (particularly technological knowledge). The need for and form of such linkages differs according to sector. As productive activities grow more complex, linkages and networks deepen and widen, as do the institutions shaping and regulating them.
- The development of TCs in enterprises, industries and economies follows an evolutionary and idiosyncratic path. Investments in knowledge, skill and capability are cumulative and path-dependent. Easier capabilities and activities are mastered first. At the enterprise level, individual firms operate with the technological knowledge they have accumulated, depending on the technologies they use and the modifications they have made.

2.4.2 Implications for Government Policy

In most neoclassical approaches, government intervention is justified only when there is market failure: the textbook cases are externalities, public goods and non-competitive market structures. These market failures are not based on information deficiencies; they are narrowly circumscribed and therefore correctable without affecting incentives and efficiency. Most economists admit that markets are never perfect in the textbook sense. However, for all practical purposes departures from the optimum are taken to be either negligible or easily correctable. Where this is not the case, incompetent and corruptible governments are assumed invariably to make things worse.

Regarding industrial policy,[27] the debate revolves primarily around the role of the government in the most successful industrializing countries, the East Asian newly industrializing economies (NIEs). The neoclassical literature in the late 1970s and early 1980s argued that East Asian success was a triumph of economic liberalism. The NIEs followed the dictates of endowment-based comparative advantage by adopting neutral (later equated with free market) policies, their success a demonstration of the validity of textbook models. Other developing countries should follow course, liberalizing their markets by reducing government involvement in the economy.

Following increasing criticism of the argument that NIEs had followed free market policies, many neoliberal writers admitted that NIE governments had in fact been rather more interventionist than initially suggested.[28] However they did not accept that there was a direct causal relationship between the degree and nature of intervention and the kind of industrial structure and capabilities that were developed in the different NIEs. Their response attempted to preserve certain central tenets of neoclassical theory while granting that some market failures did exist, and that many successful countries did intervene. This was based on breaking down market failures into different types, and classifying their remedies as desirable or undesirable according to whether they influenced resource allocation between different directly productive activities.

Let us take the arguments of the World Bank as the leading spokesman of the neoliberal school. The World Bank (1993a) drew a distinction between two sorts of market failure:

- *Generic* market failures, calling for 'functional' interventions that strengthen the working of markets without directly affecting resource allocation. These are called 'market friendly' policies, and the success of the NIEs is traced to them.
- Market failures that call for *specific* interventions. These are 'selective' interventions favouring particular activities, and so result in a different pattern of activities and resource allocation than in the free market. Such interventions are not market friendly and are not recommended.

It should be noted that neoclassical economics itself gives no reason for such a distinction. In theory, any intervention that corrects market failure should be regarded as 'market friendly'. It is well known from economic theory that investments in knowledge and skills are likely to suffer from market failure due to factors such as externalities, fixed costs and non-appropriability.[29] However the advice given by the World Bank was that functional interventions would be sufficient to overcome such failures and stimulate growth and development. This assumes that the skills and technologies needed for industrial development are generic rather than specific. There are, in other words, no activity-specific capabilities that have to be acquired.

While there is certainly a case for functional interventions in certain types of human capital, theory provides a case for selective policies to address specific market failures. The World Bank (1993a, pp. 90–2) lists a number of market failures that may call for selective interventions. These are:

- Capital market deficiencies.
- Indivisibilities in investment arising from scale economies.
- Externalities arising from the imperfect appropriability of investments in knowledge, technology and skills, which make it difficult for economic agents to coordinate their investment decisions. These problems are exacerbated in the presence of 'diffuse' externalities.[30]

However the World Bank study suggested that in practice selective interventions should be avoided. The rejection of selectivity as a part of industrial strategy was based on two arguments: that selective interventions did not appear to have promoted industrial development in East Asia; and that most governments lacked the capability to intervene successfully in a selective way. The statistical interpretation of these 'facts', though, is ambiguous.[31]

The World Bank (1993a) study was greeted with widespread criticism.[32] For our present purposes, the most important one is that it used a *restrictive definition* of market failure in assessing the need for industrial policy. This definition was a static one, based on a optimisation framework in perfect markets from which deviations had to be remedied to restore an allocative optimum. It continued with certain simplifying assumptions about micro-level technological phenomena.[33] The 'market friendly' strategy depended crucially on a setting where enterprises optimized and industries deepened and developed without engaging in a complex and risky learning process with enormous externalities. Without a realistic micro-level theory of the development of industrial capabilities, however, it is not possible to understand what happened in the more industrialized NIEs (and Japan). It is thus not feasible to derive meaningful policy conclusions for other countries.

The TC approach suggests a very different role for governments. Given that the process by which firms in developing countries become efficient can be complex, costly and technology specific, free-market-driven allocation will lead to underinvestment in relatively 'difficult' technologies, relatively slow deepening of the industrial structure and stunted development of local technological capabilities. The protection or promotion of industry can then improve resource allocation.

Note that the approach does not say that *no* industry will take root without supporting intervention, only that entry into activities with high learning and coordination costs will be deterred. Interventions to promote industrial deepening and the exploitation of industrial linkages cannot be functional – since technologies differ in their learning needs and externalities, they have to be selective. The evidence on differing patterns of industrial development in the NIEs bears out precisely the effects of different forms, extents and levels of selective interventions.

The TC approach suggests that protection should be counterbalanced by strong incentives to achieve international competitiveness. There are many possible ways of combining interventions with stimuli for capability development: protection that is strictly limited in time; performance requirements; pressures for early entry into export markets while maintaining domestic protection. The latter was the strategy followed by Korea and Taiwan. That of Singapore was different. There, investment was guided by pressures other than protection, by giving incentives to enter particular activities, by creating specific skills and information in government-targeted sectors. This strategy was highly dependent on direct foreign investment.

Policies promoting industrial and technological development, according to the TC approach, should include three elements: interventions that are *selective* wherever learning costs and risks, vertical linkages between activities and other externalities require it; an *integrated* set of interventions addressing interlinked market failures in both product and factor markets; and selective promotion of all forms *offset* by incentives and performance pressures.

What, then, does the TC approach imply for the phasing and nature of the liberalization process? Unlike the neoclassical school, it suggests that the ideal liberalization process should not be uniform. As with the protection of infant industries, it should take account of the needs of specific productive activities. However a grace period has to be matched by offsetting incentive measures to ensure that capability development does take place. This could be achieved by credibly fixing the period over which protection or subsidies are to last. Once the adjustment of existing activities is complete, the government should retain the promotion tools to ensure the further diversification and deepening of the industrial structure and technological capabilities. Moreover, the integration of factor market improvement with import liberalization is crucial to the success of reform: if liberalization outpaces the rate at which appropriate inputs are provided to enterprises, many potentially viable concern will be forced to close down. This is the way in which most Asian countries have 'opened up' to international markets, by a gradual and controlled process of liberalization that was matched by factor market improvements and performance pressures, and which left further scope for industrial policy.

To conclude, the TC approach gives the following picture of the liberalization process:

- *Rapid and sweeping liberalization*: this can lead to deindustrialization, affecting potentially viable activities. While activities that are already competitive (based on natural resources or industries that have developed technologically during the import-substituting period) may do better than before, it is unlikely that new industrial activities with difficult learning needs will emerge unless selective policies are adopted to promote and support them. The possible exceptions are activities driven by foreign direct investment, mostly attracted by cheap labour. Even in these cases, though, industrial policies may be required in order to develop local capabilities.
- *Halting and slow liberalization*, driven by a reluctance to open up and restructure rather than by a strategy of fostering the growth of competitive enterprises. Such a process is likely to result in inefficient activities, without remedying the deficiencies that hold back their upgrading. The absence of supply-side measures to provide the skills and technologies for improving efficiency in line with liberalization is likely to hold back the emergence of dynamic new activities.
- *A gradual process of liberalization that addresses market failures and strategic needs, and is integrated with supply-side improvements*: this is likely to produce the best results in terms of restructuring existing activities and giving rise to competitive new ones.

The country studies in this book illustrate mixtures of the first two kinds of liberalization experience. But before we come to them, we will describe in greater detail the nature of technological capabilities.

2.5 CATEGORIES AND DETERMINANTS OF TECHNOLOGICAL CAPABILITIES

2.5.1 Categories of TC

This section describes a simple functional categorization of the technological tasks facing a manufacturing firm. The tasks fall into three broad categories: investment, production and linkages.[34]

Investment capabilities are the skills and information required to identify feasible investment projects, search for and buy suitable technologies, and manage the construction and start-up of the plant. Industrial technology is not perfectly codified, and choice of technology or technique is not costless or automatic. Markets for technology or technological capability are likely to be imperfect because they are markets for information.

Contracting out investment functions (to foreign consultants) solves some of the problems. But the technology being provided is likely to be a 'turnkey' operation in which the recipient is passive and likely to remain reliant on outside assistance. The experience of Japan and the Asian NIEs shows that domestic investment capability greatly reduces costs and enhances participation, and therefore stimulates subsequent learning and capability development.

Production capabilities are the skills and knowledge required to operate a firm and improve the production process. This involves process technology, product technology and industrial engineering, and include functions such as quality management, maintenance and process optimisation, as well as efforts to adapt and improve the technology (sometimes referred to as 'minor innovation'). The development of 'routine' capabilities often requires considerable time and effort, even when technologies are acquired rather an being created by the firm. As the production process is adapted, the firm develops more sophisticated capabilities and often starts carrying out basic R&D-type activities. These become more important as the firm improves its capability to absorb technology.[35]

Industrial engineering refers to the organization of production. Industrial engineers continuously monitor and seek to improve production processes. 'Just-in-time' systems, for example, call for different forms of shop-floor layout and work organization. A variety of statistical and programming techniques are applied to this task.

The amount of technological effort requires differs by industry and depends on the technology being used.[36] Engineering industries tend to focus on product design and the improvement of manufacturing methods. 'Process industries' (such as chemicals) place more emphasis on process optimization. Differences in technologies are reflected in different skill requirements.

Linkage capabilities are the skills required to establish, maintain and exploit production and technological links with other firms and institutions. In industrialized and developing countries alike, there is often a dense network of cooperative relationships between firms.

This involves the sharing of certain types of technical information, which requires the capability to share and make use of this sharing. In developing countries, supplier networks and institutions are often inadequate to the task of achieving competitiveness. Firms may have to 'coach' suppliers as well as establishing links with existing enterprises.

Technological development is to a significant extent path-dependent. The nature of the learning process results in firms developing along particular trajectories determined by their initial positions, entrepreneurial strategy and capabilities.[37] Firms may become 'locked in' to these trajectories, once they have been established, and this may well be inefficient from a long-term, dynamic point of view.

2.5.2 Determinants of Technology Development

2.5.2.1 The Incentive Framework

The extent to which a firm invests in developing its capabilities depends on the economic environment, the institutional setting and government policies.

The macroeconomic environment and prospects regarding the growth of markets (both domestic and foreign) influence firm-level decisions to invest in capability development. As with other investment decisions, a stable, high-growth environment is the most conducive. Macroeconomic issues, although not the focus of this study, will be mentioned in the country chapters: the lack of macro stability shows up as an important factor in our studies. Global technological progress also affects the pace of domestic technology development in any country. Increased openness following liberalization means that competitiveness is ultimately judged by international criteria. Indigenous technological capabilities, however, are critical to absorbing knowledge, and have to be developed before the advantages of openness and increased competition, can be realised.

2.5.2.2 Human Capital, Finance and Institutional Support

The supply response of firms depends on three main factors (apart from physical infrastructure): the availability of appropriate human capital (skills), the availability of investment finance, and access to technical support and information.

The significance of human capital for technology development is evident. Basic skills such as literacy and numeracy appear to be essential for development, whether industrial or social. As industry moves into more sophisticated products, more specialized skills are needed.

Even seemingly simple industries (such as garments or footwear) require some specialized skills in order to be internationally competitive. The industrial success of the NIEs has been closely linked to their investment in human capital, especially in engineering and technical education.[38] Firms also 'create' specific human capital and skills themselves. These activities may create external benefits for other firms, and are therefore likely to be underprovided; the government can attempt to address these failures, as it has done in many of the NIEs.

The availability of investment finance for the development of capabilities is a critical factor especially as more sophisticated and specialized investments can no longer be financed internally, and is likely to be more so during structural adjustment when fiscal policies tend to be very tight. At higher levels of industrial development the provision of technology finance, especially but not exclusively for smaller enterprises, becomes an important area for policy intervention. All the NIEs have intervened heavily in financial markets to provide venture capital and other sources of technology finance, with Korea and Taiwan using such finance to guide the technological effort in particular directions that are considered essential for long-term industrial development.

Local informational support for technology development comes partly from other enterprises and partly from the science and technology (S&T) infrastructure. This varies with the stage of development. Early on, simple testing, standards and information services are the most important needs. Simply informing enterprises of the need to invest in technological capabilities may already be a critical function of S&T institutions. As firms enter export markets and develop more sophisticated products, standards become more demanding and the entire production process has to be set up to conform to the exacting levels demanded by importing countries.

2.6 METHODOLOGICAL ISSUES: THE TECHNOLOGY INDEX (TI)

The three country studies each use a technology index (TI), which was developed in order to evaluate and compare the technological activities that firms have undertaken and the technological capabilities they possess. In the Kenya and Tanzania studies, this summary index of technological capability was used in econometric analysis; in the Zimbabwe study, the index was used in non-parametric statistical analysis (rank correlation).

The idea of using such a composite index to evaluate a wide variety of firm-level processes and activities has been used by a number of authors and institutions concerned with technological capabilities in developing countries. Lall (1990) has developed a matrix of firm-level technological capabilities, and most studies use variants of such a matrix or list. Of particular interest are works by Westphal *et al.* (1990), SRI International (1992), Gonsen (1995), Romijn (1996), Deraniyagala (1995) and Wignaraja (forthcoming), all of which have developed indices that are suited to their particular studies. It is important to note that, in spite of slight methodological differences, the basic idea remains the same: to attempt a quantification, however tentative or cautious, of firm-level technological behaviour. These indices are then, as in the case of the present study, evaluated with reference to qualitative information from firm-level interviews. The TI is therefore a convenient shorthand summary rather than a comprehensive indicator, and represents an instrument to be deployed in quantitative and statis tical analysis. Such quantitative analysis, however, cannot entirely replace a more detailed case-study approach, which must, of necessity, rely heavily on verbal exposition.

The TI incorporates information on technology and technological activity, broadly defined to include investment in plant and equipment, process and product improvements, improvements or changes in areas such as maintenance or inventory control, as well as technological linkages. In short it includes quantitative as well as qualitative information that is thought to be necessary for assembling as comprehensive a picture as possible of technology and technological processes in our sample firms. Although there is a certain subjective aspect to evaluating technological capabilities (particularly when the information collected during interviews is of a very qualitative nature), the comparison *between* firms in any particular country study can still be undertaken consistently since most of the analysis is concerned with relative values. Throughout this study we have aimed at a high level of conformability and comparability of scores and indices, from the conceptual and methodological stage through to the country and cross-country evaluations.

In the Zimbabwe and Tanzania case studies, the sample firms were given scores of 0 or 1 depending on whether or not they had carried out a particular activity or possessed a particular capability (for example, whether or not they had implemented a quality control system, carried out a feasibility study prior to investment, had made improvements to existing products, or exploited informational and technological links with other firms or institutions). In the Kenya study, the firms were given scores of 0, 1 or 2 in order to distinguish further between those firms with a limited capability in a particular activity (1) and those with a more significant capability (2).

The factors included in the TI are broadly the same in the different country studies, whereby each team was data-constrained in country-specific ways that are reflected in the slight differences between the separate indices. Each country team attempted to incorporate as much firm-level information as possible into its TI. In the course of our work, though, we found that the different measures of the TI tended to give very similar results: 'capable' firms tend to have high scores in a wide range of different technological activities (the correlations between different measures of the TI are usually around 0.95). 'Technological capability' appears to be a systemic phenomenon affecting the entire firm rather than just constituent parts of it, at least in developing countries in which the overall level of technological capability is rather low. In sum, the country-specific differences in the TI are not likely to affect the overall evaluation in any significant way.

In Chapter 6, the country-study TIs are made more comparable by including only information that is common to all the separate studies, and by expressing all the separate factors entering the index in binary form only. The index used in Chapter 6 is therefore a 'lowest common denominator' TI, which to a certain extent abstracts from some of the more detailed information in the individual country studies. In this context it is important to emphasize that the individual country studies in Chapters 3, 4 and 5 are self-contained and are not merely preliminary to the cross-country analysis in Chapter 6. The micro-level analysis of technology and technological capabilities is the main focus of this study, since the activities of individual firms have often been ignored in studies of technological development and growth.

Notes

1. See Stiglitz (1994) for an excellent discussion and criticism of the Arrow–Debreu model underlying neoclassical reasoning. The extreme informational requirements of the Arrow–Debreu model are seen as particularly relevant to questions of technological change and innovation.
2. This is the so-called 'Greenwald–Stiglitz theorem' (Greenwald and Stiglitz, 1986). Stiglitz (1989) outlines the economic role of the state, and instruments of government coordination and intervention. For a more recent exposition see Stiglitz (1996a).

3. As Lerner (1953) puts it, 'The constructions ... apply to any kind of trade, between individuals, towns, regions, countries and continents as well as between social classes or between people at different points in time; and ... it is only historical accident of the development of economic theory that all these problems are called "international trade" (quoted in Dosi *et al.*, 1990, p. 24).
4. For an early model in which the world is divided into technological leaders and followers, see Krugman (1979). For an introduction to issues of technological change in international trade, see Krugman (1995).
5. The leader–follower dynamic in these models is analogous to what is described as a red queen effect in biological evolution: the leader has to run just in order to stay in (relatively) the same place.
6. However, as Helpman and Krugman (1985) pointed out, this division is arbitrary: if interindustry linkages existed and were strong, specialization could become more aggregative by spilling over and leading to the formation of industrial complexes (or clusters of industries) where activities supported each other. Such clustering adds a further element of arbitrariness in specialization.
7. The new political economy is best described as a 'public choice' or 'rational choice' approach to government, which employs an optimizing methodology and is therefore particularly suited to neoclassical purposes. It has a neoliberal (if not libertarian) bent, and draws inspiration from writers such as Hayek and Polanyi. Prominent theories in this tradition include rent-seeking and directly unproductive activities, and leading theorists include Krueger, Bhagwati and Bates. For an overview and debate, see Meier (1992). It has been labeled 'negative political economy' by its critics.
8. In this context it is important to point out that, as long as the model has been correctly and completely specified, the outcome can only be 'optimal' from the point of view of agents in the model. Constructing a model in which the government is able to perform certain coordinating functions to improve on economic outcomes will of necessity imply that the same model *without* a government is not likely to be 'optimal' any more. In the extreme, this position leads to an 'Austrian' outlook, in which the 'spontaneous order' emerging from complex interactions among individuals acquires a special sanctity: this conclusion is not based on the logic of modeling, but on implicit assumptions regarding individual economic and political liberty.
9. Evolutionary theory derives mainly from Nelson and Winter (1992). For a good exposition of the policy implications of evolutionary theory see Metcalfe (1995).
10. Dosi *et al.* (1990).
11. Krugman (1991); Rodrik (1996).
12. A neoclassical response to the Stiglitz model would be to point out that externalities could be internalized by private agents with much less government intervention than is required here, once a property rights framework has been established. Stiglitz deflects this criticism by asserting that many of the externalities involved are 'diffuse' or 'atmospheric' and are therefore much more likely to lead to coordination failures.
13. Cf. Krugman (1991).
14. Hodgson (1998).

15. See the chapters by Pack, Bliss, Bruton and Balassa in Chenery and Srinivasan (1991) and Bardhan and Rodrik in Behrman and Srinivasan (1995).
16. This is particularly true of World Bank publications such as Michaely *et al.* (1991), Thomas and Nash (1991a and b) and Havrylyshyn (1990).
17. For a structuralist critique of these assumptions, see Chenery *et al.* (1986).
18. The belief in an inevitable mechanism linking the liberalization of markets to greater efficiency, improved welfare and greater individual freedom has been aptly christened 'Hayek's wager' by Gray (1995).
19. See Taylor (1993).
20. However Helleiner (1992) and Rodrik (1992a) argue that the discussion is muddied by confounding trade policy *proper* (changing relative prices for long-term resource reallocation) with macroeconomic policies (which also affect relative prices in seeking to balance economic aggregates).
21. It is again important to note that rigorously this can only be an argument relating to *static* efficiency: [Relative-price] distortions affect *relative* profitability across industries and sectors. If learning in some sectors is adversely affected by intervention, others must be left better in shape. Consequently, even if changes in a sector's profitability could be presumed to have unambiguous consequences for innovative activity (which they do not), the *net* change in economy-wide innovation would still be unpredictable (Rodrik, 1995, pp. 2933–4).
22. Lucas (1988) explicitly criticizes neoclassical development economists such as Krueger, arguing that, under standard (Solow) neoclassical assumptions, static optimization (as resulting from trade liberalization) cannot explain sustained differences in growth between economies. In a conventional model with two factors of production and diminishing marginal returns to capital, there is a convergence of growth rates across economies. Those that have liberalized markets cannot then consistently enjoy higher growth than others – they only have a once-and-for-all rise in incomes. Lucas and other proponents of 'new' growth theory explain higher growth rates by introducing productive factors (skills and technology) that do not suffer from declining marginal returns. Since these factors also generate significant externalities, there is the possibility of market failures in resource allocation and a theoretical case for intervention. However endogenous growth theory treats skills and technology at an aggregate, abstract level, rather than as firm-specific factors that involve costly and uncertain decision making. Technical change continues to be viewed in neoclassical terms as 'major' innovation, rather than as a wide ranging of technical effort, including that involved in mastering existing knowledge. The policy needs that emerge from these models are therefore directed at remedying 'generic' market failures in skill and technology markets, not at particular activities or firms with specific technological processes and needs. Thus interventions have to be general ('functional') rather than selective.
23. For a representative sample see Bell *et al.* (1984); Bell and Pavitt (1993); Dahlman *et al.* (1987); Enos (1992); Katz (1987); Lall (1996, 1987, 1992b); Pack (1992).
24. Note that this effectively inserts a level of behavioural analysis between investment and performance: a distinction is made between *capacity* and *capability*.

25. Such aspects are referred to as 'emergent properties' of systems.
26. See Lall (1990) for a taxonomy of TCs that distinguishes between basic and advanced capabilities.
27. 'Industrial policy' is defined broadly here to include all interventions that promote the industrialization process, rather than narrowly to cover only selective interventions in capital markets and trade.
28. This response is represented by, among others, the World Bank in its *1991 World Development Report* and its 1993 study *The East Asian Miracle*.
29. For an overview of the peculiar role of information and knowledge in economics, see Stoneman (1983, 1995); Dasgupta and Stoneman (1987).
30. Stiglitz (1987).
31. The evidence adduced in World Bank (1993a) to show that selective interventions were ineffective was based on comparing total factor productivity growth estimates over time and between activities. These estimates do not address the relevant issues of specific market failures at all, and the econometric methods used are suspect. See Cappelen and Fagerberg (1995); Kwon (1994); Lall (1994); Rodrik (1994).
32. See Cappelen and Fagerberg (1995), *World Development*, April, 1994, and Fishlow *et al.* (1994).
33. There is also a wider question of whether the 'market failure' terminology is appropriate for analysing issues that go well beyond achieving a static optimum. Government interventions can go beyond correcting for existing market deficiencies to changing the parameters within which markets function, by creating new factor endowments, institutions and market structures. It is difficult to describe the latter set of interventions as remedying 'market failures' in the neoclassical sense, that is with reference to a competitive equilibrium. In principle, markets can clear *within* a given set of endowments and parameters, even if these occur at low levels of income and growth. The conventional market failure approach has little to say on changing those endowments and raising the economy beyond 'low level equilibrium'. Yet changing endowments and developing new market structures is what development policy is all about. Most governments seek to dynamise their economic growth, create new sources of comparative advantage, deepen the industrial structures and expand their base of technological capabilities. In addition they often aim to develop specific industries and enter into new groups of activities that are believed to be more conducive to growth, competitiveness and technological progress than others. Thus a distinction may be drawn between 'strategic' and 'tactical' interventions, with the former dealing with broad issues that the market failure approach does not address, and the latter with narrower issues that can be considered as remedying market deficiencies. For ease of exposition, this book uses 'market failure' to refer to both sorts of policies, but the distinction is an important one and needs further exploration.
34. For a more detailed analysis see Lall (1992b).
35. On the absorptive functions of R&D, see Cohen and Levinthal (1989).
36. See Katz (1984).
37. The classic exposition of evolutionary theory is Nelson and Winter (1982). This theory forms the analytical basis of much of the recent work on technology development in developing countries.
38. See Lall (1990, 1992b).

3 Adjustment, Technological Capabilities and Enterprise Dynamics in Kenya

Ganeshan Wignaraja and Gerrishon Ikiara[1]

3.1 INTRODUCTION

In the mid 1960s Kenya launched an import-substituting industrialization strategy, with high levels of protection for manufacturing and a large role for the public sector in industry. By the 1980s it had achieved a high level of industrialization by SubSaharan African standards – the share of manufacturing in GDP averaged 12.3 per cent in 1975–80 compared with about 10.0 per cent for the region as a whole. However, after an initial spurt, manufacturing growth began to slow down, from 11.6 per cent per year in 1970–75 to 4.9 per cent in 1975–80; the share of manufactured products in total exports stagnated at 16.0 per cent during 1975–80.

Most studies placed the blame for this slowdown on the inward-oriented trade strategy, which was blamed for distorted resource allocation, constricted foreign competition and restricted technology inflows from abroad.[2] By the late 1970s there was increasing recognition of the need for a change in strategy. Kenya introduced import liberalization measures in 1980–84 as part of a World Bank structural adjustment programme (SAP), one of the first countries in SubSaharan Africa to do so.[3] The new policies emphasized exports and the private sector, and sought to stimulate industrial competitiveness. The liberalization process was, however, halting and intermittent, at least until the most recent phase of opening up to import competition. This chapter examines the impact of the most recent liberalization on the acquisition of technological capabilities by Kenyan manufacturing enterprises, and the technological responses of different types of enterprises. The analysis is based on a survey of 41 manufacturing enterprises in the garments and engineering industries in early 1995. Divided evenly between the two industries, the sample covers some of Kenya's leading foreign and Asian enterprises as well as several African enterprises.

3.2 ECONOMIC BACKGROUND

3.2.1 Recent Industrial Performance

Kenya's *manufacturing growth rate* since the start of adjustment in 1980 – 4.1 per cent – has been relatively good by regional standards.[4] While lower than the rate in South Asia (6.3 per cent), it was higher than in SubSaharan Africa as a whole (0.9 per cent) and Latin America (0.8 per cent). The figure is, however, lower than the 4.9 per cent achieved by Kenya during 1975–80 and hides considerable variation between sub-periods: 4.2 per cent in 1980–85, 5.4 per cent in 1986–91 and 2.0 per cent in 1992–94. The slowdown since 1992 coincides with the period of most stringent liberalization (see below), but may also be traced to two factors not directly related to adjustment.[5] First, a severe drought caused water and electricity shortages, prompting energy-conservation measures in 1992 (a six-hour daily power cut for the manufacturing sector, later replaced by self-rationing whereby firms agreed to cut consumption by 30 per cent). Second, access to imports was constricted because of a suspension of foreign aid in 1991. Coupled with weak export growth, this reduced capacity utilization in manufacturing significantly, on one estimate from 65–70 per cent to 40–45 per cent over 1992–93 (World Bank, 1993a, p. 24). Nevertheless the liberalization itself may have been responsible for some of the slowdown, as the evidence below suggests.

Overall Kenyan manufacturing performance masks differences in the growth of individual industries. Take garments and engineering, the two sample industries considered in this study. Data from UNIDO suggest that the growth rate of the garment industry deteriorated significantly after the recent liberalization from −0.6 per cent to −3.3 per cent between 1980–90 and 1990–93 (estimated from UNIDO, *Industry and Development Global Report*, 1995). Engineering did worse than garments and went into decline after growing in the 1980s (from 2.1 per cent to −3.7 per cent between 1980–90 and 1990–93). The poor performance of garments is due to several factors, including power cuts and restricted access to imports, but as discussed below, a large part of the explanation lies in the impact of second-hand imports, which began in the 1980s and accelerated thereafter. The downturn in engineering is attributed to a decline in demand for engineering products due to a domestic recession in the 1990s as well as to power shortages and reduced access to imports.

Kenya underwent a modest degree of *structural transformation* during 1980–94. By 1994 the share of manufacturing in GDP had risen by one percentage point to 13.6 per cent, compared with 11.0 per cent for SubSaharan Africa as a whole.[6] Table 3.1 shows the structure of MVA in Kenya in 1980 and 1993, divided between light and heavy industry. The structure reflects an essentially early stage of industrialization: light industry accounted for 64 per cent of MVA in 1993,

Table 3.1 MVA structure in Kenya by light and heavy industry, 1980 and 1993 (% of total MVA)

	1980	*1993*
Light industry	60.6	64.0
311 Food products	23.4	26.3
313 Beverages	7.4	10.7
314 Tobacco products	2.5	1.6
321 Textiles	7.9	6.6
322 Wearing apparel	2.3	1.7
323 Leather and leather products	0.8	0.4
324 Footwear	1.2	0.9
331 Wood and wood products	2.7	1.7
332 Furniture and fixtures	1.2	1.0
341 Paper and paper products	4.5	4.7
342 Printing and publishing	2.9	3.3
355 Rubber products	3.3	4.5
361 Pottery, china and earthenware	0.1	0.1
362 Glass and glass products	0.4	0.5
Heavy industry	39.4	36.0
351 Industrial chemicals	3.3	2.0
352 Other chemicals	5.2	7.6
353 Petroleum refineries	2	0.7
354 Misc petroleum products	0	0.0
356 Plastic products	1.9	2.9
369 Other non-metallic minerals	2.6	5.1
371 Iron and steel	1.6	0.0
372 Non-ferrous metals	0	0.0
381 Metal products	7.3	6.3
382 Non-electrical machinery	0.8	0.6
383 Electrical machinery	5.3	5.1
384 Transport equipment	8.5	3.8
385 Professional and scien. equip.	0.1	0.2
390 Other manufacturing industries	0.8	1.6
Total MVA (%)	100	100
Total MVA ($US million)	755	806

Source: UNIDO (1995).

up from 61 per cent in 1980. It was dominated by food, beverages and tobacco, with a combined share of 39 per cent in 1993 (33 per cent in 1980), and by paper, printing and publishing, with a combined MVA share of 8 per cent (7 per cent). Textiles and garments, another important activity, experienced a fall in share from 10 per cent to 8 per cent. Heavy industry suffered a fall in its share in manufacturing over the period, from 39 per cent to 36 per cent, with the capital goods industries falling faster than other activities, from 19 per cent to 15 per cent. The engineering sector is underdeveloped and constitutes an important weakness in the industrial sector, resulting in a high dependence on imported components, equipment and technology.

Manufactured export growth has been disappointing since adjustment. It was respectable earlier, at 10.4 per cent per year during 1965–80 (compared with 5.5 per cent for SubSaharan Africa). However there was a marked reversal between 1980 and 1991, with a *decline* of 10 per cent a year,[7] from \$191.3 million to \$146.5 million (this is in current US dollars, so the decline was higher in constant terms). The structure of Kenyan exports also changed little during adjustment. Primary products (coffee, tea and other agricultural products) continued to dominate merchandise exports, as they have done for over a quarter of a century. In 1991, primary products and fuel re-exports accounted for 87 per cent of total exports, and manufactures for only 13 per cent (down from 14 per cent in 1980).

Table 3.2 shows Kenya's manufactured exports in 1980 and 1991 by 'low-skill' and 'high-skill' items. The skill classification, following a methodology used commonly in the empirical trade literature, is based on wages per employee in Kenyan industry.

Kenya's manufactured exports were evenly split between low- and high-skill products, though the former increased at the expense of the latter between 1980 and 1991. A handful of 'low skill' exports dominated the total. Leather items were the largest manufactured export, increasing from 6 per cent to 18 per cent of the total; this was closely followed by textiles, from 3 per cent to 11 per cent, and printed matter, from nil to 9 per cent. Three other items (garments, plastic and rubber manufactures) also experienced increases in share but, taken together, only accounted for 8 per cent of exports in 1991. The remaining low-skill items declined in share. Among the high-skill exports iron and steel products registered the largest increase in share, from 4 per cent to 14 per cent. Other activities that recorded increases were metal manufactures, medicines, perfumes and plastic materials. The equipment manufacturing industries (that is, machines for special industries, general

Table 3.2 Manufactured export structure in Kenya by low- and high-skill activities, 1980 and 1991

	Export value (US$ mn)		*% of manufactured exports*	
	1980	*1991*	*1980*	*1991*
Low skill	84.7	74.1	44.3	50.6
61 Leather, dressed fur etc.	12.3	25.9	6.4	17.7
62 Rubber manufactures	0	2.3	0.0	1.6
63 Wood, cork manufactures	4.2	0.0	2.2	0.0
64 Paper and paperboard	19.2	7.3	10.0	5.0
65 Textiles, yarn, fabrics etc.	6.3	15.4	3.3	10.5
66 Non-metallic minerals	32.9	0.0	17.2	0.0
84 Clothing and accessories	0.5	4.0	0.3	2.7
851 Furniture	4.6	0.0	2.4	0.0
892 Printed matter	0	13.2	0.0	9.0
893 Articles of plastic	4.7	6.0	2.5	4.1
High skill	106.6	72.4	55.7	49.4
52 Inorganic chemicals	3.5	2.4	1.8	1.6
53 Dyes, tanning etc.	8.1	0.0	4.2	0.0
54 Medicine, pharm. products	11.1	9.3	5.8	6.3
55 Perfume, cleaning products etc.	13.4	16.0	7.0	10.9
58 Plastic materials etc.	0	2.5	0.0	1.7
59 Chemical products etc.	10.4	4.4	5.4	3.0
67 Iron and steel	7.3	20.1	3.8	13.7
69 Metal manufactures	13.1	11.0	6.8	7.5
72 Machines for special industries	4.7	1.7	2.5	1.2
74 General industrial machinery	7.6	1.2	4.0	0.8
76 Telecommunications sound equip.	0	1.1	0.0	0.8
77 Electrical machinery	6.1	1.5	3.2	1.0
78 Road vehicles	21.3	1.2	11.1	0.8
Total	191.3	146.5	100	100

Source: UN (1983, 1995).

industrial machinery, telecommunications sound equipment, electrical machinery and road vehicles) experienced a decline in share, falling from 21 per cent to 3 per cent.

Two explanations have been put forward for this poor export performance since adjustment.[8] First, the break-up of the East African Community (EAC) and the virtual cessation of trade with

Tanzania. Access to EAC had been an engine for the expansion of Kenya's exports since independence, and in 1970 over two thirds of Kenya's exports went to Uganda and Tanzania (World Bank, 1987b, p. 31). However by the mid 1980s this had fallen to less than one third. The collapse of the EAC in 1977, coupled with a political disagreement with Tanzania that closed down bilateral trade for four years, triggered a sharp decrease in exports. By the 1990s, Kenya's exports had been unable to recover to their pre-1980 levels in the former EAC countries.

Second, inadequate trade liberalization and macro instability (N'geno, 1991; World Bank, 1993b; Mwega, 1995). Kenya's liberalization was not sustained and appropriate macroeconomic policies were not put in place. Insufficient exchange rate adjustments undermined import liberalization and inefficient fiscal adjustment prevented a substantial investment response. The net result was an anti-export bias in the trade regime that persisted well into the early 1990s.

While there is considerable validity in these explanations, they do not fully explain the weak export performance of the 1980s. A third explanation needs to be added, *viz.* competitive deficiencies arising from weak technological capabilities. This is discussed below.

3.2.2 Import Liberalization

Prior to the introduction of the SAPs, Kenya had a highly restricted import regime, with high tariffs and a cumbersome and discretionary licensing mechanism. Effective protection was high, leading to a strong anti-export bias. Import liberalization started in a modest way in mid 1980, when import bans were replaced by tariffs and two broad categories of imports were created to improve the classification system: Schedule I for unrestricted licensing items and Schedule II for quota-restricted ones.[9] There was a rise in the export compensation rate from 10 per cent to 20 per cent for a selected number of exports, and a simplification of the export compensation procedures. However, due to the failure to devalue the shilling and reduce the budget deficit, the balance of payments deteriorated and the import liberalization process could not be sustained. By the end of 1982 some import restrictions had been reinstated (World Bank, 1993, p. 37). A second episode of import liberalization took place in mid 1987, when more items were transferred from restricted to unrestricted schedules and tariffs were reduced. In addition, exporters were provided with duty-free access to imported inputs and export marketing support.

In both phases the implementation of liberalization was slow, halting and reluctant, leading donors to suspend aid to Kenya in late 1991. The Kenyan authorities accelerated the pace of reform, and in the third phase (1992–95) made substantial progress in trade and other economic reforms. All price and exchange rate controls were removed, import tariffs slashed, domestic trade liberalized, privatization embarked on, parastatal enterprises restructured, the civil service trimmed and political reforms launched. Donors responded by restoring aid in 1993–94.[10] Thus the third phase marked a break from the past as far as import liberalization was concerned.

Several indicators can be used to assess the progress of import liberalization:

- Coverage of quantitative restrictions on imports.
- Nominal tariffs.
- Effective rates of protection.
- Import to GDP ratios.

3.2.2.1 Coverage of Quantitative Restrictions (QRs) on Imports

Table 3.3 shows the evolution of QRs in Kenya since 1984. QRs declined between the mid 1980s and the early 1990s, with the coverage of items falling from 71 per cent in 1984–85 to 0.8 per cent in 1994–95. Restricted imports as a share of domestic production fell from 79 per cent to 10 per cent between 1988–90 and 1994–95. However import restrictions as a proportion of total import value rose slightly in the last two years.

Table 3.3 Coverage of QRs, 1984–95 (per cent)

Fiscal year	*Coverage of items*	*Import value*	*Domestic production*
1984–85	71.0	n.a	n.a
1986–87	32.2	4.8	79.0
1988–89	23.5	5.1	47.0
1990–91	15.4	3.5	0.0
1991–92	0.2	0.0	0.0
1993–94	0.1	3.0	5.0
1994–95	0.8	5.1	10.0

Sources: UNDP/World Bank (1993); information since 1993 from Ministry of Finance, Nairobi.

Table 3.4 Import tariffs in Kenya, 1987–96

Fiscal year	*Number of tariff bands*	*Highest tariff rate (%)*	*Unweighted average tariff**
1987/88	24	170	39.9
1988/89	16	135	41.3
1989/90	11	135	46.3
1990/91	15	100	44.3
1991/92	12	70	37.9
1992/93	10	60	35.5
1993/94	8	50	31.7
1994/95	7	45	26.4
1995/96	6	40	20.9

* *Ad valorem* tariff including duty-free tariff.
Source: Ryan (forthcoming).

3.2.2.2 *Nominal Tariffs*

Table 3.4 provides information on the number of tariff bands, the highest tariff rate and the unweighted average between 1987–88 and 1995–96. It also shows a fall in protection. The unweighted average tariff, which rose slightly from 39.9 per cent to 46.3 per cent between 1987–88 and 1989–90, fell sharply thereafter to reach 20.9 per cent in 1995–96. There was also a reduction in the dispersion of tariffs. The number of tariff bands declined from 24 to 12 between 1987–88 and 1991–92 and to 6 in 1995–96. The latest six-band system had the following tranches: 0 per cent, 5 per cent, 10 per cent, 15 per cent, 25 per cent and 40 per cent. Of the 5742 CCCN items in 1995–96, only 23.6 per cent were in the 40 per cent tariff category and another 11.7 per cent were in the 25 per cent tariff category. The highest tariff also fell from 170 per cent to 70 per cent between 1987–88 and 1991–92 and to 40 per cent in 1995–96. While no data are available for manufacturing alone in 1987–88, unweighted average tariffs declined substantially from 41.2 per cent to 26.4 per cent for this sector between 1990 and 1994.[11]

3.2.2.3 *Effective Rates of Protection*

The change in the trade regime appears less marked in terms of effective rates of protection (ERP). Estimates of the ERPs differ: according to Sharpley and Lewis (1990) they rose from 38 per cent to 51 per cent during 1968–85, while according to Keyfitz and Wanjala (1991) they rose from 66 per cent to 164 per cent during 1976–85. Table 3.5 shows the World Bank's ERP estimates for 1985, 1990 and 1992. These suggest that the average ERP for manufacturing in 1985 was very high (107 per cent), but it had declined to 48 per cent by 1990 and 45 per cent by 1992. Thus trade liberalization started to 'bite' only in the 1990s.

In 1985 several sectors had very high rates to protection – metal products (312 per cent), non-metallic minerals (248 per cent), chemicals (21 per cent), textiles and garments (126 per cent) and food preparations (111 per cent). Between 1985 and 1990, the ERP fell in food preparations, textiles and garments, leather and footwear, chemicals, non-metallic minerals and metal products. Nevertheless protection remained high in most cases.

The liberalization process started to slow down as the Kenyan authorities responded to pressure from industrial lobbies in 1990–92. Take the case of garments and engineering. Between 1990 and 1992 there was an increase in the ERP for garments from 77 per cent to 100 per cent, while the ERP for textile raw materials fell from 41 per cent to 36 per cent and that for finished textiles from 60 per cent to 58 per cent. The ERP

Table 3.5 Effective rates of protection in Kenyan manufacturing, 1985, 1990 and 1992

	1985	*1990*	*1992*
Food preparations	111	51.0	44.1
Beverages	38	40.9	36.8
Textiles and garments:	126	59.6*	64.4*
Textile raw materials	n.a.	41.1	35.9
Finished textiles	n.a.	60.0	57.5
Garments	n.a.	77.1	99.7
Leather and footwear	80	43.0	40.5
Paper and wood products	6	47.3*	42.1*
Chemicals:	211	45.2*	40.6*
Rubber products	n.a.	47.1	45.2
Paints and detergents	n.a.	43.7	37.5
Other chemicals	n.a.	44.8	39.3
Non-metallic minerals	248	36.5	30.9
Metal products	312	46.9	40.4
Mean	107	47.9	44.5

*Simple average of sub-sector within broad category.
Sources: World Bank (1987b); UNDP/World Bank (1993).

for metal products also declined, from 47 per cent to 40 per cent. Though there are no ERP estimates after 1992, the evidence suggests that the metal products sector had an increase in protection during 1993–95 as a result of rises in import duties on rails, wire made from iron and non-alloy steel, while the tariffs on the textiles and garments sector were reduced.[12] Therefore import liberalization continued slowly and erratically in engineering and more rapidly in textiles and garments. Despite its uneven incidence, in general there has been marked liberalization of imports after 1992.

3.2.2.4 Import to GDP Ratios

Import to GDP ratios reflect both import liberalization and the availability of foreign exchange. Table 3.6 shows Kenya's non-fuel imports for 1980 and 1994. The ratio of non-fuel imports to GDP nearly doubled in this period, suggesting that the economy had become more 'open'. The shares of consumer goods and intermediates increased slightly, while that of capital goods fell, indicating a greater reliance on finished product imports and greater use of existing capacity than additions to new capacity.

In sum, we can identify three shortcomings in liberalization policies since 1980.

First, *speed and intensity of reform*. Kenya reformed gradually and rather hesitantly. Though quantitative restrictions have now been replaced by tariffs, with greater transparency in the trade regime and a reduction in protection, at the time of the study overall protection for the manufacturing sector remained high and variable. In the first two phases the implementation of liberalization measures was slow and

Table 3.6 Non-fuel imports into Kenya (percentage shares)

	1980	*1994*
Consumer goods	32.3	34.7
Intermediate goods	39.3	46.9
Capital goods	28.1	18.4
Total	100.0	100.0
Imports to GDP ratio (per cent)	15.4	30.0

Source: Central Bureau of Statistics, *Economic Survey*, various.

intermittent, with weak commitment on the part of policy makers. In addition, rent-seeking behaviour was pervasive. In the third phase the implementation of liberalization measures was better because of pressure from aid donors. In all three phases there was no coherent strategy of liberalization linked to increasing the efficiency of the manufacturing sector. Prolonged protection was maintained for many activities without a clear rationale, and its reduction also lacked a rationale. There was no preannounced timetable for reducing protection linked to the adjustment needs to the activities concerned. Levels of protection were arbitrarily adjusted, with some activities witnessing increases and others sharp reductions. Kenyan firms were not supported in their restructuring efforts, and insufficient attention was paid to supply-side measures (that is, finance, skills, information and technology institutions) to support upgrading. In spite of the liberalization undertaken in the third phase, the future pace and nature of trade reform still remains unclear, making long-term planning by industry difficult.

Second, *credibility and sustainability of reform*. Credibility has an important influence on the sustainability of trade reform: when liberalization is viewed as lacking credibility, enterprises tend to concentrate on non-tradables and imports and put off long-term investments in upgrading their own competitiveness or cultivating export markets. Kenya has suffered from this. Reinikka (1993) concludes that neither the 1980 nor the 1987 phase was credible and consequently ended in reversals. In his study of the post-1992 episode, Mwega (1995) finds that this is also unlikely to be credible, given the government's poor record on import liberalization. However he argues that, unlike previous phases, the current phase may be sustained because of pressures from aid donors and a recovery in coffee prices.

Third, *export push*. In view of the gradual approach to import liberalization, a strong set of export incentives was required to offset the inward bias in the regime.[13] However Kenya's export promotion was extremely weak during the period of adjustment. A recent study listed the following findings on export schemes (UNDP/World Bank, 1993):

- The two schemes that provided exporters with duty-free access to imported inputs – the export compensation scheme (ECS) and the manufacturing-under-bond scheme (MUB) – suffered from drawbacks. The ECS was hindered by long delays and only a handful of exporters were covered by it. The study noted that 'the scheme applied a flat 20 per cent rebate rate, which meant that producers were either under- or over-compensated since tariffs on intermediate and raw material imports ranged from 0 to 80 per cent. The scheme used a positive list to define eligibility (currently 1250 items), which implied that access to duty-free imports was not available for all potential exports' (UNDP/World Bank, 1993, p. 48).[14] The MUB scheme was found to be equally flawed. Among other things it had high operating costs (in terms of license fees, bonding costs and customs costs) and prohibited the domestic sale of rejects.

- Several commercial and state banks provided exporters with working capital loans, but there were long delays in accessing these loans and large firms had preferential access.
- The Kenya External Trade Authority (KETA), which was responsible for export marketing, provided weak support. It suffered from a bureaucratic orientation and a shortage of financial resources. It lacked a well-developed export tracking system, rarely organised the participation of local firms in overseas trade fairs and did little to encourage the entry of foreign buyers.

3.2.3 Foreign Direct Investment

Reforms to Kenya's foreign investment policies since adjustment resemble the import liberalization programme in speed and intensity. In the mid 1980s Kenya's policy environment was distinctly unfavourable to foreign direct investment (FDI). The World Bank's 1986 report described the FDI policies as follows:

> The Government's attitude has been ambivalent, desiring the inflow of funds and associated skills and entrepreneurship, but at the same time, wanting Kenyanization by participation in ownership and management. At the moment there are five major impediments to new inflows of direct foreign investment. First, repatriation of the initial capital is limited to the original Kenya shilling equivalent of the foreign investment, regardless of intervening inflation and exchange rate movements; any capital gain may be repatriated only after a five-year waiting period during which it must be placed in a blocked capital account earning a low interest rate. Second, dividends may be repatriated up to an amount equal to 10 per cent per annum of the original investment, though this limit has been applied with flexibility. Third, there are restrictions, graduated by extent of foreign ownership, on the amount of domestic borrowing, thereby limiting expansion. Fourth, majority foreign owned firms are subject to a higher rate to income tax at (52.5 per cent) than domestic firms

(45 per cent). Fifth, permission to employ expatriate personnel has become increasing difficult to obtain (World Bank, 1986, para 3–34).

The government attempted to improve the FDI regime in the 1990s. The 1990–91 budget lowered the corporate tax rate from 42.5 per cent to 40.0 per cent. An export processing zone (EPZ) was established in 1990, offering 10-year tax holidays for export activity, a 10-year exemption from withholding tax on dividends for non-resident investors, VAT exemption, duty free access to inputs, the right to establish foreign currency bank accounts and work permits fir expatriate employees. An Investment Promotion Centre (IPC) was established in the late 1980s to provide a one-stop facility for foreign investors. Foreign investments were guaranteed against nationalization and all after-tax profits were repatriable under the Foreign Investment Protection Act.

FDI inflows have been modest (Table 3.7), and Kenya has not realized its potential as a host for FDI.[15] Inflows more than doubled between 1981–85 and 1986–90, but declined sharply thereafter. In 1991–94 they accounted for less than 1 per cent of domestic investment, a low figure even by SubSaharan African standards.[16] The bulk of FDI (95 per cent) went into manufacturing and services. As far as export-oriented FDI is concerned, EPZs were only a modest success. By the end of 1994, 18 enterprises had begun production in the three functioning EPZs, with total employment of 3000 and exports of US$10 million.[17] EPZ firms spanned a number of industrial sectors, including garments, textiles, food processing, printing and light engineering.

The increase in FDI inflows between 1981–85 and 1986–90 is traceable to preferential treatment of Kenyan exports in EU, US and Japanese markets (because of its membership of the ACP Lomé Convention and the Generalized System of Preferences); a relatively large domestic manufacturing base; an early commitment to a SAP that promised increased foreign aid and an upturn in economic growth; well-developed physical infrastructure by African standards; and political stability. However

Table 3.7 FDI inflows

	1981–85	*1986–90*	*1991–94*
FDI inflows ($US million)	15.9	39.0	9.0
FDI as % of gross domestic investment	1.1	2.4	0.7

Source: UNCTAD (1995).

these factors were eroded after 1990 by high relative wage costs, deteriorating growth prospects, the persistence of an unfavourable policy environment for FDI, weaknesses in supply-side factors and growing political uncertainty.

Kenyan wages are quite high compared with locations in Asia: monthly wages in garment manufacture are around US$67 in Kenya, US$60 in Sri Lanka and US$28–50 in India.[18] Wages in Bangladesh, Indonesia and China are likely to lie between the Sri Lankan and Indian levels.

On the policy environment for FDI, a 1991 report highlights some current deterrents to foreign investors:

> the encouragement of Kenyan participation, the need for case-by-case screening of licensing agreements with royalties/fees of over 5 per cent of sales, the persistence of delays on remittances of dividends and capital repatriation; discrimination in access to local finance; restrictions on expatriate employment. There is still considerable scope for ad hoc decision making, e.g. on tariff protection, license screening, employment, which could lead to corruption, delays and discrimination (Lall, 1991, p. 98).

Weaknesses in supply-side factors, such a deficiencies in skills (especially technical manpower), infrastructure, supplier support and institutions also deter foreign investors. Some of these will be taken up below.

Finally, there is increased political uncertainty. In the 1990s, in response to donor pressure Kenya has embarked on a process of transforming its political regime from a single to a multiparty system, although it is unclear whether the present government will continue in power. In addition ethnic peace has been shattered by violent tribal clashes in the Rift Valley Province. In combination these factors have increased Kenya's political risk rating with international credit agencies.[19]

3.2.4 Technology Infrastructure

By African standards, Kenya has a large technology infrastructure. Four sets of institutions provide technology support to the manufacturing sector: the Kenya Bureau of Standards, the Kenya Industrial Research and Development Institute, the Kenya Textile Training Institute and the universities.[20]

The Kenya Bureau of Standards (*KBS*) was set up in 1974 to establish quality standards and upgrade process quality in manufacturing. It provides a variety of service, including guidance on quality control systems, training programmes in standards and quality control, seminars on standardization and quality control, machine calibration, and laboratory facilities for testing raw materials. The KBS has the capacity to calibrate instruments to international norms and perform laboratory tests on a wide range of products and raw materials. By the end of the 1980s the KBS had established standards for about 450 products. However the KBS facilities are not effectively utilized: only a small proportion of Kenyan firms demand its services or interact with it in other ways. Two factors may account for this. First, the average enterprise (particularly in the SME sector) is not sufficiently aware of the importance of product quality for domestic and international competitiveness. For instance in the mid 1980s about 90 per cent of Kenyan enterprises had not established their own minimum standards (*Business Age*, December 1984, p. 19). Second, The KBS has an inflexible bureaucratic approach to service provision. Firms that have tried to use KBS services complain of long delays.

In the last few years the KBS has been encouraging Kenyan firms to adopt ISO 9000 quality standards as a way of making their products attractive to European buyers. The response has been encouraging, with an estimated 30 firms having begun the process of implementing ISO 9000, and 10 having obtained certification by mid-1995.

The Kenya Industrial Research and Development Institute (KIRDI) was established in 1979 to identify and develop appropriate process and product technologies; facilitate technology transfer through design and development of equipment, instruments and processes; develop waste treatment methods; establish pilot plants to demonstrate technologies developed by the institute; provide consultancy services to Kenyan manufacturers; and generally develop local technological capabilities.[21] KIRDI's activities are organized into four divisions: (1) the analytical testing division for both public and private sector enterprises; (2) the design and engineering division, which develops indigenous designs for products and machinery, provides advisory services on improvement to industrial machinery, and undertakes laboratory studies to develop products based on local raw materials; (3) the process and product development division, which improves existing processes and products through laboratory experiments; and (4) the project studies and development division, which undertakes market research and feasibility studies for enterprises.

The institute has six laboratories specializing in food technology, construction, engineering and metals, leather, ceramics and analytical chemistry, and by the late 1980s it employed 30 professionals. KIRDI's research gave priority to agro-industries, engineering and metals, chemicals, building materials and energy. However the bulk of its resources was allocated to construction materials, which accounted for almost 69 per cent of its research budget in the 1984–88 programme. This was followed by metals and engineering, with a share of 13.6 per cent of the research budget.[22]

The government established *the Kenya Textile Training Institute (KTTI)* in 1987 to help textile and garment enterprises that were providing inadequate training because of its cost and the extensive poaching of trained workers. However it suffers weaknesses in terms of equipment and trained staff, and its outdated equipment is not suited to training in modern technologies. In addition to the state-owned KTTI, which is based in Nairobi, there is a private sector textile institute in Eldoret (300 kilometres from Nairobi). Raymond's Textile Training Institute (RTTI), which is owned by the country's largest privately owned (foreign) integrated textile firm, trains its own staff as well as applicants from elsewhere, who are free to join other firms after graduation.

Kenyan *universities and colleges* are largely oriented towards general art and science, with technical and engineering enrolments constituting a small part of the total. The three premier institutions for technical manpower are the Kenya Polytechnic and the departments of engineering at the University of Nairobi and the Jomo Kenyatta University of Agriculture and Technology (JKUAT). Both universities produce a small number of engineering graduates. The University of Nairobi's total number of graduates in engineering increased from 154 in 1980 to 237 in 1994, while that of the JKUAT rose from 128 in 1990 to 144 in 1994. Before 1990 the JKUAT was producing diploma holders. For middle-level technical manpower the Kenya Polytechnic is dominant, producing diploma holders in the mechanical, electrical, automobile, aeronautical, telecommunication, building and civil engineering fields: between 1980 and 1994 the annual number of graduates rose from 748 to 1640. Apart from training, most of these technical institutes hardly provide any research or technical services to industry.

3.3 SAMPLE CHARACTERISTICS AND PERFORMANCE

3.3.1 Background

Table 3.8 shows the distribution of the sample.[23] The garment firms are characterized by a fairly homogeneous set of production technologies.

Table 3.8 Sample characteristics

	All firms	*Garments*	*Engineering*
No. of firms	41	20	21
Size (% distribution)			
Small	36.6	40.4	33.3
Medium	26.7	15.0	38.1
Large	36.6	45.0	28.6
Ownership (% distribution)			
Foreign	12.2	5.0	19.0
LNA	48.8	50.0	42.9
LA	39.0	45.0	38.1
Age (% distribution)			
Below 15 years	65.9	55.0	71.4
Over 16 years	34.1	45.0	28.6

The majority (17) are in the assembly stage, using manual sewing machines. There has been little expansion into the more skill-intensive design stage of garment manufacturing.

The engineering firms are heterogeneous, covering activities with different degrees of technological complexity, including fabricated metal products (eight firms), heavy structural steel items (two firms), non-electrical machinery (five firms) and electrical items (six firms). There is essentially a dualistic production structure. One group of firms, consisting of large foreign-owned and large local firms, are part of the formal engineering industry, and are largely involved in the final assembly of imported parts and components. The other group, consisting of small-scale enterprises, are in the informal part of the industry and make a range of simple items including agricultural equipment, grills, gates, hand tools and buckets. With one or two exceptions, their process technologies involve traditional metal-working skills and know-how, with low capital and scale intensity. None of the leading firms have moved into full automation or use advanced, numerically controlled machine tools.

Of the 41 firms in the sample 15 are small (36.6 per cent), 11 medium (26.7 per cent) and 15 large (36.6 per cent). Most of the large firms are foreign or local non-African owned.[24] The size distribution of firms in our sample is similar to that of the World Bank's recent Regional Program on Enterprise Development (RPED) survey, which was based on a larger sample, and is probably fairly representative of the country's industrial structure.[25]

As for ownership, a distinction is made within private firms between local African (LA) ownership, local-non African (LNA) ownership (of Indian or European origin) and foreign ownership. Five of the firms have some proportion of foreign equity, twenty firms some proportion of LNA equity, and sixteen are wholly local African owned.[26] Four of the foreign-owned firms are in engineering and one is in garments. The sample includes four of the largest foreign affiliates in the country (Eveready, Philips and Holman Brothers in engineering and Sunflag Textiles in garments), four of largest African-owned enterprises (Eva Modell and Kega Fashions in garments and Naciti Engineering and Beta Engineering in engineering), several large Asian firms (including Bedi, Alpha Knits and Loundra in garments) and a host of Asian and African SMEs.

Nearly two thirds of the sample firms existed before the initial liberalization of 1980. The bulk of the foreign and LNA firms falls into the preliberalization category. Most of the firms set up after import liberalization are of local African origin, probably due to the entry of civil servants who were retired after 1978 and by similar retrenchment in the private sector in this period.

3.3.2 Market Performance

How has the performance of the sample firms been affected by liberalization? Since it proved difficult to acquire performance information for the early 1980s, we shall focus on the latest episode, 1989–94. Table 3.9 provides the five measures of performance that could be calculated: (1) sales growth rates, (2) capacity utilization rates, (3) percentage of firms with high profitability in 1994 than in 1984, (4) number of exporters, and (5) export ratios for exporters in 1994.

Both industries have contracted since 1989. Overall growth rates (measured in current US dollars) are positive in garments, but only 30 per cent of the garment firms have actually expanded sales. If the largest garment firm is excluded, the industry has contracted by 1.0 per cent per annum. Foreign and LNA firms have grown faster (2.5 per cent) than African ones (−7.0 per cent). The average capacity utilization rate has fallen sharply, in garments from 80 per cent to 48 per cent and in engineering from 63 per cent to 52 per cent. Only 10 per cent of garment and 48 per cent of engineering firms had higher profits in 1994 than 1984.

Export activity has responded favourably to the new incentive environment. The number of exporters increased from five in 1989 to 13

Table 3.9 Performance of sample firms

	Garments	*Engineering*
1 Sales growth		
Av. Annual growth rate 1989–94 (%)[1]	1.9[2]	−3.2
% of firms with positive sales growth, 1989–94	30	42.9
2 Capacity utilisation rate		
Average 1989 (%)	80.0	63.0
Average 1994 (%)	48.0	52.0
% of firms with higher profits in 1994 than in 1984	10.0	48.0
3 Exports		
No. of exporters in 1989	2	5
No. of exporters in 1994	4	9
Av. export share in 1994, exporters only (%)	63.9	9.7
Main market	Africa	Africa

Notes:
[1] Current US dollar.
[2] Excluding the largest firm, this becomes −1.0% per cent per annum.

in 1994. In the latter year, nine of the exporters were engineering firms, and only four were in garments; however the garment exporting firms tended to be larger than those in engineering. The average value (per exporting firm) of garment exports was US$2.0 million compared with US$0.3 million for engineering. The average export ratio for exporting firms reflects this: 69.3 per cent for garments and 9.7 per cent for engineering; the average export ratios including the non-exporting firms were 24.1 per cent for garments and 6.6 per cent for engineering. All the garment and engineering exporters are either Asian or foreign-owned: none of the African firms had managed the transition from domestic market-oriented to export production in this period.

Over half of the exports from the sample firms were destined for the regional African market. In the case of garments, a high proportion of the export business with African markets seems to have been aided by strong relationships between Asian business families and other ties. In the case of engineering, intra-African trade reflects the transport cost for heavy items such as structural steel products, Land Rover bodies, metal signs and agricultural machinery.

3.3.3 Import Competition

The evolution of protection in garments and engineering reflects the generally haphazard pattern of liberalization. In garments there was a reduction in protection between 1985 and 1990, an increase between 1990 and 1992 and then a sharp reduction after 1992. In engineering there was a reduction between 1985 and 1990, a further reduction between 1990 and 1992 and an increase between 1992 and 1995. Thus garments appear to have become more 'open' than engineering by 1995.

It is useful to report entrepreneurs' perceptions of their competitive environment. The sample firms were asked to rank their perception of the competition faced from imports in 1984, 1989 and 1994 on a scale of one to five.[27] The individual firms' scores were normalized on a scale of zero to one, with increasing competition indicated by scores closer to one. The results are shown in Table 3.10.

The macroeconomic information on protection in the first two phases of liberalization is confirmed by the firm-level data. Both industries reported limited import competition in 1984 and a modest increase by 1989. Between 1989 and 1994 there was a sharp increase in import competition in both industries, with the degree of exposure being higher in garments than in engineering.

The haphazard nature of liberalization is illustrated by the authorities' ambivalent attitude towards illegal second-hand ('*mitumba*') garment imports. Second-hand garments, largely outerwear, consist of end-of-runs, factory rejects and used clothing. Before 1989 there was a trickle of *mitumba* into the country, but these flows increased

Table 3.10 Entrepreneur's perception of the degree of import competition faced since 1984*

	1984	*1989*	*1994*
Garments	0.21	0.25	0.95
Engineering	0.20	0.27	0.39

* The entrepreneurs' scores are normalized along a scale of 0 to 1, in which competition ranked close to 0 is least intensive and that ranked close to 1 is most intensive. The figures are averages for all firms.

markedly in the 1990s. Local firms believe that they come from two sources. In the main, the end-of-runs and factory rejects come from South-East Asia (particularly China), while used garments originate from charities in Europe and the United States. It is also possible, however, that *mitumba* include 'normal' garment imports from Asia that are evading the full rate of import duty. The bulk of the second-hand clothes found in Nairobi markets lack labels and other details of origin, so it is difficult to verify this.

Mitumba have had a significant impact on local industry. They are sold at much lower prices than garments made by local firms. Table 3.11 compares the retail prices of four common types of garment in 1995 (obtained from the interviews with garment firms). On average, the prices of *mitumba* garments were 37 per cent of the prices of local garments. Local firms suggest that importers of second-hand garments either evade duty altogether or pay low duty by undervaluing the landed cost.[28] They also argue that, unlike local garments, *mitumba* garments are not subject to KBS inspection and therefore could be sub-standard.

Thus local garment firms face intense, often destructive competition from second-hand imports. Of the 20 garment firms in the sample, 16 said that they had been negatively affected by recent imports of second-hand garments. One was on the verge of closing down in early 1995, and another six said that they would be forced to close down by the end of 1995 if nothing was done to stop such imports. While both Asian and African garment firms were negatively affected by second-hand imports, the latter, being smaller and specializing in low-quality garments, seemed less able to cope.

Even though garment firms have presented their case to the government through business associations (notably the Kenyan Association of

Table 3.11 Prices of local garments and second-hand imports, 1995

	T-shirt	*Men's trousers*	*Ladies' dress*	*Boys' suit*	*Average*
Local retail (US$)[1]	2.90	10.04	17.86	4.02	8.71
Second-hand imports[2] (local retail = 100)	38	67	19	22	37

Notes:
[1] Local retail price refers to the price at which local firms' products are sold to consumers.
[2] Second-hand imports are end-of-runs, factory rejects and used clothing.

Manufacturers and the Federation of Kenyan Employers), there has been no official investigation, nor has any action been taken to curtail these imports. The government has adopted a passive wait-and-see attitude because of the benefits that cheap clothing brings to consumers and the political influence of *mitumba* importers. The danger is that this policy may put the import liberalization programme at risk by affecting its credibility.

The strategies adopted in response to import competition can be grouped into two types:

- *Offensive*, where enterprises respond 'head on' to import competition by undertaking one or all of the following: moving into exports, upgrading product quality, introducing new products, buying new technology or seeking out a foreign partner.
- *Defensive*, where enterprises 'retreat' in the face of import competition by shifting into non-tradable activities, cutting costs by reducing wages or employment, or lobbying for protection.

In garments, four firms (20 per cent) had adopted an offensive strategy. As import competition intensified in the late 1980s, these domestic market-oriented firms began diversifying into exports. Two firms (Alpha and Bedi) sought out foreign buyers from the US/UK, bought new technology and upgraded their products; foreign buyers assisted by transferring technology and sending their technicians to train workers. The other two were less international; they bought new equipment through relatives in the UK and started to export Uganda and Tanzania. The remaining 16 garment firms responded defensively. A common strategy was initially to cut costs by firing employees – the 16 firms shed an average of 10 per cent of their workers during 1989–94. In general, however, this proved insufficient to counter import competition, particularly from *mitumba* imports. A secondary strategy entailed one of the following: a shift into a niche garment market (such as the production of school uniforms), a move into a non-tradable sector (such as construction), opening a shop to sell *mitumba* clothes, or a passive 'do-nothing' approach.

The engineering sample exhibited a different response pattern, in part reflecting their more gradual exposure to import competition. Most engineering firms were sheltered from direct import competition by the nature of their product and had little need to respond.[29] Of the 14 firms that had some exposure to import competition, seven responded offensively by introducing new products, increasing exports to the regional market, improving their domestic after-sales services and buying new equipment and technology. Interestingly, none of the firms was able to tie up with a new foreign partner, although two or three tried. The remaining seven engineering firms adopted a largely defensive posture and either sacked workers or moved into non-tradable sectors.

3.4 ASSESSMENT OF TECHNOLOGICAL CAPABILITIES UNDER LIBERALIZATION

This section attempts to 'map out' the technological capabilities (TCs) of the sample firms. To the greatest extent possible, it attempts to indicate both the current level of technological capabilities and the change during the latest phase of import liberalization. The breakdown of technological capabilities falls under three main headings: process technology, product technology and linkages with firms and institutions.[30] The discussion begins with a brief review of the 'initial conditions' for industrial technological development firms in terms of TCs, characteristics of plants, technology and skills.

3.4.1 Past TCs, Characteristics of Plants, Technology and Skills

3.4.1.1 Past TCs, Characteristics of Plants and Technology

Little systematic information is available on the nature of TCs in Kenya during the import substitution period. Interviews suggest that import substitution had resulted in a typical pattern of significant but distorted learning.[31] High and indiscriminate import protection induced the acquisition of industrial capabilities for home market production, including those to substitute local raw materials for imports, to stretch and maintain equipment and to introduce simple new products. Production technologies became obsolete over time as most forms of imported technology were restricted by foreign exchange controls. Enterprises did not generally develop the competitive capability to penetrate international markets. Among other things, there was little emphasis on cost reduction, productivity improvement, quality control, inventory control and layout changes. Industrial engineering as a distinct function was absent. Design capabilities were inadequate. These weaknesses contributed to poor industrial performance during the import substitution period. After an initial spurt, enterprise growth slowed down and exports were sluggish.

Table 3.12 shows the average age of equipment in 1995, the proportion of firms that set up with used equipment, the average replacement value of equipment, the average number of investments since

Table 3.12 Plant and equipment

Industry	*Average age of equipment in 1995 (years)*	*% of firms that began with used equipment*	*Average replacement value of equipment per employee (US$)*	*Average no. of investments since 1984 per firm**	*No. of firms investing more than US$100 000 (more than US$1 million)*
Garments	13	55.0	4183	4.7	6 (1)
Engineering	15	47.6	12 955	3.6	5 (3)

*Major investments are defined as those above US$500.

1984, the number of firms investing more than US$100 000 and the number investing more than US$1 million.

The equipment in both sectors is fairly old, the average age being 13 years in garments and 15 in engineering. While both industries contain firms with fairly new as well as old equipment, the engineering sector has a higher proportion of firms with old equipment. There is a high propensity to set up with used equipment: 55 per cent of garment and 48 per cent of engineering firms.

As expected, engineering firms are more capital-intensive than garment firms. The average value of equipment per employee in the former is US$13 thousand compared with US$4.2 thousand in the latter. This value rises with firm size, and is over 10 times higher in very large firms than in small ones. In garments, the average value for the large firms is US$8310 and for small firms US$480. In engineering, these figures are US$14 680 and US$1361 respectively.

The average number of investments by garment firms since 1984 (4.7) is slightly higher than those by engineering firms (3.6). Nevertheless there have been relatively few large investments: only 11 firms invested more than US$100 000 each and only four firms invested more than US$1 million. Most new investments were small replacement purchases.

Formal imports of technology are very low. Table 3.13 shows foreign licences, technical assistance contracts and foreign consultants. There were only three foreign licences in force in 1995, all in engineering; two were held by one foreign affiliate. Technical assistance was similarly low. The use of foreign consultants was more widespread. One garment and four engineering firms employed foreign consultants in 1994. Of these, three were foreign affiliates and two were local firms. The garment firm spent 0.11 per cent of its sales on this while the average

Table 3.13 Contractual technology imports, 1995

Industry	*No. of licences*[1] *(1995)*	*No. of technical assistance contracts*[2] *(1994)*	*No. of technical consultants*[3] *(1994)*
Garments	0	0	1
Engineering	3	3	4

Notes:
[1] The engineering firms have had two licences in the last decade.
[2] Three engineering firms spent 6.0 per cent, 1.6 per cent and 10 per cent of sales on TACs, respectively.
[3] The expenditure on technical consultants by the single garment firms was 0.11 per cent of sales while the average for four engineering firms was 0.31 per cent.

for the engineering firms was 0.3 per cent. The local firms began to employ consultants after import liberalization, but the foreign affiliates had engaged consultants in the preliberalization period.

There thus seems to be some impact of import liberalization in terms of increasing technology contracts, but in general the data suggest low capabilities and a relatively passive approach to technological upgrading. This stands in sharp contrast to enterprises in Asian industrializing economies, where in the same period there was a very rapid increase in formal technology imports, along with large purchases of new equipment.

3.4.1.2 Skills

A crucial factor in technological development is the stock of trained employees and additions to this stock by training, both in-house and externally. Data are available on the education level of the entrepreneur, the number of technical workers and the extent of internal and external training (Tables 3.14–3.16).

One of the striking features of Table 3.14 is the high proportion of entrepreneurs with tertiary-level education[32] and the low incidence of entrepreneurs with only primary education. This rather high educational background is surprising given the simple nature of the technology involved in both industries, and also in terms of the relatively low higher-education enrolments in Kenya (Chapter 1). The influence of entrepreneurial education on technological capabilities will be examined in Sections 3.5 and 3.6.

Table 3.14 Education levels of entrepreneurs 1994

Industry	*% with primary education only*	*% with up to secondary education only*	*% with tertiary education*
Garments	0.0	55.0	45.0
Engineering	14.3	23.8	61.9

Table 3.15 Technical manpower indicators

	Engineers & technicians (% of employment) (1994)	*Engineers only (% of employment) (1994)*	*% of total number of engineers employed by the 3 largest firms (1994)*	*Weighted average monthly worker wage (US$) (1995)*
Garments	2.2	0.4	66.7 (8)	67
Engineering	7.0[1]	3.6[2]	75.0 (57)	127[3]

Notes:
[1] Excluding the two small firms with high technical ratios, this falls to 5.3 per cent.
[2] Excluding the two small firms with high technical ratios, this fall to 2.4 per cent.
[3] Excluding the two large MNCs, this falls to US$103.

Table 3.15 shows the share of engineers and technicians in employment. This is, as may be expected, low in garments but quite high in engineering. However, if two small firms with high technical manpower ratios are excluded, the technical manpower ratio for the engineering industry falls from 7 per cent to 5.3 per cent. Most of the technical manpower consists of technicians rather than engineers. The proportion of engineers only is 3.6 per cent in engineering and 0.4 per cent in garments; this figure drops to 2.4 per cent in engineering if the two outliers are excluded.[33] By size of firm, the largest firms tend to have the highest proportion of engineers. The largest three firms in engineering employ a total of 57 engineers (75 per cent of all engineers in the industry) while those in garments employ eight (67 per cent).

Wages may be used as a rough proxy for skills levels of firms. The weighted average monthly wage in the engineering industry (US$127) is higher than the garments (US$67). If the two large multinationals, which are special cases in terms of their technology

Table 3.16 External training

	No. of firms with external training programmes	*Share of personnel sent on external training in Kenya and abroad (per cent of employment*	
	(1994)	*(1989)*	*(1994)*
Garments	4	0.27	0.47
Engineering	8	0.60	1.21

and size, are excluded, the average for engineering falls to US$103. This ranking is in line with the technological characteristics of the two industries – garments typically require lower levels of skill than engineering.

In terms of training, firms in both industries provide limited formal training. Only five firms in each industry have an in-house training programme and few firms have independent training budgets. The training budget averaged 0.13 per cent of sales in 1994 for the three engineering firms that maintain records. Unfortunately no information is available on the nature of their internal training programmes. Table 3.16 shows the numbers of employees sent on training outside the firm in Kenya and abroad in 1989 and 1994. External training is carried out by very few firms (12 in total), mostly in engineering (eight). Interestingly, there seems to have been a rise in external training since liberalization. The share of employees sent on external training courses has increased from 0.27 per cent to 0.47 per cent in garments and from 0.60 per cent to 1.21 per cent in engineering, although most of this training is in management or accountancy rather than in technical areas. Kenya suffers from a shortage of technical training institutions (for quality control, maintenance, production supervision and product design) in specific industries. The problem seems particularly severe in the garments industry.

These data support an earlier firm-level survey by Teitel (1993), which included garments and engineering firms. In Teitel's study, only 25 per cent of the firms paid for training of technical personnel outside the firm – including studies towards a technical degree, management and computer training, production and tool room training as well as short seminars. The bulk of such training was provided in Kenya rather than overseas. Teitel concluded that on-the-job and off-the-job training programmes are weak in Kenya.

3.4.2 Process Technology

3.4.2.1 Quality Control

There is considerable variation in the attention paid to formal quality control in garment firms. At one end there are firms with formal systems for quality control (based on final inspection), with a full-time quality-control department and reject rate data. At the other end there are firms where the entrepreneur does *ad hoc* checks on the finished products and the reject rates are not recorded. Nine firms have a full-time quality control department and eight keep track of the reject rates. Table 3.17 shows the share of full-time quality control employees in employment and the average internal defect rates for the main product in 1989 and 1994.

The data suggest that import competition has had a positive impact: there has been a rise in quality control efforts since 1989. Between 1989 and 1994 the share of full-time employees in quality control increased from 1.5 per cent to 1.7 per cent and the average internal defect rate fell from 2.6 per cent to 1.8 per cent. However, even these figures for quality control manpower in the Kenyan garment industry are low by the standards of other developing-country garment manufacturers.[34]

Only one garment firm has received ISO 9000 quality certification. Another garment firm began to implement the ISO 9000 system in the late 1980s but soon abandoned it because the cost of implementation was too high. The remaining 18 Kenyan garment firms seem to be unaware of the existence of the ISO 9000 quality management certificate and its growing significance in export activity.

Formal quality control has been traditionally a fairly low priority in engineering firms. In 1994, for instance, only seven firms had a full-time

Table 3.17 Quality control

	Full-time QC manpower (% employment)		*No. of firms recording defects*	*Average internal defect rates for main product**	
	(1989)	*(1994)*		*(1989)*	*(1994)*
Garments	1.5	1.7	8	2.6	1.8
Engineering	0.7	1.9	4	8.0	3.3

*Internal defect rates are the percentage of finished products that are rejected at final inspection.

quality control department and only four kept track of reject rates. The majority of the engineering firms relied heavily on *ad hoc* visual inspections of the final products by the entrepreneur or the foreman. Specialized tools and equipment for dimensional checking (that is, the shape of the final product) were rare and only one firm (an MNC) had a laboratory to analyse the quality of raw materials and components. As with garments, liberalization has led to an intensification of quality control. Since 1989 proportion of full-time employees in quality control has more than doubled (from 0.7 per cent to 1.9 per cent) and the average internal defect rate has more than halved (from 8.0 per cent to 3.3 per cent). This is in the context of fairly simple technological requirements. None of the engineering firms has obtained ISO 9000 certification, and most are unaware of its existence. Two firms (both MNCs) said that they were aware of the system but had no plans to introduce it in Kenya while the local firms had no awareness of it.

3.4.2.2 Maintenance

There is considerable variation in maintenance efforts between garment firms, ranging from those that have a regular routine for maintenance and servicing and a full-time maintenance department to those that only undertake repairs when equipment breaks down and rely on contract maintenance services. Only 10 garment firms have a full-time maintenance department with qualified employees and specialized equipment. Table 3.18 shows the share of full-time maintenance employees in 1989 and 1994 and the number of average monthly equipment breakdowns per firm in 1994. These data also indicate some (albeit marginal) improvement in maintenance since liberalization started: the share of maintenance manpower increased from 1.1 per cent to 1.3 per cent. The average number of monthly equipment breakdowns, however, remains quite high, at 5.5 times per month.

Table 3.18 Maintenance and breakdowns

	Full-time maintenance manpower (% employment)		*Average monthly equipment breakdowns*
	(1989)	*(1994)*	*(1994)*
Garments	1.1	1.3	5.5
Engineering	1.8	4.0	1.9

Maintenance capabilities in the engineering firms have traditionally been quite good. In several firms, the equipment has operated trouble free for a decade or more. The equipment is serviced regularly and spares are replaced according to manufacturers' schedules. About 10 firms have a full-time maintenance department and 13 have a maintenance shop with specialized equipment. There has been a significant improvement in maintenance efforts in the engineering firms since 1989, and the proportion of full-time employees in maintenance has more than doubled. In addition, the average number of monthly equipment breakdowns is quite low, at only 1.9 times per month.

3.4.2.3 Inventory Control

Table 3.19 shows the number of firms that have a system for continuous inventory control and the average number of working days of inventory kept by the sample firms. In 1994, 10 garment firms had a system of continuous inventory control, however the bulk of these firms use manual rather than computerized systems. There has been an improvement in inventory control over time, with a reduction in the average number of working days of inventory held from 146.3 to 80. This probably reflects easier access to imported inputs rather than a conscious improvement in inventory control efforts. It is impossible to disentangle the two effects with the available information.

Limited attention is paid to inventory control in engineering firms. In 1994 only seven firms had a continuous system for inventory control. Of these, four had upgraded from a manual system to a computerized one. The remaining firms accumulate stocks of raw materials but lack an organized system and trained personnel to keep track of them. This unnecessarily ties up valuable working capital and sometimes

Table 3.19 Inventory control

	System of continuous inventory control[1]		*Average no. of working days of inventory kept*	
	(No.)	*(per cent)*[2]	*(1984)*	*(1994)*
Garments	10	50.0	146.3	80.0
Engineering	7	33.3	143.5	117.6

[1] Raw materials only.
[2] Percentage of firms using computers for inventory control: 20% in garments and 23.8% in engineering.

causes disruptions in production because of scarcities of important raw materials. There has been an improvement in inventory control since 1984, with a reduction in the average number of working days that inventory is held from 143.5 to 117.6. Again, this may be due to the easier availability of imported inputs rather than to improved efficiency consequent on liberalization – we cannot say.

3.4.2.4 Process Improvement

There is evidence of improvements to equipment and processes in the sample firms. Three garment firms adjusted their layout every time they shifted product patterns. In addition, seven firms said that they had implemented energy saving measures that had resulted in a notable reduction in their energy bills. Both these types of process improvements occurred after 1989. The nature of the data prevented us from tracing similar earlier efforts.

None of the engineering firms carry out formal process development. Even the large MNC affiliates do not conduct research and development. The improvements to equipment and processes in the sample firms take the form of minor adaptations to save energy and modify machinery. Three firm have adopted energy-saving measures that have led to some reduction in the total energy bill. Only one firm (an MNC) has conducted a comprehensive energy audit of its plant and improved its processes (for which it relied heavily on technical assistance from its parent), resulting in a 15 per cent reduction in its energy bill. The other three firms have under taken more modest projects, for example installing capacitors on lathes, milling machines and so on to correct for the power fluctuations (sudden power losses in the workshops' power supply).

Modifications to equipment are more widespread. Five firms said they have turned out jigs, fixtures and other mechanical attachments for their main tools. This has permitted them to undertake heavier jobs or specialized tasks. These activities have only been undertaken since liberalization, suggesting that increased competition has led to greater efforts to upgrade installed technologies.

3.4.3 Improvements in Product Technology

Product technology includes assimilating foreign product designs and making modifications to meet market needs, as well as the more demanding tasks of design improvement and new product introduction. There is little evidence of independent design capabilities in the garment firms.

As in much of South and South-East Asia (but unlike the better exporters in East Asia), the four exporting firms rely heavily on their foreign buyers for new products and designs.[35] Specialist pattern makers employed by each exporter create copies of the product in accordance with the foreign buyer's 'master pattern'. The exporters feel that they have the capacity to introduce standard, low-quality products for the African market but have yet to demonstrate this in practice (see below). The non-exporting firms rely on a variety of sources for products and designs, including local buyers, catalogues, imports and occasional visits to foreign trade fairs. Only two of the non-exporting firms employ specialist pattern makers. In most cases the design efforts are undertaken by the entrepreneur or the foreman.

Table 3.20 shows the number of firms with product designers (that is pattern makers in garments), the number of firms with a computer-aided design (CAD) system and the number of new products introduced between 1989 and 1994. The data suggest little improvement in product design capabilities since liberalization. The garment firms introduced less than one new product each during 1989–94 and only one firm had adopted a CAD system to design logos for T-shirts. Probably the most important change has been the establishment of links by some local firms with foreign buyers. However the benefits of buyer–seller relationships have yet to spill over to the firms' design capabilities. There has been little attempt on the part of the local firms to ensure that this happens.

There is considerable variation in the design capabilities of the engineering firms. The four foreign-owned firms obtained new products and designs from their parent companies. This enabled them to introduce more than double the number of new products than large local firms but the foreign-owned firms have not invested in independent product design capabilities in Kenya.[36] Local firms copy imports or tailor their products to customer demands. Only four of the local firms have full-time design departments. The rest rely on the management

Table 3.20 Designers, CAD and new products

	No. of firms with full-time designers (1994)	*No. of firms with CAD systems (1994)*	*Average number of new products introduced (1989–94)*
Garments	7	1	0.8
Engineering	5	3	1.2

to introduce new products. In contrast there is some evidence of improvements in product design capabilities in the engineering firms since import liberalization. The engineering firms introduced an average of 1.2 new products each during 1989–94. Four firms introduced three or more products during this period. In addition three firms had recently adopted CAD systems.

In general, design capabilities are quite weak in both industries: this is to be expected, because new product design tends to be technologically very demanding. Nevertheless the sample firms are able to produce a range of simple products by copying imports (reverse engineering of complex products is also quite difficult). Given the entry of second-hand items this is not sufficient to compete in the local market and is inadequate for export expansion. MNCs rely heavily on their parent companies for new products, and local exporters, particularly garment exporters, rely on foreign buyers. While there is little evidence of independent design capabilities having emerged since liberalization, it seems that other types of product technological capabilities have improved slightly.

3.4.4 Linkages between Firms and with Technology Institutions

Interfirm and interindustry linkages – relationships between firms that result in the conscious transmission of information and skills – are a vital feature of industrialization. They permit increasing specialization and are an effective way of diffusing technology and information from large to small enterprises. They allow for a greater deepening of the industrial structure, and hence they reduce dependence on imported parts, components and services. In addition, institutions that provide technical information, training and other technical services can enhance technological capabilities by undertaking activities with infrastructural (public goods) characteristics and filling in any gaps left by deficient markets.

We begin by considering interfirm linkages. Table 3.21 shows the percentage of firms that subcontract. It also shows the firms' average ranking of the quality of service provided by the subcontractors in terms of price, quality of output and delivery deadlines.

The Kenyan sample firms undertake very little subcontracting. Of the 41 firms, only nine (22 per cent) subcontracted in 1994. As expected, the engineering sector displays a higher incidence of subcontracting than garments (about 33.3 per cent compared with 10 per cent in garments). Import liberalization again seems to have had a positive effect: there has been an increase in subcontracting since 1989, when none of

Table 3.21 Subcontracting

	% of firms subcontracting		*Satisfaction rating (ranked 1, very poor, to 5, very good)*		
	(1984)	*(1994)*	*Price*	*Quality of output*	*Delivery deadlines*
Garments	0	10.0	3.5	4.0	4.0
Engineering	14.3	33.3	2.6	2.9	3.0

the garment firms subcontracted and only 14.3 per cent of engineering firms did so.

None of the multinational affiliates in the sample subcontract to locally owned firms. Instead they rely heavily on their parent companies and imports for their inputs as well as for information, technology and so on. All the subcontracting arrangements in the sample involve Asian and African firms: typically a medium to large Asian firm subcontracts work to one or two small African firms located nearby. In the main, these arrangements tend to be *ad hoc* and are short-lived. They also tend to be arm's-length relationships that rarely involve a significant transfer of information, skills and technology. The net result is that there are few technological capability spillovers from large to small firms. There is also little impetus to deepen the industrial structure and hence to reduce dependence on imported parts, components and services.

There are few linkages with technology institutions in the Kenyan sample (Table 3.22). However there has been a recent increase in institutional linkages: 15 firms used a technology institution in 1994 compared with six in 1989. It is not clear that this indicates greater technological activity, since the linkages remain highly skewed towards the Kenya Bureau of Standards (KBS). The KBS is used by the largest number of firms in both industries – 30 per cent of garment firms and 33.3 per cent of engineering firms in 1994 – mainly for material testing.[37] There is evidently greater attention to quality, but not to improving technologies in other ways. None of the other technology institutions were used by any of the garment firms, while the Kenya Industrial Research and Development Institute (KIRDI) and the Department of Engineering at the University of Nairobi were each used by 14.2 per cent of the engineering firms. The Jomo Kenyatta University of Agriculture and the Kenya Polytechnic were each used by only 4.8 per cent of the engineering firms.

Table 3.22 Percentage of firms using technology institutions

	KBS[1]		*KIRDI*[2]		*Uni. Nairobi*[3]		*JK Ag. Uni.*		*Ken. Poly.*	
Industry	*(1989)*	*(1994)*	*(1989)*	*(1994)*	*(1989)*	*(1994)*	*(1989)*	*(1994)*	*(1989)*	*(1994)*
Garments	10	30	0	0	0	0	0	0	0	0
Engineering	14.3	33.3	0	14.2	4.8	14.2	4.8	4.8	4.8	4.8

Notes:
[1] Average ranking for KBS: 9 garment firms (2.3), 12 engineering firms (1.8).
[2] Average ranking for KIRDI by four engineering firms (1.5).
[3] Average ranking for University of Nairobi by three engineering firms (2.7).

The average ranking of the quality of service provided by different technology institutions (1 = worst, 5 = best) shows that none of them was rated by the sample firms as 'good' (4) or 'very good' (5). The best rating was recorded by the Department of Engineering at the University of Nairobi – the average rating for the three engineering firms that provided this information was 2.7. This was followed by the KBS (with an average rating of 2.3 for nine garments firms and 1.8 for 12 engineering firms). The worst rating was recorded by the KIRDI (an average of only 1.5 for four engineering firms).

Only a few firms seem to be fully aware of the type and range of services available in technology institutions. These firms said that technology institutions lack the technical manpower and equipment to conduct the technical activities they need, and have failed to develop links with other institutions to share equipment and manpower. They have also done a poor job of selling themselves to enterprises and are bureaucratic and inflexible in their approach to service provision.[38] In addition there appears to be an element of size bias in the provision of technical services. Large and medium firms seem to have benefited most while small firms rarely have access to these services.

3.4.5 Summary Evaluation of Technological Capabilities

Kenya's import substitution strategy has resulted in some learning in the manufacturing sector, though its pattern and extent have been distorted by high and indiscriminate import protection. The incentive regime has mainly induced Kenyan manufacturing to acquire the capability to substitute local raw materials for imports, maintain equipment and introduce some simple products. Foreign investment and other forms of technology imports have been restricted and have contributed to obsolete production technologies. Kenyan industry has lacked the requisite competitive capability to penetrate international markets.

There is a high propensity to obtain used equipment when setting up a firm and machinery used by most firms is over ten years old. Most firms specialize in technologically simple, mature products. There have been several new investments since import liberalization but, with a few notable exceptions, most tend to be very small. There is a surprisingly high proportion of entrepreneurs with secondary and tertiary-level qualifications. However weaknesses still remain in other aspects to skill formation. The employment of engineers is quite limited and highly concentrated in the largest firms. There is little emphasis on in-house or external training, although some increase has occurred since 1989.

Given the low overall level of technological capability, there have been signs of improvement since the start of the third liberalization phase. Both industries have upgraded their quality control procedures and equipment maintenance, and other forms of technological activity have increased. While this is encouraging, it appears that very few are reaching the international levels of 'best practice' that would enable them to grow and export in a fully competitive environment. There is too little use of foreign technology contracts and most firms purchase technology embodied in used equipment. Quality control systems are week by the standards of Asian countries. Few firms have systems for continuous inventory control. The capacity to develop new products is weak and none of the firms carry out formal R&D. Industrial engineering as a separate function is notably absent. Linkages with other firms or technology institutions are rare.

There are differences in the pattern of technological capability improvement between firms in the two industries. Engineering firms seem to have made more improvements than the garment firms, with better quality control and maintenance and the development of sub-contracting linkages and relationships with technology institutions. Garment firms have shown some improvement in quality and inventory control capabilities. They have also made some minor process improvements, particularly in order to save energy. However their ability to select new technologies, maintain equipment and design new products is extremely weak. In addition there seems to have been little attempt to forge local sub-contracting linkages or to make use of technology institutions. They are far less competitive, except for the large exporters; most are badly affected by *mitumba* imports and may not survive in terms of exposed products.

3.5 DETERMINANTS OF TECHNOLOGICAL CAPABILITIES AND ENTERPRISE PERFORMANCE

Two types of econometric investigation are undertaken in this section: (1) an analysis of the determinants of the technology index (TI) and (2) an examination of the determinants of enterprise performance. The modelling was based on the full sample of 40 Kenyan firms, using cross-section data largely for 1994.[39]

3.5.1 The Technology Index

The technology index (TI) was introduced in Chapter 2 of this study. This scoring and ranking system groups technological capabilities into three sets of technical functions: investment, production and linkages. The TI scoring system used for the Kenyan firms is presented in Table 3.23. The largest category, production, is represented by 14 separate technical activities, and is followed by linkages with seven and investment in six.

The frequency distribution of the capability scores for the sample firms is shown in Table 3.24 as 'TI1'. For purposes of comparison, the table also shows the frequency distribution for another index (TI2), which includes equipment purchase as well as some other components (see Chapter 4). The two technology indices are highly correlated ($r=0.92$), suggesting that either could be used in the statistical analysis. TI1 is used here while TI2 is used in the Tanzania case study and the comparative analysis.

3.5.2 Determinants of the Technology Index

The present analysis tests for the influence of firm size, ownership, technical manpower, entrepreneurial education, employee training and industry membership on TI. Technology imports were excluded from the model because only a handful of Kenyan firms use formal technology contracts.

The linear model is:

$$\text{TI1} = b_0 + b_1\ \text{SIZE} + b_2\ \text{OWNER} + b_3\ \text{ENTEDU} + b_4\ \text{ENG} + b_5\ \text{TRAIN} \qquad (3.1)$$

The independent variables are as follows:

- SIZE: total sales in 1994 (US$). This is expected to have a positive relationship with TI. The returns from capability acquisition are

Table 3.23 Technology index for the Kenyan sample

Investment capabilities		*Production capabilities* — *Process engineering*		*Production capabilities* — *Product engineering*		*Production capabilities* — *Industrial engineering*		*Linkages capabilities*	
Feasibility study		Quality awareness		Copying		Inventory reduction		Subcontracting linkages	
None	0	None	0	None	0	None	0	None	0
Rough	1	Low	1	*Ad hoc*	1	Little	1	*Ad hoc* technical transfer	1
Complete	2	High	2	systematic	2	A lot	2	Systematic technical	2
Search for		Maintenance		Improving existing		Productivity		transfer	
equipment		awareness		products		improvement		S&T (trouble shooting)	
No search	0	None	0	None	0	None	0	None	0
Local search	1	Only repair when	1	Some	1	Some	1	*Ad hoc*	1
Local and	2	Preventive system	2	Considerable	2	Systematic	2	Long term	2
overseas search		Changing layout[1]		Introducing new				S&T (testing)	
Assessment of		None	0	products				None	0
equipment		Little	1	None	0			*Ad hoc*	1
None	0	A lot	2	Some	1			Long term	2
Rough	1	Calibration of		Considerable	2			S&T	
evaluation		equipment[2]		Licensing product				None	0
Complete	2	None	0	technology				*Ad hoc*	1
evaluation		Little	1	None	0			Long term	2
Training		Frequently	2	*Ad hoc*	1			S&T (new product)	
No training		Substitution of		Systematic	2			None	0
programme	0	local products						*Ad hoc*	1
Very limited		None	0					Long term	2
Systematic	1	Little	1						
(local/overseas)	2	A lot	2						

Involvement of firm in detailed engineering		Energy saving						Systematic receipt of tech. from buyers	
None	0	None	0					None	0
Very limited	1	Little	1					*Ad hoc* tech. transfer	1
Systematic	2	A lot	2					Systematic tech. transfer	2
Improvement stock capability		Upgrading existing equipment						Systematic receipt of tech. from equip. suppliers	
None	0	None	0					None	0
Little	1	Little	1					*Ad hoc* tech. transfer	1
A lot	2	A lot	2					Systematic tech. transfer	2
		Buy new equipment							
		None	0						
		Little	1						
		A lot	2						

Notes:
[1]Garments only.
[2]Standards in garments; metrology.

Table 3.24 Frequency distribution of technology indices

	TI1		*TI2*	
TI Class	*Percentage of total garment firms*	*Percentage of total eng. firms*	*Percentage of total garment firms*	*Percentage of total eng. firms*
0.0–0.20	45.0	28.6	45.0	33.3
0.21–0.40	25.0	38.1	20.0	38.1
0.41–0.60	20.0	23.8	10.0	10.0
0.61–0.80	10.0	9.5	20.0	9.5
0.80–1.00	0.0	0.0	5.0	4.8
Total	100.0	100.0	100.0	100.0

higher where a firm has a larger volume of sales to spread the fixed costs of capability acquisition and large firms can have more specialized technical manpower. Moreover capital market imperfections confer an advantage on large firms in securing finance for risky technological activities, and size is correlated with the availability and stability of external funds.

- OWNER: the share of foreign and local non-African equity in 1994. This is expected to be positively correlated to TI. There are two *a priori* reasons for this:[40] First, the owner may have had a lengthy industrial experience. Foreign affiliates and some of the Asian families have been in manufacturing for several generations and may have accumulated technological capabilities that new African entrants lack. Second, the owner may have better international connections to access capital and technology or larger markets internal to the particular business community.
- ENTEDU: the number of years of schooling attained by the entrepreneur or CEO. We expect this to have a positive sign since educated entrepreneurs are expected to be more technologically dynamic in various ways, for example in buying new equipment, forging links with foreign investors and hiring technical manpower.
- ENG: the share of engineers in employment in 1994. This is expected to have a positive sign. Engineers can play a major part in technological capability acquisition through search, experimentation, training and formal R&D activities, though it is mainly relatively complex activities that need engineers for technology absorption.

- TRAIN: the number of employees sent on training courses outside the firm as a percentage of employment in 1994. This is expected to have a positive sign.

The results are as follows (*T* statistics in parentheses):

$$\begin{aligned} \text{TI1} = & -0.106 + 0.001\ \text{SIZE} + 0.002\ \text{OWNER} + 0.022\ \text{ENTEDU} \\ & \ (-0.8) \qquad (3.0)^{*} \qquad\qquad (2.9)^{*} \qquad\qquad (2.3)^{*} \\ & -0.002\ \text{ENG} + 0.008\ \text{TRAIN} \\ & \qquad (-0.3) \qquad\quad (0.9) \end{aligned} \tag{3.2}$$

Adjusted $R^2 = 0.53$

*Denotes statistical significance at the 5 per cent level

Following diagnostic testing, the results are considered.[41] The adjusted R^2 (0.53) is quite high for a cross-section study based on a small sample.[42] Three of the five independent variables are significant at the 5 per cent level and have the expected sign. Firm size, non-African ownership and entrepreneurial education have a positive and significant relationship with TI.

The positive sign on the firm size variable suggests that both explanations for the size effect are valid. The positive sign on the foreign/non-African ownership variable suggests that firms with overseas connections have access to inputs for capability building. The positive sign on the entrepreneurial education variable indicates that highly educated entrepreneurs act as a pivotal 'technology catalyst' in managing capability acquisition.

Engineering manpower surprisingly has no significance. One explanation may be that the engineers employed do not contribute to the acquisition of TCs (that is, they may be involved in marketing or administration activities rather than technological activities); this is more widespread in large local firms than MNC affiliates. In addition, employee training has no effect on TI. This may be because the measure for employee training is fairly crude and excludes formal in-house training programmes and on-the-job training, which may be far more important.

The above econometric work is based on the full sample of firms. The small size of the industrial groupings precluded estimating Equation 3.2 separately for each industry. As an alternative, a dummy variable for industry was added to Equation 3.2 but this did not prove significant,[43] perhaps because of the small sample.

The econometric analysis suggests that the *nature of ownership* was an important influence of TI. To shed further light on this, some characteristics of foreign/LNA and African enterprises were compared. Table 3.25 provides the results of T-tests on the means of several features of the two groups on which data were available. Unfortunately the small size of the sample prevented the use of more powerful econometric techniques. The main findings are as follows:

- Foreign/LNA firms have significantly higher levels of technological capability (the means for the technology indices are 0.42 and 0.18 respectively). This does not mean that their ownership *per se* matters for technological performance, but that the experience acquired by early entry into manufacturing and access to overseas sources of capital, technology and marketing are significant influences on TI.
- Sales growth in 1989–94 is significantly higher in foreign/LNA firms (the means are 2.5 per cent and −7.0 per cent respectively). In African garment firms, this reflects the impact of second-hand clothing imports, and in African engineering firms, the fall in domestic demand following the downturn in industrial growth since 1992.
- Foreign/LNA firms are significantly larger than African firms (the means are 164.8 and 15.9 employees respectively). As mentioned above, this suggests that the returns from capability acquisition are higher where a firm has a larger volume of sales to spread the fixed costs of capability acquisition. Moreover capital market imperfection may confer an advantage on large firms in securing finance for technological activities.
- There is a significant difference in capital per employee between the two groups (the means are US$138 000 for foreign/LNA and US$2300 for African firms). This is expected, given the larger size of the foreign/LNA group.
- There is a significant difference between the age in production of the two groups (the means are 27.3 years for the non-African and 12.9 years for the African firms).
- The average wage paid by non-African firms is significantly higher (the means are US$104 and US$64). This may indicate that non-African enterprises hire workers with higher skill levels, pay higher wages to retain them and provide them with better training, though it may also be due to other factors such as larger size or labour market distortions.

Table 3.25 T-test to compare the means of foreign/non-African and African firms

	Technology index	*Sales growth 1989–94 (%)*	*Employment (no.)*	*Capital per employee (US$)*	*Age in production in 1995 (years)*	*Av. wage (US$)*	*Entrep. education (years)*	*Scien., eng. & tech (% of emp.)*	*Eng. only (% of emp.)*	*Quality control/ mainten. manpower (% of emp.)*
Non-African firms[1]										
Observations	23	23	23	23	23	23	23	23	23	23
Mean	0.42	2.5	164.8	13.758	27.3	104	14.6	4.5	1.7	7.0
African firms										
Observations	17	17	17	17	17	17	17	17	17	17
Mean	0.18	−7.0	15.9	2311	12.9	64	12.8	5.3	2.6	1.4
T-statistic[2]	5.15*	2.22*	3.33*	3.73*	5.74*	2.86*	2.11*	−0.33	−0.66	2.59*

Notes:
[1] Non-African firms = MNC affiliates and Asian firms.
[2] T-critical at the 5% level is 2.02 with 38 degrees of freedom.

- There is a small but statistically significant difference in entrepreneurial education between foreign/LNA and African firms (the means are 14.6 years and 12.8 years respectively).
- Foreign/LNA firms have a significantly higher share of quality control and maintenance manpower in their workforces than African firms, the mean being 7.0 per cent for the former and 1.4 per cent for the latter. However the ratios of scientists, engineers and technicians in employment and engineers only in employment do not show any statistically significant difference.

Thus African firms tend to be smaller and have less production experience, lower levels of technical manpower and less educated entrepreneurs: these seem to be features of late entry into industrial activity rather than of African ownership as such. However, while time may take care of these differences, to the extent that there are factor market distortions that favour established firms there may be a need for appropriate remedial policies.

It is interesting to examine the features of the four most technologically capable African enterprises, two in garments and two in engineering (Table 3.26). The technological performance of these firms is well above the average for all African enterprises (the average value of the technology indices are 0.38 and 0.18 respectively). Superior technological performance appears to be associated with superior market performance. The sales growth of three of the leading African firms (6.8 per cent for Beta engineering, −0.1 per cent for Eva Modell and −5.0 per cent for Kega Fashions) is better than the average for all African firms (−7.0 per cent). It is striking, however, that only one of these firms (Beta Engineering) recorded positive sales growth during this period. Beta Engineering's good performance is partly due to the fact that it was not directly exposed to import competition. Of the three declining firms, the two garment firms were severely affected by second-hand clothing imports while the engineering firm was affected by domestic recession. Even the most capable African firms had difficulty coping with the competitive pressures induced by import liberalization. None moved into export markets and two of them said that if things did not improve they would quit manufacturing altogether.

The superior technological and market performance of the four African enterprises appears to be due to firm size and entrepreneurial characteristics. Three of them are medium-sized (21–50 employees) and one is large (over 51 employees). The average number of employees is

Table 3.26 Features of four leading African firms

Firm/industry/size (G=garments; E=engineering)	*Technology index*	*Sales growth 1989–94 (per cent)*	*Age of entrepreneur (years)*	*Entrepreneur's highest education level (location)*	*Entrepreneur's previous previous work experience (years)*
Eva Modell (G) (35 employees)	0.43	−0.1	38	BSc textile technology (overseas)	Garment buying house (11)
Kega Fashions (G) (40 employees)	0.38	−5.0	55	BSc electrical engineering (overseas)	Civil service (30)
Naciti Engineering (E) (60 employees)	0.35	−9.9	48	MSc mechanical engineering (overseas)	Kenya Railways workshop (11)
Beta Engineering (E) (29 employees)	0.35	6.8	44	BSc mechanical engineering (Kenya)	Engineering firm (4)

41 compared with 15.9 for all African-owned enterprises. All the entrepreneurs are relatively young and well educated. Their average age is 46 years, and three are university graduates and one is a post-graduate. Technical education is another distinguishing feature. Three have an engineering background, one is a textile technologist, and all but one graduated from foreign universities. Three of the entrepreneurs have some experience of working in the same line of business as their present one. These characteristics have important implications for technological development in Kenya. Entrepreneurial success in among Kenyans is clearly associated with high levels of technical education, overseas exposure and relevant work experience. Such characteristics probably provide entrepreneurs with better access to segmented factor markets, a better appreciation of technological factors and a willingness to search for information and hire qualified technical manpower.

3.5.3 Determinants of Firm Performance

3.5.3.1 Export Performance

The econometric analysis of export performance here is based on similar work in other developing countries. This literature suggests that firm-level export performance is influenced by factors such as capital, skills, ownership, technology and firm size.[44] There is little previous work on Kenyan manufacturing enterprises.[45] The linear model is:

$$\text{EXSH} = b_0 + b_1 \text{ CAPITAL} + b_2 \text{ SKILL} + b_3 \text{ TI1} + b_4 \text{ OWNER} + b_5 \text{ SIZE} \qquad (3.3)$$

The independent variables are as follows:

- CAPITAL per worker: the dollar replacement value of capital in 1994. Within a given activity, a higher level of physical capital in the form of modern equipment is likely to give a firm a competitive export advantage. Thus a positive relationship is expected between capital per employee and export performance.
- SKILL: the average dollar wage in 1995. Within a given activity, a higher level of skill is likely to give a firm a competitive export advantage and is expected to have a positive effect on export performance.
- TI: the technology index. We expect the acquisition of technological capabilities to be positively associated with export performance.
- OWNER: the share of foreign and local non-African equity. We expect foreign ownership to have a positive influence on export performance.
- SIZE: total employment in 1994. This is expected to have a positive effect on export performance. A common argument is that exporting

allows large firms, particularly in small economies, to exploit economies of scale in production by counteracting the disadvantage of the small home market.[46]

The results are as follows:

$$\underset{(0.2)}{\text{EXSH}=0.890}+\underset{(0.2)}{0.022\,\text{CAPITAL}}+\underset{(2.6)^*}{0.168\,\text{SKILL}}+\underset{(0.5)}{0.028\,\text{OWNER}}+\underset{(2.0)^*}{0.092\,\text{TI1}}+\underset{(3.0)^*}{0.066\,\text{SIZE}} \quad (3.4)$$

Adjusted $R^2 = 0.61$

*Denotes statistical significance at the 5 per cent level

Diagnostic testing for multicollinearity and heteroskedasticity show that neither poses a problem. The R^2 is quite high (0.61) and three of the five independent variables are significant and have the expected sign. TI, SIZE and WAGE are significant and positive.[47]

Ownership and capital were not found to be significant. One possible explanation for the former may be that because the sample is relatively small the ownership effect may not show up. Further work is needed to find an explanation for this result. In the case of capital, it suggests that a higher level of physical capital has no influence on export performance. This may be explained by measurement error; in firm-level research capital is often difficult to measure (Wilmore, 1992). Again a dummy variable was used to capture industrial effects, but did not show up as significant.

3.5.3.2 Sales Growth

We estimated a model of sales growth, using the CAPITAL, SKILL, SIZE, TI and ENTEDU as arguments. The dependent variable in this model, SGR, is the sales growth rate between 1989 and 1994 in current US dollars. The independent variables are CAPITAL per worker (the replacement value of capital in 1994 in US dollars), SKILL, SIZE, TI and ENTEDU (all defined above).

For the reasons discussed, all the independent variables are expected to have positive signs. The results are as follows:

$$\underset{(0.6)}{\text{SGR}=6.177}-\underset{(-0.6)}{1.419\,\text{CAPITAL}}+\underset{(1.7)}{0.691\,\text{SKILL}}-\underset{(-0.9)}{0.017\,\text{SIZE}}+\underset{(2.9)^*}{63.865\,\text{TI1}}-\underset{(-1.4)}{0.971\,\text{ENTEDU}} \quad (3.5)$$

Adjusted $R^2 = 0.20$

*Denotes statistical significance at the 5 per cent level

The overall results of the estimation are disappointing. The R^2 (0.20) is low and only one of the independent variables has turned out to be significant with the expected sign. Interestingly, this is TI, supporting the importance of technological capabilities in firm performance.

Thus the econometric work on the determinants of enterprise performance in the Kenyan sample yielded useful results, the most being that TI has a positive effect on firm performance in both models. In addition, skills and firm size are positively associated with export shares. In the case of sales growth, however, none of the other explanatory variables is significant.

3.6 CONCLUSION

Kenya's liberalization has been slow, intermittent and largely reluctant, and has been accompanied by an unfavourable environment for foreign investment and weak institutional support. Manufacturing growth since adjustment has been reasonable by historical standards but there are few signs of dynamism; in fact there has been a marked slowdown since 1992. There is little sign of the export-led growth of labour-intensive industries that spearheaded the rise of the East Asian NIEs.

Both the industries studied here have become more exposed to import competition, but garments far more so than engineering. The general response to competition has been rather passive. Of the 41 sample enterprises, only four garment and seven engineering firms have responded offensively by buying new technology and moving into exports. The remainder have adopted a defensive approach, reducing employment, moving into non-tradable products or doing nothing. Both sectors contracted during 1989–94, the contraction being more severe in garments than in engineering. There has been as increase in the number of exporting firms, but the numbers involved are small and most exports and directed at the regional African market rather than at the much larger global market.

Most Kenyan firms have obsolete technologies: they started with used equipment and the average age of the equipment is quite high. There have been some new investments since import liberalization but most have been small. While there are several entrepreneurs with secondary and tertiary-level qualifications, the employment of engineers is limited and concentrated in the largest firms. Moreover in-house and external training efforts are weak, confined to a few large local firms and MNC affiliates.

While capabilities are low by international standards, import liberalization has led to technological improvements in both industries. However important gaps in competitive technological capabilities remain, and it is not clear whether the improvements will be sufficient to allow liberalization to proceed without severely disrupting industrial production and employment. In particular, the use of foreign technology is low, with little use of foreign technology contracts or direct investment. Quality control systems and quality management standards are insufficient to attract major European and American buyers. Few firms have systems for continuous inventory control or productivity improvement. The capacity to develop new products is weak and none of the firms carries out formal R&D. Industrial engineering as a separate function is absent. There are few linkages with other firms or technology institutions.

In econometric terms, TI has a positive effect on sales performance, while TI, skills and size have a positive effect on export performance. TI itself is positively related to ownership, the entrepreneur's education level and firm size. African owned firms are generally smaller and younger, and use less capital-intensive techniques as well as less technical manpower than other firms: this shows up in their lower levels of technological competence and weaker response to import liberalization.

There are important differences in the patterns of technological capability improvement between the two industries. Engineering firms have undertaken more improvements in technological capabilities than garment firms since import liberalization. Emphasis has been placed on process improvement in the form of better quality control and maintenance and the development of subcontracting linkages and relationships with technology institutions. However improvements in these areas have not spilled over into areas such as product design and industrial engineering. Garment firms have also shown some improvement in quality and inventory control capabilities, and have undertaken some minor process improvements (particularly in order to save energy). However their ability to select new technologies, maintain equipment, and design new products is extremely weak. Certainly, few firms are able to withstand the onslaught of cheap imports from East Asia, or to seek markets in developed countries to offset their troubles at home.

In the end, therefore, we are left with misgivings about the impact of import liberalization. While the extent of liberalization is not clear, where it has really 'bit', as in garments, the effects are devastating and the technological response of firms, with a few exceptions, inadequate. Where its effects are milder, firms are responding positively but the extent of the in response may be insufficient to sustain them in a really open competitive environment. There are complex processes of technological development to be undergone before Kenya can really benefit from liberal trade policies, and these need to be directly addressed by adjustment policies. Current strategies are not doing this.

Notes

1. We would like to thank Wilfred Nyangena for research assistance and John Kuriya and Simon Ihiga for arranging interviews with Kenyan firms. We also owe a debt to the numerous firms and institutions that provided us with information and hospitality. The views expressed in this chapter are solely our own and should not be attributed to the Commonwealth Secretariat or the University of Nairobi.
2. World Bank (1987b); Sharpley and Lewis (1990).
3. World Bank (1994).
4. The information on manufacturing growth is from Central Bureau of Statistics, *Economic Survey, 1980* and *1995*, while those on other regions is from the World Bank, *World Development Report 1995*.
5. See World Bank (1993b).
6. Central Bureau of Statistics, *Economic Survey*, various; World Bank (1994); World Bank *World Development Report 1995*.
7. The manufactured export growth rates in 1980–91 (1987 prices) are compound growth estimates. Data after 1991 are lacking .
8. See World Bank (1987b); N'geno (1991); UNDP/World Bank (1993); Mwega (1995).
9. A detailed account of the process of import liberalization in Kenya can be found in Swamy (1994). This account, however, does not cover the 1992–93 episode.
10. At the Paris Club meetings in 1993 and 1994, donors pledged US$390 million to Kenya.
11. Falls were also recorded for agriculture (from 41.9 per cent to 28.5 per cent) and services (from 30.6 per cent to 18.6 per cent) between 1990 and 1994. See UNDP/World Bank (1993); Republic of Kenya, *Importer information Tables 1995*.
12. To quote the Central Bureau of Statistics, *Economic Survey, 1995* (p. 146): 'the continued importation of textiles and clothing resulted in the poor performance of the sector and substantial declines were recorded in the manufacture of textiles.... Production of bed sheets, pullovers, knitted fabrics among others all recorded significant declines. Other significant declines were noted in the production of suits for both men and boys while the production of dresses also decreased significantly.'
13. This would have involved measures such as immediate and automatic access to duty-free imported inputs, working capital loans and strong institutional support for export marketing.
14. The ECS was abolished in 1994 after allegations of misuse of the scheme. These arose from the so-called 'Goldenberg scandal' in which it is claimed

that KSH 9.5 billion was paid to support non-existent exports of gold and diamonds.

15. The World Bank's 1986 CEM on Kenya noted that 'in 1981, majority foreign-owned firms accounted for only 9 per cent of total employment in large scale (fifty plus employees) manufacturing enterprises. Since 1979, direct foreign investment has been static in nominal terms, declining in real terms, and virtually all of it is from re-invested earnings rather than new equity' (para 3.33). Also see Wignaraja (1996).
16. According to UNCTAD (1995), 21 SubSaharan African countries received higher annual FDI inflows than Kenya during 1991–94. The top five destinations were Nigeria (US$780 million), Zambia (US$97 million), Namibia (US$76 million), Côte d'Ivorie (US$63 million) and Gabon (US$57 million). The bulk of the FDI was directed at natural resource extraction activity, for which these countries are better placed than Kenya.
17. By the end of 1994 over 40 enterprises had been approved by the EPZ Authority but only 18 translated into actual projects. The government sought to establish a total of nine EPZs in Kenya in the 1990s. At the end of 1994, three had attracted foreign investors and six more were in various stages of construction and operation. The number of entreprises in the three EPZs was as follows: Sameer Industrial Park (12), Anicit (EPZ) Ltd (3), and East African Molasses (3). Information from interviews with the EPZ Authority, February 1995 and from Central Bureau of Statistics, *Economic Survey*, 1995.
18. These estimates are for wages only and exclude social security payments. The figure for Kenya for 1995 is from the firm-level survey discussed in Section 3.5. The estimates for Sri Lanka and India for 1996 were obtained from interviews with leading MNCs in Sri Lanka by one of the authors.
19. See Dunn and Bradstreet (1995).
20. Apart from these, there are some other technology institutions that are less directly relevant to industrial technology, including the Kenya Industrial Property Office and the National Council for Science and Technology. Useful accounts of technology policy in Kenya can be found in Ikiara (1988); Mwamadzingo (1994); Enos (1995). King (1996) analyses the vocational education and training sector in Kenya.
21. Ikiara (1988).
22. Ibid., p. 243.
23. The firms are located in and around Nairobi and Nakuru.
24. The average number of employees is 134.7 in garments and 65.1 in engineering. The largest firms are Bedi (700 employees), Alpha Knit (600 employees), Eveready (340 employees) and H. Young (250 employees). The first two are Asian-owned garment firms while the others are foreign-owned engineering firms. The largest two African firms are Naciti engineering (60 employees) and Kega Fashions (40 employees). Section 3.5 contains an analysis of the technological and market performance in these and other African firms.
25. The 222 firms in the Regional Program on Enterprise Development (RPED) 1993 survey were distributed as follows: small (36.9 per cent), medium (23.5 per cent) and large (39.6 per cent). The employment size groupings in the RPED survey are comparable to those used here. See University of

Gothenburg Department of Economics and University of Nairobi Department of Economics (1994).

26. The extent of foreign ownership in our sample is similar to that the RPED survey: 14.0 per cent of the firms in the latter had some proportion of foreign ownership. Unfortunately no information was provided on breakdown of Kenyan private ownership into LA and LNA ownership.
27. This method was first used by Levy (1993) in the context of SMEs in Tanzania and Sri Lanka.
28. See Federation of Kenyan Employers (1991) for an elaboration of this point.
29. King makes this point in his work on technology development in small, informal sector 'jua kali' enterprises in Kenya. He argues that 'the *jua kali* engineer entrepreneur ... is very aware that there are niches in the local market where products can be designed that have a comparative advantage over what can be imported. The zero-grazer is perhaps one of the best examples. But other, relatively bulky, but not complex machines such as maize-mills, and block-making machines are also obvious candidates for the local *fundis* to take on (King, 1996, p. 67).
30. This functional classification of technological capabilities is based on Lall (1992b).
31. Also see Bennell (1984); King (1996).
32. There was a particularly high incidence of university-level training among entrepreneurs in the sample firms. About 33.3 per cent of entrepreneurs in engineering and 30 per cent in garments had first-class degrees. In addition, 14.3 per cent in engineering and 5 per cent in garments had a Masters degree. This is well above the levels found in many other African countries. A recent study of 268 SMEs in Tanzania, Malawi, Mali and Ghana found that only 20 per cent of entrepreneurs in Tanzania and Ghana had some form of post-secondary education, while in the other two countries the share was much smaller. See Parker, *et al.* (1995).
33. The proportion of engineers in the Kenyan engineering industry is low compared with Asian developing countries. According to Lall and Wignaraja (1996) the ratio for engineers in employment in Malaysia is 7.6 per cent and in India 6.5 per cent.
34. A survey of 11 export-oriented garment firms in the late 1980s in Sri Lanka, for instance, found that the average share of quality control manpower in employment was 4.7 per cent while the average internal defect rate was under 1.0 per cent. The top three Sri Lankan firms, of which two were local, employed 9.5 per cent, 8.4 per cent and 5.9 per cent of their respective workforces as quality controllers (Wignaraja, forthcoming).
35. See Egan and Mody (1992) for an account of buyer–seller relationships in the footwear industry. Lall and Wignaraja (1994) discuss theoretical and empirical aspects of buyer–seller relationship in the garment industry and provide a case study of a sustained technology transfer between a German buyer and a Sri Lankan garment firm.
36. Only one of the foreign-owned firms has set up a design department with trained designers (who account for 4.0 per cent of total employment).
37. A similar finding was reported by the Regional Programme on Enterprise Development's (RPED) 1993 survey. Of the 214 firms drawn from textiles

and garments, engineering, wood working and food processing that responded, only 26.6 per cent had used the services of the KBS, only 1.4 per cent had used KIRDI services and only 2.8 per cent had used other technology institutions. See University of Gothenburg Department of Economics and University of Nairobi Department of Economics (1994), p. 115.

38. On the lack of cooperation among public technology institutions, the RPED survey reported that KIRDI has limited collaborative research programmes with the country's universities, leading to underutilization of both equipment and manpower in these institutions (see University of Gothenburg Department of Economics and University of Nairobi Department of Economics, 1994). See Mwamadzingo (1994) and Enos (1995) for a more detailed evaluation of the capacities and budgets of technology institutions in Kenya.
39. The statistical analysis involved 19 garment firms and 21 engineering firms. One of the garment firms, which turned out to be an outlier on the verge of closing down, was dropped.
40. See Lall *et al.* (1994) for a fuller discussion of the theoretical aspects of this issue and an empirical analysis of the influence of ownership on technological performance in Ghanaian manufacturing firms. Himbara (1994) and Weinstein *et al.* (1992) have undertaken preliminary work on Kenya.
41. The model was appraised for multicollinearity using the tolerance of the variable and the variance inflation factor and for heteroskedasticity using the Park–Glejser test. The results indicated that neither posed a problem for the estimated equation.
42. Another study based on a small sample of Sri Lankan firms also found a high R^2 but somewhat different results. Wignaraja (forthcoming) estimated an econometric model of the determinants of technological capabilities for a sample of 27 Sri Lankan manufacturing enterprises. He found that firm size (total sales), technical manpower (share of engineers and technicians in employment) and technology transfer from foreign buyers (number of technical visits by buyers to the firm) were significant and positive in sign. Meanwhile, other factors such as foreign ownership and entrepreneurial education had no effect on technological capabilities. The overall adjusted R^2 was 0.41.
43. To test the robustness of Equation 3.2 we dropped some of the outliers and reran the model several times, but the results were broadly similar to the above.
44. There is a growing body of econometric literature on firm-level export performance in developing countries. Recent work includes Wilmore (1992) on Brazil; Kumar and Siddarhathan (1993) on India; and Wignaraja (forthcoming) on Sri Lanka.
45. One of the few studies that has examined the determinants of export performance at the industry level in Kenya is Lall *et al.* (1987).
46. Size is represented by employees rather than sales. Simple correlation analysis suggests that employees are more highly correlated with export shares than total sales.
47. There was no evidence of multicollinearity between the TI index and the average wage. The correlation coefficient between the two was 0.40.

APPENDIX 3.1 TECHNOLOGY INDEX FOR THE KENYAN FIRMS

	Technology index (TI)				*Size 1994*	*Performance 1989–94*	*Exports 1994*
Firm	*Investment*	*Production*	*Linkages*	*Overall index*	*(no. of employees)*	*Sales growth (%)*	*% of sales*
Garments							
Bedi	1.00	0.75	0.43	0.73	700	21.6	100
Alpha Knits	0.75	0.68	0.29	0.57	600	8.4	50
Loundra	0.75	0.39	0.29	0.48	320	−3.5	0
Sunflag Textiles	0.83	0.71	0.36	0.63	290	25.4	65
Vajas Manufac.	0.67	0.36	0.14	0.39	205	3.1	0
Uzuri Manufac.	0.58	0.64	0.36	0.53	170	1.2	62
Intersilk	0.33	0.36	0.07	0.25	100	−15.3	0
Silver Star	0.50	0.29	0.14	0.31	80	−6.1	0
Interfashions	0.25	0.14	0.00	0.13	60	−14.2	0
Denamal	0.33	0.21	0.00	0.18	41	−10.0	0
Kega Fashions	0.67	0.32	0.14	0.38	40	−5.0	0
Eva Modell	0.58	0.57	0.14	0.43	35	−0.1	0
Muasia	0.25	0.18	0.07	0.17	13	−8.3	0
Kianga	0.58	0.25	0.07	0.30	9	3.0	0
Joy Fabrics	0.42	0.11	0.07	0.20	9	−9.2	0
Munyaka Fashions	0.00	0.14	0.00	0.05	8	−17.2	0
Atieno	0.17	0.14	0.00	0.10	5	−28.2	0
Maggy Fashions	0.08	0.14	0.07	0.10	4	−13.3	0
Twins Fitters	0.25	0.14	0.14	0.18	4	−19.0	0

Oz Fashions	0.25	0.21	0.00	0.15	1	−20.9	0
Average garments	0.46	0.34	0.14	0.31	134.7	1.9*	24.1
Engineering							
Eveready	0.92	0.92	0.14	0.66	340	−2.2	1
H. Young	0.92	0.81	0.14	0.62	250	3.0	25
CMC Engineering	0.67	0.35	0.14	0.39	150	0.9	5
Datini	0.75	0.46	0.36	0.52	125	2.2	3
Holman Brothers	0.58	0.38	0.21	0.39	70	−19.8	0
Naciti Eng.	0.50	0.35	0.21	0.35	60	−9.9	0
Zenith Steel	0.83	0.62	0.14	0.53	50	6.8	26
Karimbhai	0.75	0.42	0.07	0.41	50	−1.5	10
Pelican	0.75	0.46	0.21	0.48	45	13.2	10
Philips	0.67	0.42	0.21	0.43	43	−7.9	1
Marshall Fowler	0.50	0.46	0.14	0.37	35	−2.0	6
Mughal Eng.	0.42	0.23	0.07	0.24	30	0.6	0
Sehmi Eng.	0.42	0.23	0.14	0.26	25	−2.3	0
Beta Eng.	0.50	0.35	0.21	0.35	24	6.8	0
28 Shed	0.00	0.19	0.00	0.06	20	−3.5	0
Novus Eng. Works	0.50	0.23	0.14	0.29	12	56.1	0
Samuel Mwangi	0.00	0.08	0.00	0.03	11	3.0	0
Rimpex	0.25	0.19	0.00	0.15	10	−9.2	0
K.J. Tools	0.25	0.08	0.00	0.11	8	−1.5	0
Samuel Njenga	0.00	0.08	0.00	0.03	6	−1.5	0
Githua Metal Works	0.08	0.15	0.00	0.08	4	−5.0	0
Average engineering	0.49	0.36	0.12	0.32	65.1	−3.2	6.6

*The growth rate for the garment firms becomes −1 per cent if the largest firm is excluded.

4 Trade Liberalization, Firm Performance and Technology Upgrading in Tanzania

Sonali Deraniyagala and
Haji H. H. Semboja[1]

4.1 INTRODUCTION

After nearly two decades of trade restrictions, Tanzania launched a series of trade liberalization measures in the mid 1980s. Economic and manufacturing growth, which had collapsed in the 'crisis years' prior to liberalization, recovered modestly thereafter. This chapter examines the extent to which manufacturing firms responded technologically to trade liberalization, and whether their performance in the post-liberalization period can be explained in terms of their relative technological efforts and capabilities. It also sheds light on micro-level supply-side factors that determined the capacity of firms to upgrade technology and improve economic performance under the conditions of trade liberalization. The analysis deals with two subsectors – engineering and garments – and is based on a cross-section survey of 65 firms.

Section 4.2 provides background information on trade policy and economic performance in Tanzania, and Section 4.3 on the sample of firms used in the study. Section 4.4 examines the extent to which firms responded to liberalization by upgrading their technology and technological capabilities. In Section 4.5 we present an econometric analysis of the impact of this technological behaviour on several performance indicators. Section 4.6 undertakes an econometric analysis of the characteristics of high-technology/high-performance firms, and Section 4.7 presents the conclusions of the study.

4.2 BACKGROUND: TRADE POLICY AND ECONOMIC PERFORMANCE IN TANZANIA

4.2.1 Trade and Industrial Policy

There have been three phases in the evolution of Tanzania's trade policy since the early 1970s. The first, between 1970 and 1985, was one of trade restrictions, with systematic increases in quantitative restrictions, culminating in severe controls between 1980 and 1985. Prompted by a temporary commodity boom, there was some (not sustained) liberalization in 1978–79. An Open General Licence for imports was introduced in the early 1970s, but all imports were subjected to licence by 1980. An import-substituting basic industrialization strategy was launched to promote domestic manufacturing.

The period between 1985 and 1988, the second phase, was one of partial trade liberalization (Ndulu and Semboja, 1994). After 1985 the exchange rate was devalued and the importation of selected consumer, intermediate and capital goods with 'own' foreign exchange was permitted. The third phase, from 1988 to the present, has been a period of 'serious' liberalization, with the dismantling of import restrictions and the reduction of tariffs. The complex tariff structure has also been rationalized: in 1980 there were 18 main tariff categories, with wide dispersions rating from 0–200 per cent, but in 1992 there were five categories with rates ranging from 0–40 per cent (Ndulu and Semboja, 1994).

A broad indication of changes in effective protection rates is given in Table 4.1 for the period 1986–93. While these figures are not continuous measures of protection, they provide snapshots of the effective protection levels in various years. The effective rates of protection declined after 1986, and by 1993 had declined by more than half in eight of the ten industrial sectors for which they were computed. Quantitative restrictions on imports were also substantially reduced and import licensing virtually scrapped. The introduction of the New Open General License (NOGL) for selective imports expanded the proportion of imports subject to automatic licensing from 19.4 per cent in 1984 to 55.3 per cent in 1991. Since 1988 the NOGL has been changed from a positive list to a small negative list.

The exchange rate regime continued to be liberalized, with a steep real depreciation of 85 per cent between 1987 and 1994. The General Retention Scheme of 1986 allowed exporters to retain foreign exchange for essential imports. In early 1992 the Exchange Control Act was

Table 4.1 Effective rates of protection in Tanzania

	1986	*1989/90*	*1993*
Beverages and tobacco	83.8	63.7	35.0
Food products	65.1	38.1	39.1
Textiles and apparel	55.1	36.1	24.6
Tanneries and leather	41.3	40.1	2.48
Plastics and rubber, pharmaceuticals	45.4	n.a.	2.64
Iron, steel and metal products	28.1	19.2	14.1
Agriculture	24.0	31.7	35.0
Machinery and transport equipment	25.0	17.6	8.0
Rubber, glass, wood, paper	27.9	9.42	2.8
Chemicals and fertilizers	1.6	−2.0	27.3

Source: Ndulu *et al*. (1995).

amended to allow residents legally to hold foreign currency. This was accompanied by the introduction of foreign exchange bureaux, which bought and sold foreign exchange at market-determined rates. The official and bureaux exchange rates were unified in 1993.

From the early 1980s several export promotion measures were introduced, mainly targeting non-traditional exports. In the preliberalization period, measures such as an export rebate scheme, export retention schemes and preferential credit facilities had been introduced to counteract the disincentive effects of currency overvaluation. In the post-liberalization period, export taxes were abolished and export finance schemes, for example a export credit guarantee scheme, were introduced.

4.2.2 Economic and Industrial Performance

The annual growth rate of Tanzanian GDP averaged 3.9 per cent in real terms between 1966 and 1975 (Table 4.2). While agricultural growth in this period was modest (around 2.3 per cent), average manufacturing growth rates reached 4.8 per cent. This period was also marked by an increase in investment, with the ratio of fixed capital formation to GDP increasing from an average of 16.5 per cent between 1966 and 1970 to an average of 20 per cent between 1970 and 1975. Despite the investment drive linked to the basic industrialization strategy, output growth slowed in the second half of the 1970s. The ratio of fixed investment to GDP rose slightly to 22 per cent between 1976 and 1980, while the real rate of growth of GDP fell to around 2.8 per cent

Table 4.2(a) Performance indicators for Tanzania

	Average annual growth rates in constant prices			
	GDP growth	*Manufacturing growth*	*Agricultural growth*	*Fixed capital formation (per cent of GDP)*
1971–75	3.9	4.8	2.5	20.5
1976–80	3.8	2.7	1.8	22.2
1981–85	0.7	−4.7	0.4	15.7
1986–93	2.8	3.5	1.2	31.7

Table 4.2(b)

Share of manufacturing in GDP		*Share of manufactured exports in total exports*	
1976	12.9	1976–80	15.6
1980	11.4	1981–85	13.0
1986	7.9	1986–91	21.0
1993	9.1	1992–94	14.0

Table 4.2(c)

	Growth rates of selected subsectors (real annual average growth of MVA)	
	Clothing	*Engineering*
1980–88	−16.6	−8.8
1989–94	−22.3	5.3

per annum. Agricultural growth declined, averaging 1.8 per cent between 1976 and 1980. Although manufacturing received much of the increased investment in this period, its growth rate also fell to an average of 2.7 per cent, indicating a decline in investment productivity (Ndulu and Lipumba, 1991). The export orientation of manufacturing declined steadily from the mid 1960s, the share of exports in manufactured output falling from an average of 12.4 per cent in 1970–75 to 9 per cent in 1976–80.

The period of severe trade restrictions (1981–85) was also one of a sharp downturn in economic performance. GDP growth fell to

0.7 per cent per annum during these 'crisis years'. Investment rates declined due to a fall in both domestic and foreign savings. The share of fixed capital formation in GDP fell from 22 per cent in 1976–80 to 15.7 per cent in 1981–85. Manufacturing performance also deteriorated sharply, with a real average annual rate of decline between 1981 and 1985 of 5 per cent. A process of 'deindustrialization' took place, with the share of manufacturing in GDP falling from 12.9 per cent in 1976 to 7.9 per cent in 1985. The share of exports in manufacturing output fell further to 4.6 per cent in 1981–85 (Ndulu and Semboja, 1994).

The post-liberalization period (1986–94) witnessed improved performance, but GDP growth rates were still low (at 3 per cent per annum), lower than the population growth rate. The decline in manufacturing growth was reversed, with growth rates averaging around 3.5 per cent per annum; the performance of the agricultural and service sectors in this period was, however, superior to that of manufacturing, with growth rates of 5 per cent and 4.2 per cent respectively. Investment increased sharply, with the ratio of fixed capital formation to GDP rising to 32 per cent in 1986–92, due more to external financing than to domestic savings. This increased investment was mainly directed at agriculture, with the share of manufacturing in fixed capital formation falling from 24 per cent in 1981–85 to 13 per cent in 1986–92.

The relaxation of import and exchange rate restrictions generated an expansion of imports. Estimates of import demand functions show that, while the tightening of import and exchange rate controls between 1980 and 1985 had resulted in a contraction of real imports at an average annual rate of 18 per cent, the relaxation of these measures between 1986 and 1993 caused real imports to rise at an average rate of 9.5 per cent.

Export performance also improved. The ratio of exports to GDP (in constant 1987 prices) increased from 12.3 per cent in 1986 to 15 per cent in 1992. Export growth averaged 9 per cent per annum in real terms between 1987 and 1992, reversing its negative growth during 1980–86. There was also significant diversification of the composition of exports: the share of non-traditional goods in total exports increased from 24 per cent in 1985 to 41 per cent in 1989. Manufactured exports constituted a major part of this diversification, with the share of manufactures in total exports increasing from 13 per cent in 1980–85 to 21 per cent in 1986–91. However these rates should be considered in light of the very small values involved: total manufactured exports only totalled $43 million in 1991, half of the $86 million achieved in 1980 (see Chapter 1).

The manufacturing activities whose exports increased most were paper and paper products, textiles, sisal fabrics, food products, leather and leather products and machinery and transport equipment (Bank of Tanzania, 1992). With the exception of paper products, these subsectors were all established prior to trade liberalization. There was some tendency for manufactured exports to shift towards less processed products, for instance from finished to grey cloth. This export growth was not sustained, however, and the share of manufactures in total exports fell to 14 per cent in 1992–94. This was due to the failure of firms to improve their production and technological capabilities to meet the efficiency and quality standards of export markets (Ndulu and Semboja, 1994). Thus it seems that while the more established firms were able to respond to the improved incentives for exporting in the short term, this could not be sustained due to weak export capabilities.

4.2.3 The Engineering and Clothing Industries: Performance Trends

The engineering industry includes fabricated metal products and machinery (including electrical machinery and transport equipment). In Tanzania this industry is largely a product of early import substitution and experienced some expansion in the 1970s and early 1980s. Most engineering firms in Tanzania produce simple, basic products using relatively unsophisticated production technology, and the industry is dominated by small and medium-sized firms: over 85 per cent of engineering firms employ fewer than 100 people. In 1992 the industry accounted for around 11 per cent of total manufacturing employment in Tanzania. The industry performed poorly in the crisis years of 1980–85; in real terms its value added declined by 8.8 per cent per annum. Capacity utilization levels were low for much of this period, as low as 20 per cent in some subsectors. There were severe technological deficiencies in industry, compounded by excess capacity, low levels of investment and lack of access to imported capital goods and spares. These resulted in foundry technology as well as activities such as precision forging, metal cutting and heat treatment being inefficient and underdeveloped (MEIDA, 1992).

The performance of the engineering industry has improved since liberalization, with a positive growth rate of 5 per cent between 1988 and 1994. While the export orientation of the industry is low, there was some increase in exports. The share of exports in the engineering output increased from 2.2 per cent in 1980 to 5 per cent in 1990.

Engineering exports accounted for 4 per cent of total manufacturing exports in 1990, an increase from 1.7 per cent in 1980.

The clothing industry consists largely of informal sector microenterprises and small and medium-sized firms producing almost wholly for the domestic market; the modern garment industry, in particular large firms with a modern organizational structure and equipment serving world markets, has not reached Tanzania (one exception is noted below). The number of clothing firms expanded fairly rapidly until the early 1980s. Since then the industry has contracted sharply, with the number of formal sector firms (with over 10 employees) falling from around 75 in 1980 to 28 in 1994. The industry's share in total MVA declined from 2.8 per cent in 1980 to 0.2 per cent in 1994. Production declined by 16.9 per cent per year during 1980–88, and further by 22 per cent per year in 1989–94. Capacity utilization levels have remained low since 1980, at around 25 per cent.

The poor performance of the clothing industry in the preliberalization period is attributable to shortages of imported inputs, poor production technologies and low levels of domestic demand, especially during the crisis years 1980–84. Several public sector firms were established in this period, and generally outperformed private firms due to privileged access to foreign exchange and tenders. The poor performance of the clothing industry since liberalization is mainly due to its inability to cope with import competition, especially competition from the second-hand imports noted in the other country studies. In the 1990s, imported second-hand clothing has accounted for over 90 per cent of total clothing imports. New entrants into the clothing industry in the post-liberalization period have mainly been informal sector microenterprises (with fewer than 10 employees) undertaking basic tailoring for small local markets. In view of this, it is not surprising that there is little export capability in the Tanzanian garment industry, even though this industry normally constitutes the first entry point for developing country exporters of manufactured products that are not based on natural resources.

4.3 SURVEY AND SAMPLE BACKGROUND

4.3.1 Characteristics of the Sample

The present analysis is based on a sample of 46 engineering and 15 clothing firms in Dar-es-Salaam, Arusha, Mwanza and Tanga. The sample was selected broadly to reflect the existing size distribution of firms in the two industrial subsectors, and was not intended to be random.

4.3.1.1 Products and Markets

The engineering firms manufacture a wide range of products. Most of the sample firms are engaged in basic activities such as the manufacture of simple spare parts and agricultural tools; a small group of firms, however, produces more sophisticated products such as car radiators and high-precision tools and dies. The engineering firms in our sample fall into five broad product groups: construction, transport, spares, agricultural machinery and furniture. As Table 4.3 indicates, 'spares and repairs' constitute the largest product group, accounting for 40 per cent of firms. Ginneries and textile mills, using mainly obsolete and outdated capital equipment, are some of the main customers of spare parts manufacturers. The firms in this group largely serve local and regional markets. The firms in the 'construction-related' group produce wire, galvanized steel sheets, steel bars and aluminium sheets. The 'transport-related' category includes products such as radiators, heat exchangers and brake pads. It also includes two firms engaged in the assembly of trailers and bus-bodies. Producers of construction-related and vehicle-related products typically serve the national market.

The garment firms are much more homogeneous. They mainly undertake basic tailoring of low-quality products for the domestic market. A strikingly high proportion (almost 75 per cent) produce various types of uniform, a 'niche', mainly non-tradable, market into which firms have retreated in the face of import competition. However orders for uniforms, usually put on tender, are erratic and many firms shut down for long periods of time.

Table 4.3 Engineering industry sample

	Per cent of firms
Construction-related (wire, roofing)	17
Motor-vehicle related (radiators, bus bodies)	15
Spare parts (repairs and spares)	40
Agricultural machinery and equipment	15
Other (mainly furniture and household products	11

4.3.1.2 Firm Size

Firms of all sizes are represented in the industry samples. On average the engineering firms are larger than the clothing firms in terms of employment. The mean size in engineering is 75 employees and in clothing 55. Firm size, especially in engineering, varies considerably according to type of product. The manufacture of spare parts is usually carried out in small workshops. Agricultural machinery and equipment producers are largely small and medium-sized. The firms that manufacture construction-related and transport-related products are more large scale.

The size distribution of firms in both industry samples is shown in Table 4.4, which groups firms into micro (fewer than 10 employees), small (11–30 employees), medium (31–99 employees) and large (over 100 employees). The majority of engineering firms are small and medium sized. Microenterprises and large firms account for 15 and 20 per cent of the engineering sample respectively. This size distribution corresponds broadly to industry proportions. A markedly higher

Table 4.4 Sample characteristics (per cent of firms)

	Engineering	*Clothing*
Size distribution		
<10 employees	15	33
10–30	35	27
31–99	30	27
>100	20	13
Mean size	75[1]	55[2]
Mean age (years)	21[3]	24[4]
Per cent exporters	11	13
Ownership		
Per cent foreign	7.5	6.6
Per cent domestic	92	93
(As per cent of domestic firms)		
Asian-owned	55	77
African owned	45	23
State-owned	13	0
Private	87	100

Notes:
[1] Minimum 3, maximum 550.
[2] Minimum 4, maximum 300.
[3] Minimum 5, maximum 85.
[4] Minimum 4, maximum 40.

proportion of firms in the clothing sample (33 per cent) are micro enterprises, and the proportion of large firms in this industry is lower, reflecting the structure of the industry as a whole.

4.3.1.3 Firm Age

There is little difference in the mean age of the firms in the clothing and engineering samples. The firms in both industries are, on average, around 20 years old. The majority of firms were established prior to the period of 'serious' trade liberalization (since 1988). Only three of the engineering firms and one clothing firm have been established since 1989.[2]

4.3.1.4 Ownership

Most of the engineering and clothing firms are privately owned. State-owned enterprises comprise 13 per cent of the engineering sample; there are no state-owned firms in the clothing sample. Foreign ownership in both industries is also minimal: there are three foreign subsidiaries in engineering and one in clothing. In terms of ethnicity, 40 per cent of the domestic engineering firms are African-owned, the remainder being Asian-owned. The African firms are, on average, smaller than the Asian firms. The high degree of Asian ownership in clothing in general is reflected in our sample, in which only 20 per cent of firms are African-owned.

4.3.1.5 Export Orientation

The export-orientation of firms in both industries is very low. Seven of the engineering firms (15 per cent of the sample) engage in some exporting, mainly to other African countries. There are only two exporters in the garment industry sample. One of these, which is wholly foreign owned, exports all its output on a CMT ('cut, make and trim') basis for a parent firm that has other production sites in the Middle East and Asia. It was the only firm in the country engaged in this type of exporting at the time of the survey, and was set up after liberalization. Apart from this affiliate, there has been little entry of new exporters after liberalization in either industry sample.

Five of the seven exporters in the engineering sample were established before liberalization, and had undertaken some degree of exporting; four of them increased their exports (share of exports in total output) after liberalization. The remaining two firms are new firms set up in the post-liberalization period, both exporting simple agricultural machines (for example sesame seed milling machines) to other African countries. The engineering sample also provides some limited evidence of the recent slowdown and contraction in manufactured exports noted above. For instance, one firm, a manufacturer of electrical light fittings that exported around 60 per cent of its output before 1989, switched from exports to the domestic market after liberalization, primarily due to its inability to upgrade the quality of its products to the levels needed in liberalizing neighbouring markets.

4.3.1.6 Entrepreneurship

A high proportion of the firms in both industries are sole proprietorships or family owned. Decision-making power in these firms is generally highly centralized, usually in the hands of a single entrepreneur. The entrepreneurs in the engineering sample have relatively high educational qualifications (Table 4.5), with around a third holding a university degree or professional qualification, mainly in engineering or a related technical subject. Fewer than 5 per cent of the entrepreneurs have only had primary education. The African entrepreneurs in engineering have higher educational qualifications than the Asian ones. This may, however, be specific to this sample: our sample contains 10 firms established by the Small Industry Development Organisation (SIDO), an institution set up to foster African entrepreneurship. It selects entrepreneurs for predesigned projects mainly on educational criteria. When the SIDO firms are excluded there are no significant differences in the educational qualifications of the African and Asian entrepreneurs in the sample. The entrepreneurs in the garment industry have markedly lower educational qualifications: 27 per cent have only had primary schooling, while around 26 per cent were educated beyond the secondary level.

Table 4.5 Educational background of entrepreneurs and training (per cent of entrepreneurs)

	Engineering	*Clothing*
Primary	4.5	27
Secondary	21	47
Post-secondary diploma	24	–
Undergraduate degree	28	26
Higher degree	21	–
Per cent of firms undertaking training	54	13
Per cent of firms employing at least one engineer	60	–

The previous work experience of the entrepreneurs in both industries was largely confined to the industry they currently work in. A minority (around 10 per cent in each industry) have had some experience in trade, particularly the Asian entrepreneurs, a number of whom had started to manufacture the types of product they had previously traded in.

4.3.2 Performance after Liberalization

4.3.2.1 Engineering

Sales growth. Sales growth for the sample improved after liberalization to 2.2 per cent in 1989–94, in contrast with a fall of 9 per cent per annum during the 'crisis years' years of 1984–89 (Table 4.6).

There is some variation in sales growth among the five product groups, with the manufacturers of construction-related and 'other' products displaying the highest growth rates: 2 per cent and 7 per cent respectively. These aggregate figures, however, mask substantial interfirm variations: 60 per cent of the engineering firms experienced negative growth after liberalization, with real annual average growth rates in sales ranging from −0.06 per cent to −18 per cent. The median real annual growth rate was negative – −3 per cent.

Productivity. Due to the lack of value-added data, sales per employee is used as an indicator of labour productivity. According to this measure, productivity improved after liberalization. Negative real growth rates of 12 per cent per annum between 1984 and 1989 were replaced by positive real growth rates of 2.6 per cent between 1989 and 1994. The performance of the five product groups varied, with the manufacturers of construction-related products performing best. The manufacturers of spare parts also had moderate productivity growth after liberalization. Again, these aggregate figures mask significant interfirm variation: 52 per cent of sample firms had negative growth in sales per employee in 1989–94, and another 12 per cent experienced no change.

Employment. The data on employment indicate a general contraction of the engineering firms, with the median average growth rate of employment being −11 per cent. The average number of employees per firm fell from 103 in 1989 to 75 in 1994. Around 65 per cent of the firms reduced their workforce, while 25 per cent increased employment and the rest stayed constant. This contraction in firm size contrasts with the preliberalization years 1984–89, when average firm size

Table 4.6 Performance indicators (per cent)

Indicator	*Clothing*	*Engineering*
Sales growth 1989–94	−6	2.2
Sales growth 1984–89	12	−9
Capacity utilization 1994	30	n.a.
Capacity utilization 1989	60	n.a.
Growth sales/employee 1989–94	3.1	2.6
Per cent of firms with falling employment	80	65

increased from 93 to 103, and 55 per cent of firms expanded employment. Thus heightened import competition appears to be associated with falling average firm size in this industry.

Export performance. As noted, the engineering firms have shown little tendency to increase their export orientation in the post-liberalization period. There are seven exporters (that is, firms that export some proportion of their total output) in the engineering sample; of these, three have had some growth in export revenues, while the remaining four have recorded a decline.

4.3.2.2 The Clothing Industry

The performance of the clothing firms since liberalization has been very poor. In aggregate, sales growth declined by 6 per cent per annum in real terms in 1989–94, in contrast to a growth rate of 12 per cent per annum in 1984–89 (Table 4.6). All the firms, except the export-oriented affiliate, experienced falling sales in this period. This contraction also occured in employment: some 80 per cent of garment firms have reduced their workforce since 1989, with the rest experiencing no change. Capacity utilization has declined sharply, with average levels falling from 60 per cent in 1989 to 30 per cent in 1994. Over 90 per cent of firms experienced a decline in capacity utilization in the later period.

4.4 TECHNOLOGICAL RESPONSE TO TRADE LIBERALIZATION

The impact of trade liberalization on technological dynamism is hard to predict (Chapter 2). Some analysts posit 'opening up' to have a positive and dynamic effect on technological change, with import competition spurring innovative activity. While this has an element of validity, it is based on a simplistic view of what constitutes and drives technological change at the micro level, particularly in developing countries that face severe learning costs and have grossly imperfect markets and institutions. In particular it ignores legitimate arguments for infant industry promotion. The other aspect of import liberalization, liberalization of capital goods and intermediate imports, is more widely accepted as beneficial to technology upgrading. At the empirical level, firm-level studies have documented how, under different circumstances, both trade restrictions and trade liberalization generate firm-level technological dynamism. However the evidence shows that the types of technological activity undertaken vary in the two cases, and the outcome depends on the nature of competitive pressures exerted behind protective barriers – import-substituting regimes produce less dynamism than export-oriented ones with more selective policies (Lall, 1992b).

The discussion of the technological response of Tanzanian firms to trade liberalization focuses on two interrelated issues: technology, and technological skills and capabilities. We shall examine the extent of technology upgrading and skill development since liberalization. Technology upgrading is taken to include improvements to plant and equipment, products and the organization of production. Skill development is seen as the acquisition of technological knowledge and information.

4.4.1 Technological Behaviour under Liberalization

Technological activity by developing country firms includes the adoption of new capital equipment, incremental, minor improvements to production technology and products and substantial or innovative changes to existing products and processes (Bell and Pavitt, 1993). The following discussion of technological performance in the Tanzanian engineering and clothing industries focuses on these types of technical activity. Table 4.7 presents some summary information on the various types of technological activity undertaken by the sample firms.

4.4.1.1 The Engineering Industry

The production process in this industry consists of a design stage in which product specifications and the metal transformation processes to be used are established; a machining stage where individual

Table 4.7 Technological activity

Type of technological activity	*Per cent of firms undertaking activity* Engineering	*Per cent of firms undertaking activity* Clothing
Plant and equipment		
Equipment upgrading	35.0	13.0
Introducing CAD	6.5	6.6
Introducing CNC	11.0	13.0
Organisation		
Quality control system	10.0	6.6
In-house repair shop	60.0	40.0
Inventory control	20.0	13.0
Product technology		
Formal design	15.0	–
In-house R&D	4.0	–
Introduction of new products	55.0	–

components and parts are produced; an assembly stage; and finishing and testing. As noted earlier, most of the engineering firms in our sample make products involving relatively simple technologies and organization: largely repair-type work, with limited batch production and little standardization of products, or the batch production of simple standardized products. A few are engaged in more complex operations that demand more advanced skills and technical information.

Plant and equipment. The plant and equipment used by the engineering firms in our sample is generally very basic. Cutting, bending, forging and welding operations are carried out using simple, general purpose machinery such as presses, drilling machines, milling machines, lathes and so on. The machinery used in the preliberalization period was largely obsolete. In 1989 the average age of machinery in the sample was over 30 years. While there has been some upgrading of production technology since liberalization, this has been fairly limited, confined to a small group of firms. In terms of recent equipment upgrading, the sample firms fall into three categories.

First, a small minority of comparatively advanced firms – around 11 per cent of the sample – upgraded technology by investing in fairly sophisticated machinery such as numerically controlled (NC) and computer-numerically controlled (CNC) machine tools and computer-aided design (CAD). For these firms, import liberalization has had a positive effect on technological activity. These firms are diverse in terms of size, markets and product ranges. Their products range from household appliances and high-precision machine tools to the assembly of bus bodies. While most of them are large and medium-sized, a few are small, with fewer than 30 employees. Two firms are exporters, while the rest produce for the domestic market. One firm is a subsidiary of a French multinational. These firms also undertake some minor technical activities that mainly involve substituting imported for local materials and *vice versa*, both to meet requirements of the new capital equipment and to reduce production costs.

Although they display diverse characteristics, the firms in this group have two common features. First, they have all upgraded their technology as part of a longer-term strategy to improve competitiveness. In most cases this strategy was adopted as a response both to increased import competition and to the greater availability of imported capital equipment. Second, access to foreign expertise has been important in facilitating the technological upgrading in all cases. In the case of the foreign firm, the parent firm played a key role in the selection and installation of the new technology. The domestic firms used foreign consultants or had a technical agreement with a foreign manufacturer. For instance three producers of high-precision machine tools employed resident foreign consultants when the new equipment was introduced. Two firms that assemble bus bodies had technical assistance agreements with the Far Eastern producers of the new equipment. Such foreign expertise was needed because all these firms had clearly made a considerable 'technological leap' from their preliberalization technology levels. Most firms used such external assistance mainly for selecting and operationalizing the new technology.

The second group of firms – around 35 per cent of the sample – have undertaken some replacement investment that has not involved moving to a markedly more sophisticated level of technology. These firms have mainly invested in simple general-purpose machinery. Given the obsolete nature of much of the technology used prior to liberalization, this new machinery has several new and advanced features – for example lathes with automatic feeders and loaders. The equipment has generally been purchased from domestic retailers and did not involve a lengthy search and selection process. Furthermore, much of the equipment purchased since liberalization is new, in contrast with the high proportion of second-hand machinery purchased in the earlier import-constrained environment. Unlike firms in the first group, this investment has been largely *ad hoc* and does not appear to be part of a longer-term strategy to improve firm performance. Easier access to imported capital goods clearly prompted these firms to replace their obsolete plant and equipment.

The third group, over 50 per cent of engineering firms, are technologically relatively stagnant and have made few changes to their production technology since liberalization. Most of these firms are small repair shops and service centres serving small, regional markets. The only form of investment in production technology undertaken by these firms has been minor retooling for existing machinery and equipment. The machinery used by these firms is largely obsolete, averaging over 35 years, and is kept alive by 'stretching' and 'tinkering'. Uncertainty in the face of increased competition, low levels of technical skills and high capital costs are seen as reasons for this unwillingness to invest.

Organizational activity and process engineering. Process engineering involves such functions as quality control, maintenance and stock control. Overall, these capabilities are at a basic level in the Tanzanian engineering industry, and improvements since liberalization have been very limited.

A fairly high proportion of the firms in the sample have in-house repair and maintenance facilities. Given the simple nature of the technology used, the types of repair and maintenance activities undertaken are very simple. Functions such as quality control, inventory control and materials testing are markedly underdeveloped. Only around 25 per cent of the firms employ full-time quality control personnel and 10 per cent have a formal system of quality control (sampling checks or a Kawasaki system). Around 20 per cent have systematic inventory control procedures. Only a minority of the engineering firms have made significant improvements in process engineering in response to liberalization: these are mainly the same firms that have invested in advanced machinery and equipment. These firms have increased the proportion of their workforce engaged in full-time quality control and maintenance, indicating greater attention to these tasks, though they do not aspire to advanced ISO 9000 quality management systems. In contrast to the other countries in the study, and a testimony to the weak state of capabilities in Tanzania, not a single sample firm has reached this quality level.

Despite the minor improvements noted, competence in process engineering is generally low, even among the technologically advanced firms. For instance the firm that makes precision moulds and dies for export had over 30 per cent of its orders rejected due to defects in the two years preceding the study; this was despite investments in CAD/CNC technology. Several of the other technologically advanced firms – manufacturers of machine tools and car radiators – have no system of routine, scheduled maintenance, leading to high 'machine-down' time due to sudden breakdowns. A manufacturer of light fittings that used to export a substantial proportion of its output has had to stop all exports due to its inability to implement proper inventory control procedures and meet deadlines.

Overall, it is apparent that although some firms have invested in fairly advanced capital goods since liberalization, 'best practice' levels of efficiency in the operation of this technology have not been achieved. More surprisingly, these gaps are present even in firms with an established export market (admittedly only to neighbouring countries) and should have had an advantage in locating the problems and finding the solution.

The majority of firms have shown stagnant or deteriorating competence in process engineering since liberalization. The proportion of the workforce engaged in maintenance and quality control has fallen in many of the firms: in 55 per cent of firms that employ full-time quality controllers, the proportion of quality control personnel in the workforce was lower in 1994 than in 1989. Around 40 per cent of the firms that employ full-time maintenance personnel also reduced their employee numbers in that period. This was part of the labour-shedding adopted by most firms in reaction to liberalization, but the fact that quality and maintenance were regarded as relatively peripheral is itself indicative of their attitude towards technological upgrading. Reduced attention to quality also reflects attempts to compete with imports by entering into lower-quality segments and attempting to compete on price.

Product technology. Most engineering firms in Tanzania produce simple products involving little formal design.[3] Products are usually 'rough copies' of other imported or domestically produced products, and technical drawings are rarely used. Spare parts manufacturers often work from samples that are worn out or broken, resulting in poor product quality.

A minority of firms in the sample (around 15 per cent) undertake in-house product design and development (though this does not rank as formal R&D in the normal sense). Again, these are mostly the same firms that have invested in advanced machinery and equipment. Their products are significantly more complex than those of other firms and their efforts to improve product quality have clearly increased since liberalization. Some of them have established in-house drawing offices and employed design engineers.

Around 55 per cent of the sample have introduced new products since liberalization. In many cases this was a response to increased import competition in existing product lines, but was a move *down* rather than up the technology ladder. New sources of competitive advantage were sought by moving into simpler products with very localized demand and strong non-tradable characteristics, such as some agricultural machines or repair services, or to products that are still relatively highly protected (for example electrical switchgear). In a few cases, however, efforts to introduce more complex new products are also evident, within technologies that are relatively undemanding. Such efforts are concentrated among the producers of agricultural machinery and involve changing product specifications to meet the local climatic conditions or to suit requirements of specific customers, for example a firm that adapted a sesame oil press to suit domestic conditions.

Nearly 50 per cent of the engineering firms have reacted to import competition by producing lower-quality, cheaper products. This has involved, for instance, substituting cheaper and lower-quality parts and components for better-quality ones, reducing the performance and durability of products. In some cases 'serious' product development activity has been cut back to lower costs. A manufacturer of household appliances, in the period prior to liberalization, had a formal design department that developed several new products. Since liberalization it has stopped all design work and product-centred technical activity now consists only of *ad hoc* efforts to produce lower-quality, cheaper products.

To summarize, efforts to upgrade plant and equipment, process engineering or product quality in the post-liberalization period have been limited. Only a minority of engineering firms have responded to the trade policy reforms by upgrading their technology, but their efforts are often below the levels of competence and comprehensiveness needed to sustain competitiveness in a truly liberal trading environment. In the majority of cases, trade liberalization has done little to change the technological stagnation that existed prior to liberalization. In several cases there has been a deterioration of technological competence since the introduction of the trade reforms, particularly where the level of competence was low to start with.

4.4.1.2 Clothing

The clothing industry in Tanzania operates at a very low technological level, and the technological stagnation of firms in this industry in the years since trade liberalization is very marked.

Plant and equipment. Most of the firms in the clothing industry sample use outdated industrial sewing machines; the average age of machinery in the sample is over 25 years. These machines have few new features such as under-bed thread trimmers. Only two firms in the sample use advanced technology such as operator programmable machines. Despite the greater availability of imported machinery, little new investment has been undertaken since liberalization. One firm, the export-oriented affiliate, has a computer-aided grading and marker-making system, but while this firm is relatively advanced by Tanzanian standards, it aims for the lowest-quality end of the international market. This firm was established in the wake of liberalization and has undertaken little new investment since it began. Hence there is no evidence of a wave of export-oriented garment investments.

Organizational change. The organizational competence of the clothing firms in the sample is generally low. Systematic quality control (using quality checkers) is only present in one firm. Only a minority undertake inventory control, although a higher proportion (40 per cent) carry out in-house maintenance. There have been few improvements in organizational capacity since liberalization. On the contrary, there has been a marked deterioration: six of the sample firms have reduced their maintenance staff, and two firms that used to conduct quality checks have stopped doing so in the past five years.

Product-centred activity. Product design in most of the clothing firms consists of little more than basic 'tailoring'. Garments such as uniforms are produced using very simple patterns. Few firms pay attention to matters such as fabric saving in the drawing and cutting stages. The most technologically sophisticated firm, which engages in 'cut, make and trim' (CMT) production, manufactures according to designs provided by foreign buyers and hence there is no product design activity in this firm.

4.4.2 Improvements in Technological Capabilities and Skills since Liberalization

Improvements in capabilities and skills accompany technological upgrading and are the determinants of technological dynamism. Here we examine the extent of skill development among Tanzanian firms since liberalization. Three types of capability and skill development are considered: hiring skilled personnel, training, and technological linkages with science and technology institutions and other firms.

4.4.2.1 The Engineering Industry

Formal qualifications. Some 60 per cent of firms in the engineering sample employ at least one graduate engineer. While this figure appears fairly high, it reflects the fact, noted above, that the sample contains several firms set up by the Small Industry Development Organisation (SIDO) under a scheme that favours entrepreneurs who are qualified engineers. Taking out this subsample, the proportion of firms employing at least one graduate engineer falls to 45 per cent. On average, engineers comprise around 2 per cent of the workforce in the total sample and 1.5 per cent of the workforce when the SIDO subsample is excluded. As expected, most graduate engineers are employed in supervisory and managerial positions. It is common for firms in which the entrepreneur is a graduate engineer to employ other engineers; such employers are probably better placed to evaluate the usefulness of, and use the capabilities of, trained engineers.

Only a few of the firms (around 15 per cent) have employed additional graduate engineers since liberalization. These are mainly the firms that have substantially upgraded their equipment: the additional engineers have been employed to operationalize the new technology and to improve product design and quality. For instance a manufacturer of high precision machine tools has set up a product development centre headed by a expatriate engineer – three graduate engineers have been hired with the specific aim of improving product quality and moving into export markets. However the intensity of formal engineering skills in the most sample firms has remained unchanged in the post-liberalization period.

Training. Around 30 per cent of firms provide their workforce with some form of systematic training (other than routine on-line training), in most cases involving short training programmes at domestic training institutions. Around 10 per cent of engineering firms train a few employees at foreign training centres. Such training is usually for longer courses such as MScs. In all cases training is mainly in technical subjects and management training is uncommon. Two firms have carried out special in-house training programmes in recent years. This training, mainly in the context of importing new and advanced technology, has often been conducted by foreign experts and equipment suppliers.

The majority of firms, however, provide little training of any type, and seem unaware of their skill deficiencies. Perhaps not surprisingly, liberalization has had little effect on their training efforts. There is some evidence of a decline in efforts to upgrade skills, as demonstrated by falling training expenditures, but this is limited to a few firms. Thus two firms that previously sent employees to foreign universities for technical training have stopped doing so due to low expectations of future growth in the increasingly competitive environment.

Technological linkages. Linkages with technology institutions, customers, suppliers and other firms such as subcontractors can be an important source of 'disembodied' technological information that enhances firm-level technological capabilities. In the case of the Tanzanian engineering firms, these linkages are minimal. Apart from local training centres, the only technology institution with which the firms have had some contact is the Tanzanian Bureau of Standards, used by some 35 per cent of the firms to test materials and product standards. This contact involves little technology transfer. While several other technology institutions exist in the country, for instance geared towards high-precision industries or product design and development, interaction with these institutions is limited. A small minority (4 per cent) have sought assistance and technical expertise in relation to the development of specific new products. However these have been largely 'one-off' contacts, usually relating to design problems during the early stages of product development, and have not been sustained for longer-term product improvement. Most of the firms consider that technology institutions provide poor-quality services or are irrelevant to the types of activity they undertake. Again, in general, linkages with technology institutions that were weak during the preliberalization period appear to have remained so after liberalization.

Technology transfer through subcontracting or by capital goods suppliers is also limited. As noted above, training and information transfer by capital goods suppliers and foreign consultants is undertaken by the few firms that have bought advanced machinery. While trade liberalization has prompted a substantial proportion of firms to undertake replacement investment, most of the purchases have been made from local distributors and have involved little information transfer. Subcontracting activity among firms has been limited, reflecting both the simple level of production undertaken by most firms (hence little need for subcontracting) and the lack of 'competent' firms capable of undertaking subcontracting work.

The only other significant interfirm linkage capable of facilitating the transfer of skills and information has been among the group of 10 firms that were established by SIDO. These firms, which at their inception manufactured products such as spare parts, simple machines and agricultural implements, were set up with the cooperation of a foreign 'sister firm'. The function of the sister company was to provide technical training and assistance both during the initial start-up and subsequently, and the firms are located on industrial estates with the aim of promoting the transfer of skills through close proximity and constant interaction. While cooperation with the 'sister firms' did promote some technology transfer in the early years, these relationships were largely dormant at the time of the survey. Furthermore, most of these firms have responded to trade liberalization by 'retreating' into non-tradable activities such as basic repair work, which generates few positive spillover effects in terms of skills and information transfer.

4.4.2.2 *The Clothing Industry*

Skill levels in the clothing industry are, as indicated above, low. Only one of the sample firms (the exporter to the US) employs a production manager with formal qualifications in clothing technology. There are no personnel with clothing-related training in another firm. Nor have any of the clothing firms increased the number of personnel with technical qualifications in the post-liberalization period.

Training efforts in the clothing industry are extremely limited, with no improvement evident after liberalization. None of the firms have provided their workforce with external training, although the foreign affiliate in the sample has organized special in-house training programmes, conducted by its parent firm. The contrast between this export-oriented firm and the others serves to highlight the large technological gaps that exist in most Tanzanian garment firms. Other linkages with domestic or foreign technology institutions are non-existent among the clothing firms, largely because there are no technology institutions to serve this industry in Tanzania.

4.4.2.3 *Summary*

To summarize, the engineering industry has faced some direct import competition, while the garment industry has been exposed rapidly and rather brutally. The extent of technology and skill upgrading in the engineering industry since liberalization has been limited. A small proportion of the firms have adopted fairly advanced technology (more in response to the availability of imported equipment than to meet direct import competition) and undertaken some skill upgrading. Some other firms have made minor improvements to technology (such as replacing basic machinery) and attempted limited amounts of skill enhancement. The remainder, the majority, have been largely stagnant in terms of technology and skill development since liberalization, with some regressing to lower levels of technology.

In the clothing industry, the situation is far more bleak, with little improvement in technology or skill levels in almost all the sample firms. Despite the greater availability of imported capital goods, few firms have upgraded their plant and equipment or improved product quality. This poor performance appears to be partly the result of the firms' inability to compete with second-hand imports, in the face of which most firms have moved out of clothing manufacture into trade (many of the sample firms have engaged in such trade whilst maintaining skeleton production facilities). The experience of the export-oriented affiliate shows the extent to which the rest of the garment firms are lagging behind.

4.5 THE IMPACT OF TECHNOLOGY AND SKILLS ON FIRM PERFORMANCE

In this section we relate the post-liberalization performance of the sample firms to technology and skill development.[4] We undertake an econometric analysis of the influence of technology and skills on two indicators of firm performance: labour productivity and export orientation. Given both the small size of and the lack of variation in the technological behaviour of the clothing industry sample, this analysis is confined to the engineering industry.

4.5.1 Methodology

Technology index: this econometric analysis requires a summary measure of technology. The technology index (TI) conceives of technology defined broadly, and was introduced in Chapter 2. The variables included in the TI, as used in this country study, are as follows:

- Equipment upgrading involving CAD.
- Equipment upgrading involving CNC/NC.
- Replacement investment since liberalization.
- Quality control system.
- Preventive maintenance.

- In-house repair shop.
- Inventory control system.
- Improvements in inventory control since liberalization.
- Improvements in quality control since liberalization.
- Improvements in maintenance since liberalization.
- Changes to existing products since liberalization.
- Introduction of new products since liberalization.
- Adaptive process changes.

Skill index: in order to limit the number of variables used in the econometric analysis, we also derive a simple composite variable relating to skills. This index is computed by aggregating (0, 1) values relating to various aspects of skill development:

- Employment of at least one graduate engineer.
- In-house training.
- Training at domestic training centre.
- Training at foreign training centre.
- Training at capital goods supplier.
- Use of technology institution for testing.
- Use of technology institution for design and development.

The above variables are aggregated and normalized to provide a firm-specific index of skill development. Thus the higher the value of this variable, the greater the extent of skill upgrading undertaken by the firm. The technology and skill indices are fairly highly correlated, with a correlation coefficient of 0.57, significant at the 1 per cent level. This partly reflects the fact that the greatest amount of skill development in the post-liberalization period was undertaken by the firms that introduced advanced machinery or improved the quality of their products. It also reflects the fact that a high level of skill promotes technological dynamism at the firm level. This issue is examined further below.

4.5.2 The Influence of Technology and Skills on Productivity

We estimate a single equation model of the determinants of labour productivity in order to assess the influence of the technology and skill indices derived above on labour productivity. The measure of labour productivity used is sales per employee. In addition to the technology and skill indices, several other variables conventionally used in estimations of the determinants of firm-level productivity are included as independent variables:

- TI: technology index.
- SKILLIND: skill index.
- CAPACITY: average level of capacity utilization in 1989–94.
- KL: capital/labour ratio.
- SIZE: number of employees in 1994.
- CONSTRUCT: a dummy variable taking the value 1 if the firm produces construction-related products, 0 otherwise.[5]

The results of the estimation of Model 1 are presented in Table 4.8. Both TI and SKILLIND are positive and significant at the 5 per cent level; thus both technology upgrading and skill development have a positive influence on firm-level productivity. In addition the variables CAPACITY and CONSTRUCT are positive and significant at the 10 per cent level.

The fact that the technology index appears to have a significant influence on productivity, whereas the capital intensity variable KL has no significant influence, is noteworthy. We have investigated whether this was due to the correlation between TI and KL. However, although TI contained information on investment in new capital

Table 4.8 Regression results for Model 1. Dependent variable: value added per employee (natural logarithm)

Variable	*Coefficient*	*(T-value)*
TI	0.31	(2.08)**
SKILLIND	2.23	(3.06)**
CAPACITY	0.01	(1.8)*
KL	0.0002	(0.70)
SIZE	−0.0004	(−0.278)
CONSTRUCT	1.23	(1.97)*
Constant	12.8	(24.8)***
Adjusted $R^2 = 0.55$		
$F = 8.42$***		
$n = 40$		

*Significant at the 10 per cent level.
**Significant at the 5 per cent level.
***Significant at the 1 per cent level.

investment that may be closely related to capital intensity, the correlation between TI and KL is low, probably due to the broad range of technology indicators used to derive TI. Dropping TI from the estimation does not alter the result.

The significance of TI and the lack of significance of capital intensity in the productivity estimation may be explained by the fact that the technology index is derived using several variables relating to 'minor' aspects of technical activity. These types of technical activity may have a high pay-off in terms of productivity, for several reasons. Firstly, the skills required to implement and master minor process changes may be more readily available in the firms in our sample. Secondly, these minor changes are likely to have a shorter pay-off period, thus showing up in our single period indicator of productivity. These interpretations must be treated with some caution, however, as the lack of significance of the capital intensity variable may be due to a measurement error, given the inherent difficulties involved in obtaining data on capital.

The significance of the dummy variable, CONSTRUCT, indicates that firms producing construction-related products such as steel roofing and galvanized sheets have significantly higher productivity levels then firms in other product group.[6] This may be due to the fact that this subsector uses a distinctly different type of technology (that is, continuous process) from that used in the other subsectors (discontinuous general purpose technology).

4.5.3 Which Aspects of Technology are Related to Higher Productivity?

The influence of different types of technical activity on productivity is examined by including some of the individual components of the technology index in an alternative productivity estimation. The other independent variables included in the previous estimation are also included in this model. Model 2 examines the relative influence of equipment upgrading and process engineering on productivity. Two dummy variables are used to capture this: EQUIP (a variable taking the value 1 if equipment upgrading has been undertaken, 0 otherwise) and PROCESS (a dummy variable taking the value 1 if any process engineering improvements have been undertaken, 0 otherwise).[7] The results are shown in Table 4.9.

Contrary to expectations, equipment upgrading is not related to higher productivity. This may be because most of the firms that have invested in sophisticated machinery and equipment have failed to master the efficient use of these technologies. As noted above, in many

Table 4.9 Regression results for Model 2. Dependent variable: value-added per employee

Variable	*Coefficient*	*T-value*
PROCESS	0.30	(2.1)**
EQUIP	0.17	(1.2)
CAPACITY	0.02	(2.2)**
KL	−0.0002	(−0.51)
SIZE	0.001	(0.87)
CONSTRUCT	1.34	(2.7)**
Constant	12.5	(16.6)***
Adjusted $R^2=0.41$		
$F=(4.2)$***		
$n=40$		

**Significant at the 5 per cent level.
***Significant at the 1 per cent level.

of these firms, training in the operation of the new machinery has been limited and there have been few efforts to achieve longer-term, continuous improvements in operating efficiency.

Process engineering is more closely related to higher productivity, as the variable PROCESS is significant at the 5 per cent level. Thus competence in functions such as quality control, maintenance and inventory control is a significant determinant of economic performance in this industry. This reflects the fact that these fairly minor aspects of technological dynamism are relatively easy to master, thus yielding quick returns. The relative importance of process engineering *vis-à-vis* investment in plant and equipment is also in accordance with the lack of significance of the capital intensity and vintage variables in the productivity estimations.

4.5.4 The Influence of Technology Activity and Skills on Exports

We now examine the impact of technological activity on another indicator of firm performance: the propensity to export, measured by the share of exports in total output. The dependent variable EXPORT is the proportion of exports in total sales in 1994. The results are presented in Table 4.10.

TI is significant in the estimation, indicating that technical activity is positively related to the propensity to export. This result could indicate reverse causality, with export-orientation promoting technological

Table 4.10 Regression results for Model 3. Dependent variable: exports as per cent of sales

Variable	*Coefficient*	*T-value*
SIZE	−0.01	(−0.74)
FOREIGN	7.3	(3.3)**
TI	0.45	(2.1)**
SKILLIND	0.15	(2.07)**
AGE	0.01	(0.67)
Constant	0.002	(2.89)
Adjusted $R^2=0.32$		
$F=3.8$**		
$n=40$		

**Significant at the 5 per cent level.

dynamism (for instance through interactions with foreign buyers). Nevertheless the fact that much of the technological activity captured by the TI variable was undertaken prior to 1994, the year for which exports are measured, may be taken as an indication that technological competence was a prior condition for export success. The skill index, SKILLIND, and the variable for foreign ownership, FOREIGN, also have significant and positive influences on the dependent variable.

The analysis indicates that the firms that have performed better in the post-liberalization period, in terms of productivity and export orientation, are those that have been more active in terms of technology and skill development. The minority of firms that have upgraded their technology in the post-liberalization period are largely the same firms that have recorded a relatively superior economic performance. Below, we attempt to identify the characteristics of these technologically dynamic, better performing firms.

4.6 DETERMINANTS OF TECHNOLOGICAL DYNAMISM

4.6.1 Model 4

In Model 4 we estimate the influence of several firm characteristics – size, age, ownership – as well as the entrepreneur's education level and the skill index on technological dynamism, measured using the technology index (TI). It is acknowledged that the skill index can be both a cause and result of technology upgrading. However this model only deals with the causality running from skill to technology and uses OLS estimation. Given the small sample size, alternative techniques such as two-stage least squares were not used to take account of the two-way interaction between skills and technology.

The dependent variable is TI, the independent variables are:

- SIZE: number of employees in 1989.
- AGE: age of the firm in 1989.
- FOREIGN: a dummy variable taking the value 1 if over 25 per cent equity is foreign owned, 0 otherwise.
- ENTRESKILL: a dummy variable taking the value 1 if the entrepreneur had a university education, 0 otherwise.
- SKILLIND: the skill and training index.

The results of the estimation are given in Table 4.11. ENTRESKILL and SKILLIND are positively and significantly related to technological dynamism. AGE is negatively and significantly related to technological dynamism.

Firm age: can be related to technological dynamism in several ways. On the one hand older firms may display higher levels of technological dynamism due to greater production experience or 'learning by doing'. On the other hand, long-established production methods and 'routines' in older firms may mean that younger firms are more likely to introduce technical change.

Table 4.11 Regression results for Model 4. Dependent variable: TI in the engineering industry

Variable	*Coefficient*	*T-value*
SIZE	0.024	(1.2)
FOREIGN	0.33	(0.59)
ENTRESKILL	0.25	(2.2)**
AGE	−0.03	(−3.2)**
SKILLIND	0.54	(3.6)**
Adjusted $R^2 = 0.37$		
$F = 4.6$**		
$n = 40$		

**Significant at the 5 per cent level.

The estimation of Model 4 shows that younger firms have significantly higher levels of technological activity than older ones. In order to check the robustness of this result, we examined whether it reflected the influence of a few very old or very young firms in the sample. For instance TI includes factors such as the use of computerized machinery and CAD, which are used by a minority of sample firms that are also considerably younger than the rest. In addition the oldest firms in the sample (over 80 years old) produce machinery for the declining sisal industry and have been technologically stagnant in recent years due to falling demand. Excluding these firms from the analysis reduces, but does not negate, the significance of the negative age–technical activity relationship.

Entrepreneurial skills: education was expected to have a positive influence on technological dynamism as entrepreneurs with higher levels of education should be better equipped to assess the potential pay-off from introducing new technology, as well as to identify new markets and coordinate external linkages that promote technological activity. The estimations show the education of entrepreneurs to be significantly and positively related to TI. The importance of entrepreneurship is not very surprising, given the centralized nature of decision making in most firms. We can examine the relationship between entrepreneurial skills and the individual aspects of technical activity included in TI using bivariate tests of association (Table 4.12).[8] The results indicate that entrepreneurial skill is especially important in relation to relatively complex technological activities such as the adoption of computerized machine tools and the introduction of new products. It is likely that such major decisions in a firm are strongly influenced by the technical knowledge and skills of the entrepreneur.

Skill: the variable SKILLIND has a significant and positive influence on TI, providing support for the argument that the acquisition

Table 4.12 Bivariate T-tests

	ENTRESKILL
CAD	3.5**
CNC	4.3**
New products	2.4**
Inventory control system	0.5
Quality control system	1.2

**Significant at the 5 per cent level.

of relevant skills is an important determinant of technological activity. This result is also likely to reflect the two-way causality that exists between skills and technology.

Size: a positive link between size and technological dynamism is expected because large firms have the financial ability to undertake expensive technological activity, either from internal funds or from access to external funds. Many aspects of technical activity included in the index, such as the introduction of quality control systems and stock control systems, were also mainly relevant to the larger firms. Contrary to expectations, however, firm size does not emerge as a significant determinant of TI. The lack of significance of the SIZE variable appears to be partly due to the fact that the firms in the sample that use such advanced equipment such as CAD and CNC machines are relatively small producers of high-precision products. It also partly reflects the presence of a few older and larger firms that are technologically stagnant. Excluding a few of these firms from the analysis, however, does not alter the original result.

Ownership: foreign firms may display higher levels of technological activity than local firms due to better access to financial resources and skills and proprietary knowledge. Contrary to expectations, foreign ownership does not improve TI. This may be mainly because the sample only contains three foreign firms, two of which are fairly dynamic and the other is technologically stagnant. The technologically stagnant foreign firm produces machinery for the declining sisal industry and is in the process of exiting the industry due to falling demand.

4.6.2 Model 5: Types of Training and Technology Linkages

Here we examine the effects of specific types of skill and skill acquisition on TI. This is done by using several of the individual variables used to derive the skill index in the estimation. It is assumed that the skill and training variables included in this estimation mainly have a causal effect on technology and are not themselves the outcome of the introduction of new technology. The training variables were constructed paying special attention to the regularity of training (this was possible as information relating to the frequency with which various types of training has been undertaken was obtained). Thus training that was undertaken for the specific purpose of introducing new technology is excluded, for example special in-house training programmes and training by capital goods suppliers.

The independent variables (SIZE, AGE, FOREIGN and ENTRE-SKILL) used in Model 4 are also included in this model. The new variables are as follows:

- FORTRAIN: a dummy variable taking the value 1 if the firm sends employees for training abroad on a regular basis, 0 otherwise.
- INTRAIN: a dummy variable taking the value 1 if the firm has an in-house training centre, 0 otherwise.
- DOMTRAIN: a dummy variable taking the value 1 if employees are given regular training at domestic training centres, 0 otherwise.
- STLINK: a dummy variable taking the value 1 if the firm has linkages with domestic technology institutions for information acquisition, 0 otherwise.
- ENGPROP: the proportion of engineers in the workforce.[9]

The results show that in-house training programmes (INTRAIN) and training at foreign institutions (FORTRAIN) have the strongest influence on technical performance (Table 4.13). Training at local training institutions does little to promote technological dynamism. This can be interpreted as partly reflecting the poor quality of training at domestic technical institutions. It also reflects the fact that a certain degree of endogeneity relating to training and technological activity is still present in this model. Firms that send their employees abroad for training and those with in-house training centres are likely to be the more technologically dynamic firms in the sample.

Linkages with domestic technology institutions seem to have little influence on firm-level technological capability. This may partly reflect the poor quality or services provided by such institutions in Tanzania or the inability of firms to utilize the services on offer, or both.

The influence of engineering skills on TI is examined in Model 5 using the variable ENGPROP: the number of graduate engineers as a proportion of the workforce. Contrary to expectations, this variable is not significant. The reasons for this were investigated and the following points emerged.

Firstly, the insignificance of ENGPROP was not due to the presence of technologically stagnant small firms with a very high proportion of engineers. Excluding such firms does not alter the result. Secondly, firms employing at least one engineer are not significantly more dynamic than those who do not employ any engineers. Using a dichotomous variable (0 if the firm did not employ any engineers, 1 otherwise) instead of the continuous variable ENGPROP does not alter the result. The fact that, in a large proportion of the sample firms, engineers were not employed in decision making positions may be

Table 4.13 Results for Model 5. Dependent variable: technology index, engineering industry

Variable	*Coefficient*	*T-value*
SIZE	0.04	(0.6)
FOREIGN	0.66	(1.2)
AGE	−0.02	(−2.5)**
ENTRESKILL	0.22	(1.7)*
ENGPROP	−0.002	(−0.14)
FORTRAIN	0.91	(2.1)**
DOMTRAIN	0.13	(0.49)
INTRAIN	1.1	(3.1)**
STLINK	−0.10	(−0.31)
Adjusted $R^2=0.53$		
$F=5.5$**		
$n=40$		

*Significant at the 10 per cent level.
**Significant at the 5 per cent level.

one reason for the weak relationship between formal engineering skills and TI.

To sum up, the econometric analysis in this section indicates that, in the engineering industry, the firms that display the most technological dynamism are young firms, those with educated entrepreneurs and those that provide regular, systematic workforce training. These firms are better able to respond to increased import competition as well as the greater availability of imported inputs and technologies. It was noted in Section 4.3 that that only a minority of firms have a long-term 'strategy' to upgrade technology and enhance productive efficiency. The econometric analysis in this section has identified some the characteristics that distinguish these firms from those that have been largely stagnant in the post-liberalization period.

4.7 CONCLUSIONS

The picture that emerges of technological responses to liberalization in the Tanzanian sample is not very encouraging. Their initial capabilities were poor and their reaction to liberalization has on the whole been passive or negative. In the clothing industry, the decline that began in the years prior to liberalization was exacerbated after implementation of the trade reforms. Most of the clothing firms have stagnated or regressed *vis-à-vis* technology and skill development since liberalization. Their unwillingness to invest in new technology, despite rising GDP and a greater availability of capital goods and inputs, can be attributed largely to the low technology base and intense competition from second-hand imports. The main response here has been to move out of clothing manufacture and into trading in second-hand garments; only one foreign affiliate has entered the industry with an export-oriented facility, and the difference in technological capabilities between it and the other firms clearly shows the gap that exists.

In the engineering industry, the initial technological level was generally quite low, though some firms had the ability to produce complex products. The simple, localized nature of most products gave many engineering firms a cushion against import liberalization and provided a 'grace period' for restructuring and upgrading. Moreover the rise in demand after the crisis period stimulated output. As a result there was some improvement in engineering capabilities compared with the previous period. This improvement, however, masks substantial interfirm variation: a minority of firms have done better in the post-liberalization years, but the majority have performed worse. Econometric analysis suggests that the firms that have displayed a better economic performance since liberalization are those whose initial technological capability was higher. Weak technological capability and low dynamism also helps explain the poor market performance of the majority of firms. The firms that had the highest level of technological dynamism were young firms, those with educated entrepreneurs and those that provided regular, systematic workforce training.

Notes

1. The authors wish to thank R. Kulwa, L. Luvanga and M. Sanghe for participating in the field research.
2. This cannot be taken as reflecting the true extent of new firms established in the post-liberalization period in either industry. The age structure of the samples partly reflects the procedure adopted to select the firms. The firms

chosen were a subsample of the firms surveyed in the Annual Survey of Industries and many new firms are not included in this sampling frame.
3. The intensity of formal design activity (for instance as measured by the ratio of design costs to total production costs) can be taken as an indicator of the complexity of a product.
4. Econometric estimations of firm-level technical efficiency and productivity growth have shown investment in new capital goods, R&D activities as well as organizational improvements and skills to be significant influences on these indicators (Caves and Barton, 1990; Chen and Tan, 1987). This has been corroborated by case studies of the influence of technology upgrading on productivity growth (Katz, 1987).
5. While the firms in our sample fall into five product categories, we make a distinction between construction-related products and the other four product groups. This is mainly because of technology differences in the product groups. While the four other product groups (agricultural machinery, industrial spares, motor spares and household goods) all use discontinuous and mainly general purpose technology, firms producing construction-related products use markedly different continuous process technology. The variable CONSTRUCT is therefore used in the estimation because this difference in technology is hypothesized to have a differential impact on the level of productivity.
6. Dummy variables relating to other product groups were also used, but were not significant.
7. The two variables EQUIP and PROCESS were derived by collapsing some of the variables included in the TI index. Thus EQUIP takes the value 1 if upgrading involved CAD or CNC/NC, 0 otherwise. PROCESS takes the value 1 if improvements in quality control, repair or maintenance were made following liberalization, 0 otherwise.
8. The individual aspects of technical activity are measured using the (0, 1) variables used to derive the TI index.
9. The variable ENGPROP is included in this estimation because, as noted earlier, the number of firms that have employed additional engineers when introducing new technology is minimal.

5 Technology and the Responses of Firms to Adjustment in Zimbabwe

Wolfram W. Latsch and
Peter B. Robinson

5.1 COUNTRY BACKGROUND

5.1.1 Historical Background: Industrialization in Zimbabwe

Industrialization began in Zimbabwe (then Southern Rhodesia) in the first two decades of this century, very early by African standards. By the early 1940s Rhodesia had a comparatively sophisticated industrial base, with the only integrated iron and steel plant in SubSaharan Africa and a range of consumer and producer goods industries. Manufacturing accounted for 10 per cent of GDP and around 8 per cent of exports. Further import substitution took place before, during and after the Second World War. In 1953 the two Rhodesias (now Zambia and Zimbabwe) federated with Nyasaland (now Malawi), forming a common market. Southern Rhodesia became the location for most of the manufacturing serving the region.

The Federation broke up in 1963, and Zambia and Malawi became independent under black majority rule. Southern Rhodesia declared unilateral independence from Britain, forming the state of Rhodesia under white minority rule (the so-called 'UDI' Regime).[1] Trade and diplomatic sanctions were imposed by the international community, launching a new period of intense import-substitution and inward-oriented development. The variety of products made in Rhodesia expanded enormously (mostly serving a very narrow segment of the population, the white minority) and manufacturing as a share of GDP rose from 17 per cent to 24 per cent during UDI.

During UDI there developed a comprehensive system of foreign exchange and price controls, deployed by a white industrialist community and a government that was determined to overcome the constraints inflicted by the sanctions. This highly restrictive system operated very effectively, and Rhodesia is now admitted to have been one of the few relatively 'efficient' import-substituting industrializers (World Bank, 1989). In particular the engineering sector became the locus of a wide range of minor innovations, and a wide variety of specialized (if often idiosyncratic) skills. Practically the only outlet for exports was South Africa, which did not join the sanctions.

After independence in 1980 the government retained widespread economic controls in pursuit of a different goal: spreading the benefits of development to the mass of the disfranchised population. But there was no longer the previous close rapport between government and industrialists, and the relationship became increasingly antagonistic. The government took the side of organized labour and introduced very restrictive labour legislation. Since there were almost no black entrepreneurs, measures were introduced to alleviate the inequality of productive ownership, but this did not amount to a coherent effort and more effective measures were introduced in the late 1980s.

There was a growing debate throughout the 1980s within the country (and between Zimbabwe and international institutions) about the merits of opening up and deregulating the economy. There was a stabilization programme in 1982–84 and mounting pressures from the trade balance. A World Bank study attempted to determine the competitiveness of Zimbabwe's industrial sectors, using domestic resource cost (DRC) analysis.[2] The result was surprising: although Zimbabwe had never been an 'open economy', only two subsectors were found to have DRC scores above unity, while in all the other subsectors there were many firms with scores significantly below unity (indicating a relatively competitive sector). The manufacturing sector was therefore found to be quite competitive, in contrast to most other African countries. In 1986 another World Bank study revised these figures downward and stated that Zimbabwean manufacturing was far more internationally competitive than previously thought.[3] The 1989 study confirmed these results, called the findings 'puzzling', and could only offer the explanation that the efficient firms had become so *in spite* of UDI restrictions. This was attributed to the presence of managerial and technological capability before the restrictions were applied, suggesting that the import-substituting regime had not been too harmful, or that the DRC measures were not telling the whole story.

In the late 1980s Zimbabwe decided to embark on a structural adjustment programme, with trade liberalization as a central ingredient.[4] A more competitive environment was seen as the way to higher growth and lower unemployment. The technological upgrading of the domestic industrial sector and an export-oriented supply response were hence critical to this undertaking. The liberalization programme had six components: (1) imports would progressively move into Open General Import License (OGIL), with average nominal protection to be reduced from 19 per cent in 1991 to 14 per cent in 1995; (2) the introduction of an export retention scheme (5–7.5 per cent of foreign exchange earnings); (3) decontrol of prices on goods considered luxuries; (4) a 'one stop' investment approval institution (the Zimbabwe Investment Centre); (5) a 100 per cent dividend remittance on newly approved foreign investments; and (6) the promotion of small and medium enterprises through a venture capital company. A later section deals with how this was implemented and how it affected the incentive regime of manufacturing firms in the country.

5.1.2 Economic Performance from Independence to ESAP (1980–91)

There was a wide range of controls in operation in Zimbabwe during the first ten years of independence and prior to the establishment of the Economic Structural Adjustment Programme (ESAP). These controls affected macroeconomic (exchange and interest rates) and trade policies (regulations on export earnings, import licences, invisibles and capital mobility). Overall real GDP (of which manufacturing steadily accounted for around 25 per cent) grew during this period at around 1.5 per cent (Table 5.1).

The volume of manufacturing production increased by an average of 2 per cent a year from 1980 to 1990, growing at roughly 1 per cent for the first six years of independence (Table 5.2). Improved performance during the period 1986–90 (around 4.5 per cent a year on average) may in part be explained by the incentives to increase production for export,[5] and the associated foreign currency benefits that were used to increase production for the domestic market.

Many Zimbabwean manufacturing enterprises were significant exporters for several decades. While during the UDI period their main market was South Africa, they had a considerable competitive advantage in neighbouring countries, which appears to have grown during the period of enforced isolation. With the coming of independence and improved access to other markets, manufactured exports grew steadily during the 1980s (according to World Bank data, at 13 per cent per annum), and the manufacturing sector's share of exports rose from just under 30 per cent in 1981 to just over 36 per cent in 1990. However the export 'commitment' of most Zimbabwean manufacturing firms

Table 5.1 GDP at factor cost (US$ million)

Year	*Total*	*Manufacturing*
1980	4782	1190
1981	6421	1611
1982	5065	1219
1983	4914	1303
1984	3760	982
1985	3794	907
1986	4380	1092
1987	4757	1261
1988	4855	1234
1989	4902	1298
1990	5554	1465
1991	3762	1024
1992	4131	1284
1993	3795	1110
Annual growth rate (%)		
1980–1993	−1.76	−0.53
1980–1990	1.51	2.10
1991–1995	<1 (est.)	

Sources: *CSO Quarterly Digest of Statistics*, various issues; Standard Chartered Bank, *Business Trends Zimbabwe*, June 1996.

remained low, with exports frequently sold at a loss to gain access to foreign exchange, and with prices on the (largely protected) domestic market set at a higher level to compensate. With an increase in the number of manufacturing inputs on Open General Import Licence (OGIL) and a liberalization of the foreign exchange regime, many companies ceased to export and only the 'committed' exporters expanded their export production.[6] However, as noted below, this latter category greatly boosted its export performance after 1993.

Investment figures are unfortunately not available after 1988. Investment had more or less collapsed just before independence in 1980, falling to less than 2 per cent of GDP. Recovering to around 5 per cent in 1981, it fell again to under 2 per cent in 1985, rising thereafter to a (still unsatisfactory) 4.6 per cent in 1988. This was in spite of negative real interest rates during most of the 1980s. Thus the capital stock in manufacturing (which was antiquated in 1980) has continued to deteriorate. The decline in investment was partly due to the increasingly erratic economic policy, widespread controls (particularly the uncertainty regarding foreign exchange allocations) and the neglect of public sector investment.

5.1.3 The Economic Environment and the Incentive Regime under Liberalization (1991–95)

Overall performance during the five years of ESAP was disappointing (Table 5.2). According to recent estimates,[7] real GDP growth from 1991 to 1995 was barely positive (compared with the projected growth

Table 5.2 Selected manufacturing sectors: volume index of production (1980 = 100)

	All manufacturing	*Clothing and footwear*	*Metals, metal products and machinery*	*Textiles and ginning*	*Transport equipment*
1980	100.0	100.0	100.0	100.0	100.0
1981	109.4	128.4	104.8	111.6	155.0
1982	108.7	118.6	96.4	118.8	178.4
1983	105.8	109.2	94.8	108.8	145.6
1984	100.7	99.9	89.4	124.1	114.7
1985	112.2	111.5	100.5	175.0	96.8
1986	115.4	106.6	98.2	190.4	98.8
1987	118.1	119.5	95.1	196.2	83.3
1988	123.9	120.2	100.4	202.7	103.6
1989	130.8	137.7	106.2	208.2	147.4
1990	139.1	145.0	111.4	216.6	146.6
ESAP					
1991	143.0	148.9	113.5	226.2	142.8
1992	129.9	124.5	100.6	176.5	141.0
1993	119.3	127.7	82.3	192.4	82.0
1994	130.7	129.0	93.2	217.6	134.8
1995	112.9	99.8	90.3	89.1	155.5
Change during ESAP (%)	−21.0	−33.0	−20.4	−60.6	8.8

Note: Sectoral figures for 1995 are for January to May only.
Sources: *CSO Quarterly Digest of Statistics*; *EIU Country Report*, 3/1996.

rate for the ESAP period of 5 per cent), and manufacturing declined by almost 9 per cent a year between 1990 and 1993. By December 1995 (the latest figures incorporated in this study), the overall manufacturing production index had fallen to 106.8 (1980 = 100) after peaking at 143 during 1991. The average index for 1995 was 112.9: this represents a decline in the volume of manufacturing production of 21 per cent during the ESAP period.

The sectors studied here declined in volume terms during the ESAP period: clothing and footwear by 33 per cent, metals, metal products and machinery by 20 per cent, and textiles and ginning by 60 per cent. GDP declined by around 3 per cent in 1995,[8] and manufacturing sector production plunged 13.7 per cent in 1995 alone (reaching its lowest level for a decade). On the present trend the manufacturing sector is expected to take until at least 1998 to regain the 1991 production levels. The share of manufacturing in GDP fell from a peak of 23.4 per cent in 1991 to 18.6 per cent in 1995, a substantial 'deindustrialization' that is causing grave concern in the country.

Exports declined immediately after the launch of ESAP, due to the removal of export incentives and general uncertainty. However they started to revive after 1992 (Table 5.3). The overall rate of growth during 1990–95 was below the 1980s rate of 13 per cent, but exceeded it in 1992–95, indicating a strengthening of preliberalization trends. The fastest rates of growth in the latter period came from two resource based activities, processed foods and wood products (mainly furniture). The lowest growth came from textiles, clothing, footwear, chemicals and transport equipment, with iron and steel suffering a significant decline. Engineering (metal products and machinery) performed well at nearly 20 per cent. Note, however, that our sample evidence does not capture the most recent increase in exports, which came after 1994.

Most of the recent export growth is a result of Zimbabwe's competitive advantage in neighbouring markets, and mainly involves large established firms (though some are also new to exporting). The extent to which exports are being 'pushed out' by domestic recession, as opposed to being a long-term commitment to foreign markets, is not clear; in any case, production data suggest that the growth in exports is insufficient to compensate for the low level of domestic demand. It also seems that the growth has little to do with import liberalization directly – the capabilities being exploited existed already – and its resumption was a return to earlier trends. Our case studies below suggest that real restructuring in response to import liberalization has yet to take place.

Table 5.3 Manufactured exports during ESAP ($ million and growth rates)

	Values			*Annual growth rates (%)*	
Sector	*1990*	*1992*	*1995*	*1990–95*	*1992–95*
Foodstuffs	49.9	50.3	152.5	25.0	44.7
Beverages, tobacco	6.2	7.4	14.1	17.9	24.0
Cotton ginning	85.3	26.9	44.8	−12.1	18.5
Textiles	40.4	55.1	58.4	7.6	2.0
Clothing	38.1	50.8	60.9	9.8	6.2
Footwear	5.2	9.9	13.8	21.6	11.7
Wood, furniture	10.7	16.6	47.4	34.7	41.9
Printing, publishing	5.6	6.0	14.2	20.5	33.3
Chemicals	25.0	37.3	47.4	13.6	8.3
Non-metallic minerals	13.1	9.0	14.0	1.3	15.9
Iron and steel	58.9	51.8	20.4	−19.1	−26.7
Ferrochrome	155.0	113.2	213.0	6.6	23.5
Metals, machinery	58.5	59.4	101.8	11.7	19.7
Transport equipment	29.7	21.0	24.2	−4.0	4.8
Art	5.9	7.4	17.5	24.3	33.2
Other	32.1	40.6	70.4	17.0	20.1
Total	619.6	562.6	914.8	8.1	17.6

Imports, as discussed further below, have been declining (Table 5.4) although an increase of imports from South Africa has been giving concern.[9]

Domestic demand after 1992 was adversely affected by the severe drought during the 1992–93 agricultural season as well as burgeoning inflation after 1991 (which increased to almost 50 per cent per annum). Inflation has since dropped to around 20 per cent per annum, but has further eroded real incomes in the process. Real income per capita was around 15 per cent lower in early 1996 than in 1990.[10] These general remarks lead us to a discussion of the incentive environment facing manufacturing firms at the time of our survey in early 1995.

Zimbabwe was an almost closed economy between 1965 and 1980 (excepting trade relations with South Africa), with a complete ban on competing imports. The wide variety of industrial activities seen in the country today are the legacy of that period. Nevertheless import-substitution was becoming harder during the early 1970s, and industry organizations started to press for an increased focus on exports while maintaining import protection.[11] An early export incentive was

Table 5.4 Manufactured imports during ESAP (US$ million, percentage change)

	Total imports	*Total manufactured imports*	*Textiles*	*Clothing*	*Metal products*	*Machinery and equipment*	*Transport equipment*
1990	1808.3	1631.8	36.6	7.4	41.2	279.2	284.9
1991	2171.1 (+20%)	1995.1 (+22%)	91.8 (+151%)	5.8 (−21%)	50.2 (+22%)	350.6 (+26%)	353.1 (+24%)
1992	2200.7 (+1%)	1989.2 (0%)	60.5 (−34%)	2.3 (−61%)	52.3 (+4%)	331.8 (−5%)	262.6 (−26%)
1993	1783.9 (−18.9%)	1589.0 (−20%)	63.2 (+5%)	2.3 (+2%)	37.9 (−28%)	214.9 (−35%)	242.8 (−7%)
1994	2239.1 (+29%)	2051.6 (+29%)	89.1 (+41%)	4.9 (+112%)	64.1 (+69%)	381.6 (+78%)	314.5 (+30%)
Annual average growth rate (%)	−1.2	−1.4	−0.5	−4.8	4.1	−1.4	−4.0

Source: *CSO Quarterly Digest of Statistics*, various issues.

Table 5.5 Summary of policy changes under the Economic and Structural Adjustment Programme (ESAP)

	Measure	*Exchange rate (Z$/US$)*	*Inflation (CPI) (%)*	*Int. rate (90d NCD) (%)*	*Export retention (%)*	*Premium ERS/FCA (%)*	*Corporate tax rate (%)*	*Import liberalization and protection*
September 1990	Trade liberalization policy announced. Export retention scheme (ERS) introduced	2.6	16.1	9.3	7.5	n.a.		Oct. 1990: first items on OGIL* (raw materials for packaging, textiles and cement)
January 1991	ESAP document launched	3.2	17.4	9.9	7.5	n.a.		10 per cent surcharge on OGIL imports Oct. 1991: manufacturers' rebate scrapped. Tariffs raised (30 per cent non-OGIL, 40 per cent OGIL, duty and surcharge combined)
June 1991		5.0	23.4	15.9	15.0	n.a.		
December 1991		5.0	28.8	25.5	15.0	n.a.		
January 1992		5.1	32.5	28.5	25.0			Restrictions on use of ERS removed. Tradability allowed from January 1992
June 1992	Export revolving fund removed. Inward processing introduced	5.0	43.1	32.5	25.0	60.0		SA trade agreement in abeyance
December 1992		5.5	46.3	37.0	30.0			By end of December, 45 per cent of imports free of licences

January 1993	Devaluation	6.0	45.0	38.0	30.0			Use of ERS for selected invisibles sanctioned
April 1993	Investment measures							Dividends included from May 1993
June 1993	Foreign currency accounts (FCAs) allowed for individuals	6.5	26.1	40.2	50.0			October 1993: suspension of import surtax and sales tax on a wide range of capital goods
December 1993		6.9	18.6	28.8	50.0	22.0	42.5	
January 1994	Devaluation, 2-tier ER system. Export incentive scheme and ERS scrapped. Corporate FCAs	8.1	18.5	28.4	60.0	5.0		Private imports funded by FCAs completely liberalized
July 1994	Exchange rate unified.	8.1	23.6	33.4	100	n.a.		July 1994: with unification of exchange rates, all imports and invisibles sourced through the market
December 1994		8.4	21.1	30.3	100	n.a.		Sept. 1994: duties on textile and clothing inputs reduced
January 1995	1995: Zimbabwe signs IMF Article VIII, giving commitment to maintain current account convertibility.		20.8		100	n.a.	40.0	
April 1995					100	n.a.	37.5	

* Open General Import Licence.

introduced in the mid 1970s. The trade regime was basically unaltered during 1980–90. The extent of protection was reduced by aid programmes rather than commercial competition, reinforced by the increasing trade deficits of the early 1980s. A stabilization programme in 1982–84 cut import allocations and reintroduced the export incentive that had been abolished in 1981. The latter remained in place until early 1994. Import competition was very weak, with foreign exchange allocations being cut and increased erratically in response to economic fluctuations. The system was based almost entirely on quantitative restrictions. Foreign exchange was allocated to importers according to a complicated formula related to export earnings: this acted as an incentive to enter export markets even at a loss in order to acquire foreign exchange.

Table 5.5 summarizes the changes in the policy regime under ESAP. An export retention scheme was introduced in September 1990 that gave exporters 7.5 per cent of export earnings, but the use of these funds was restricted. A number of crucial manufacturing inputs were placed on OGIL. In 1990, however, the real value of import allocations was only around 40 per cent of its 1981 level: exposure to competitive imports, as well as access to raw materials and capital goods, was considerably lower than at independence, even within an already highly restrictive regime.

By the end of 1991, 25 per cent of imports were available on OGIL, with severe restrictions remaining on non-OGIL goods (almost all competitive imports). In spite of this, imports were much higher than expected and trade liberalization started falling behind schedule, effectively coming to a standstill during 1992–93 as a consequence of severe drought. Tariffs were raised on all imports (OGIL and non-OGIL) and an additional surcharge of 10 per cent was implemented. The tariff system was streamlined, and by 1992 quantitative restrictions had been removed and replaced by tariffs for nearly all goods except clothing (the other exceptions were beverages, tobacco products and jewellery, which are not relevant to our study). In 1994 all direct foreign exchange allocations were abolished. Individuals and companies may hold foreign-exchange-denominated accounts, and complete convertibility of the Zimbabwe dollar is envisaged for the near future.

At the time of the study, clothing imports were on the 'negative list' and banned except for personal use: there was officially no import competition in the clothing sector. As in the other countries, however, there was a considerable inflow of smuggled second-hand items. The average nominal rate of protection for all manufacturing sectors in 1992 was 14 per cent (inputs) and 25 per cent (output). The corresponding effective protection rate was around 70 per cent for manufacturing as a whole, though with wide variations (see Table 5.6). Apart from a reduction in tariffs on clothing inputs and spare parts in 1994 and 1995, respectively, this was the import competition facing manufacturers in early 1995. 'With the exception of a few items, customs duties at present are set below 40 per cent, which is relatively low compared with those of similar developing countries' (Ratnayake, 1994, p. 67). But the tariff structure is still not transparent, and is fraught with exemptions and special regulations.[12]

The incentive regime facing exporters is shown in Figure 5.1, which gives the 'net export incentive' the real receipts (in Zimbabwe dollars) from Z$100 of exports. This takes into account the nominal exchange rate, inflation, export subsidies, as well as any premium from selling foreign exchange earnings (via the export retention scheme) on the market. Export retention was increased from 7.5 per cent in 1990 to 100 per cent in July 1994, when the two-tier exchange rate system was unified. There has been a decline in the export incentive since the end of 1991. Overall, the real effective exchange rate has been falling since about 1985, with erratic movements since the beginning of liberalization, as devaluations have been counteracted by inflation. Muzulu (1995), analysing the effects of real exchange rate depreciation from 1980–90, finds

Table 5.6 Average rates of protection, 1992 (per cent)

Sector or industry	*Nominal rate of protection (inputs)*	*Nominal rate of protection (output)*	*Effective rate of protection (ERP)*
Clothing	29	60	86
Basic metal industries	11	28	157
Cutlery, handtools	24	35	62
Agricultural machinery	19	24	29
Electrical machinery	18	32	60
Transport equipment	19	16	22
Fabricated metal products	21	30	52
Total manufacturing	14	25	70

Source: Ratnayake (1994).

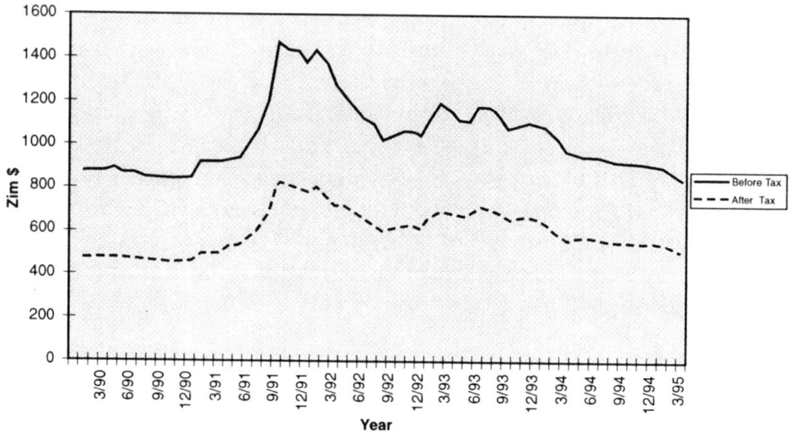

Figure 5.1 Real receipts from US$ 100 of exports (net export incentive), 1990–95

that the supply response has been very weak because of the presence of other distortions and structural problems in the economy.

Financial market liberalization and increased government expenditure (required to service debt as well as covering the increasing losses of public enterprises) led to an increase in interest rates, and from early 1993 Zimbabwe experienced consistently positive real interest for the first time since independence (Figure 5.2). High real interest rates dampened private investment as well as leading to an appreciation of the real effective exchange rate (which in turn adversely affected competitiveness). At the time of our survey, high real interest rates and an increasing burden of debt were regarded by most companies as the main problem.

5.1.4 Summary of the Incentive Regime at the Time of Survey

Clothing firms were competing against a large inflow of smuggled or semi-legal imports, which was affecting the low-quality, standardized end of the industry. Otherwise, manufacturing imports in general, and imports in our survey sectors in particular, were declining, indicating a rather low level of import competition, accounted for by a disappointing economic performance and a falling real exchange rate. However, individual firms may had been affected very differently within the broader industry groups – this will be addressed in the firm-level

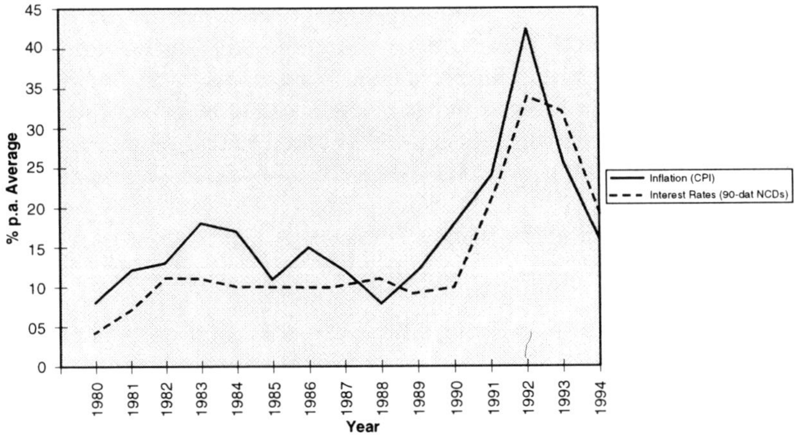

Figure 5.2 Interest rates and inflation, 1980–94

analysis. Import tariffs were modest in nominal terms, but effective protection was higher and more dispersed. Import licenses and foreign exchange allocations had been abolished.

Real export incentives had been declining, taking all taxes, subsidies, and exchange rate variations into account. This affected the clothing sector much more strongly than engineering activities since exports tended to be more important in the former. Apart from the overall export incentive (which was affected by a variety of factors), the abolition of the export incentive scheme (EIS) in 1994 was interpreted by firms as a crucial symbolic step away from a national commitment to expanding exports.

Real interest rates and interest rate volatility were high. This affected private investment plans, and existing levels of debt. High real interest rates had exerted upward pressure on the exchange rate, which further jeopardised exports and increased import competition.

Overall economic performance was disappointing, and the liberalization programme had been thrown off track by the severe drought at the beginning of ESAP, because of lagging public-sector reforms and galloping inflation due to large budget deficits. All this induced considerable uncertainty in the reform process, underlined by the changing attitude of the IMF and the World Bank towards liberalization in Zimbabwe (initially very supportive, but increasingly critical and finally, in the case of the IMF, a withdrawal of credit pending public sector reform). It was a widespread view among firms that the government had no coherent economic strategy, and political uncertainty militated against the economic factors: Zimbabwe was still an authoritarian one-party state with very limited democratic participation, and political-economic issues such as indigenization and land ownership were potentially explosive. These uncertainties and tensions were exerting a strong influence on the technological behaviour of firms, as seen below.

5.1.5 Performance of the Sample Sectors

5.1.5.1 Clothing

The clothing subsector is labour-intensive and its contribution to GDP has been consistently lower than its contribution to employment. This gap has been growing over time, since investment has been low. Informal employment is thought to be much higher than formal employment in the sector. In the formal sector there are around 250 clothing firms in Zimbabwe, and the 77 members of the Zimbabwe Clothing Council (ZCC) account for the bulk of employment. Some of these firms have over 1000 workers, a few dozen employ between 400 and 600 workers, and the rest employ between 50 and 100 workers. Most of the 'formal' non-ZCC members probably have fewer than 50 employees. Formal employment is around 20 000, informal employment probably amounts to over 350 000, with two thirds being accounted for by informal knitting, crocheting and sewing. Links between the formal and informal sectors are practically non-existent.

Exports of clothing were significant even during UDI, when trade sanctions were in place. At that time, around 20 per cent of output was exported, mainly to South Africa. This declined to less than 10 per cent after independence, due to a strong revival in the domestic market. Because of its export record, the government saw clothing as one of the sectors most likely to expand its exports under ESAP. Forecasts in 1992 envisaged around 50 per cent of output being exported by 1996. Overall turnover was projected to increase by just under 10 per cent a year between 1992 and 1996, due to export growth and revival of the domestic market after the drought. In fact clothing production declined by almost 24 per cent between May 1994 and May 1995 alone, though exports rose modestly (Tables 5.2 and 5.3). The volume index of clothing production declined by around one third between the beginning and the end of ESAP. The rise in exports was much lower than the rates achieved in this industry by other major garment-exporting developing countries, even though Zimbabwe is a very small producer and exporter in global terms – compare its $60 million of garment exports with the $1.5–2 billion by relative newcomers such as Sri Lanka, Mauritius and Bangladesh, and the much higher figures for large exporters such as India, China, Indonesia and the Asian 'Tigers'. Presumably part of the increase has been driven by low domestic demand, exacerbated by low-end competition from second-hand imports.

The liberalization of imported inputs has been slow, and many industrialists blame this, among other factors, for the relatively weak competitiveness of the sector. The import content varies between about 60 percent for export production and about 30 per cent for production for the domestic market. Zimbabwean producers must import from ACP countries in order to have access to EU markets under EUR 1, and so cannot use cheaper fabric from East Asia. Domestic fabric is generally of rather poor quality and is not well suited to the production of exports. The domestic production of textiles is heavily oligopolistic, and prices have been rising in spite of declining quality. The interests of clothing producers and textile producers therefore conflict over trade liberalization. The activity suffers from poor labour productivity and discipline (particularly in comparison with East Asian producers), which is compounded by restrictive labour legislation. In addition, Asian textile and clothing producers mostly employ women (apparently they are more nimble in the operation of sewing machines), whereas in Zimbabwe men are predominant. The physical and institutional support infrastructure (especially for export promotion) is also weak in Zimbabwe.

In terms of labour cost in 1993, Zimbabwe ranked 48 out of 58 countries. Furthermore, real wages and earnings have been declining since independence: the index of average earnings in manufacturing stood at 83.4 in 1992 (1979 = 100).[13] In 1993 its wages were higher than in China and Bangladesh (and presumably than in India, Indonesia and Sri Lanka), though much lower than in the 'Tigers' (Table 5.7). This suggests that Zimbabwe cannot sustain a competitive advantage in low-end clothing, as it cannot match the low wages in other, much larger, exporting countries that have expanded their clothing exports in the period that Zimbabwe's exports have been declining. Export growth here clearly requires a significant upgrading of quality, but this is proving difficult (see our survey below), and the main Asian competitors, with greater volumes and better access to inputs, are investing strongly in higher-quality clothing and design.

5.1.5.2 Engineering

'Metals and metal products' is the largest sector in Zimbabwean manufacturing, according to the Central Statistical Office's classification.

Table 5.7 Labour cost comparison (textile industry)

Country	*Hourly cost 1993 (US$)*	*Hourly cost 1991 (US$)*	*Change 1991–93 (per cent)*
Japan	23.65	16.37	44.5
W. Germany	20.50	18.96	8.1
USA	11.61	10.33	12.4
Hong Kong	3.85	3.39	13.6
S. Korea	3.88	3.60	7.8
S. Africa	1.64	1.64	0.0
Malaysia	1.18	0.95	24.2
Zimbabwe	0.42	0.68	−38.2
PR China	0.35	0.34	2.9
Kenya	0.31	0.58	−46.6
Bangladesh	0.23	n.a.	n.a.
Tanzania	0.22	0.32	−31.3

Note: The 1995 figure for Zimbabwe is US$0.40.
Source: Zimconsult (1995), Appendix 3.

The sample includes electrical machinery, construction-related engineering and some items included under a different subheading, transport (including agricultural) equipment. This sector, with its diverse range of products, is the legacy of intensive import substitution during UDI. Most of the production equipment is very old, but within the constraints imposed by age, production appears to be both technically and economically efficient. The age of the equipment, though, does not bode well for dynamic efficiency, particularly when it comes to expanding exports. Many engineering products are currently protected by the fact that they are either inputs into industries such as construction engineering, and protected by high transport costs, or they are not readily supplanted by imports, as in the case of custom-made spares and the servicing of old equipment. Effective protection in basic metal industries is high (157 per cent in 1993), and otherwise varies between 20 per cent and 60 per cent. Nominal tariffs on output in the sectors covered by the survey averaged 27.5 per cent in 1993.

Import penetration appears to have been low so far. Many producers have a domestic market advantage due to the robustness and appropriateness of their products, as well as their long-established links with customers. While it has been questioned whether an engineering sector of this type can be sustained, especially with increasing competition from South Africa, it seems that there will always be scope for certain smaller-scale activities (McPherson, 1991, estimates that over 30 000 people are employed in informal enterprises, compared with around 20 000 in the formal sector). What is more questionable is whether the engineering industry can experience export-led growth, except on a rather limited regional basis: this is addressed in the firm-level analysis. The volume of production in the metals and metal products sector declined by over 20 per cent during ESAP.

5.2 FIRM-LEVEL EXPERIENCE

The sample was selected to capture the wide variety of manufacturing enterprises in the two sectors in terms of size, ownership, technology and skills. Since the focus is on technology and technological capability, the section on characteristics of plant and production is the most extensive.

5.2.1 Main Features of the Sample Firms

The main features of the firms are shown in Table 5.8, and are described below.

Foreign ownership (defined as more than 50 per cent equity held by non-nationals): there are only three foreign-owned firms in the sample, all of these are engineering firms owned by UK multinationals, and most are old Rhodesian/Zimbabwean companies that were taken over. The 'entrepreneurial characteristics' refer to those of the managing director. In cases of arm's-length relationships, it is reasonable to treat managing directors as relatively autonomous entrepreneurs.

Ethnic background of owners and managers: our classification is threefold, local African (LA), local non-African (LNA) and foreign (F). In the case of foreign-owned firms, all the managers are white and male, and one is of foreign origin (British). Of the owner-managed firms, only two are run by local non-Africans not born in the country. All others are run by local Africans or local non-Africans born in the country.

Educational background: The entrepreneurs are classified as having either below or above secondary education. All have progressed beyond primary schooling, and eight have received post-secondary education, which includes diplomas and university degrees (Table 5.9). All but

Table 5.8a Selected indicators of sample firms by number of employees (clothing)

Name of firm	*Product category*[1]	*Ownership*	*Year founded*	*Employment 1994*	*Employment growth rate (%)*[2]	*Sales 1994 (US$ m)*	*Sales growth rate (%)*[2]	*Performance indicator*	*Export ratio (%)*[3]	*Technology index*	*Production system*	*Import liberal challenge*	*Response/ strategy*	*Details of strategy*
Fashion Enterprises	4	family/ LNA[4]	1960	1100	−13.9	—	—	4	45 (75)	1.0	—	1	Defensive	Rethink export strategy
Continental	1	family/ IDC[5]	1917	1100	—	—	—	4	90	0.9	In process	1	Wait and see	Reduce exports
Paramount	5	family/ LNA	1949	1000	25.7	8.54	22.5	1	55	1.0	—	1	Defensive	Specialization
Concorde	1	family/ LNA	1945	500	—	4.02	−11.1	4	25	0.8	Considering	0	Defensive	Rethink export strategy
Bernstein	4	holding company	1939	400	—	2.73	—	3	20 (40)	0.8	—	0	Offensive	Increase exports
Playtime	4	family/ LNA	1974	360	−8.3	8.2	—	5	3 (20)	0.9	—	2	Defensive	—
City Clothing	6	family/ LNA	1949	300	—	4.88	—	4	50 (60)	0.9	—	1	Wait and see	—
Delswa	2	IDC	1963	202	−9.4	0.98	−15.3	5	—	0.8	—	2	Wait and see	Consolidation

Universal Garments	5	family/ LNA	1954	200	—	1.83	1.8	3	—	0.7	—	0	Wait and see	Diversification outside sector
Boss Fashion	2	LNA	1980	150	—	1.22	21.0	4	90	0.3	—	0	Wait and see	—
Chiratidzo	5	LA	1982	117	−12.5	—	—	5	—	0.4	—	1	Defensive	Diversification outside sector
Escapades	2	LA	1990	85	—	0.49	26.7	2	—	0.7	—	2	Offensive	Improve quality
Milford Clothing	5	family/ LNA	1979	69	—	0.55	—	3	—	0.2	—	0	Wait and see	—
Doma Enterprises	5	LA	1983	50	5.7	0.04	−0.9	3	—	0.4	—	0	Wait and see	—
Sprogz	3	LNA	1992	18	—	0.03	—	1	—	0.5	—	0	Offensive	Improve quality, increase exports
Cactus Clothing	2	LA	1978	16	−14.5	0.03	−15.8	4	—	0.4	—	2	Defensive	Uniforms and workwear

Notes:
[1]Product categories (1) menswear; (2) ladies wear; (3) children's wear; (4) mix of 1 3; (5) workwear; (6) mix of 1 3 and 5.
[2]Average Annual Growth Rate 1989/90 – 1994 (where applicable or available).
[3]Percentage of sales generated through exports; the numbers in brackets refer to 1989 where different.
[4]Acquired by foreign company during survery period.
[5]Industrial Development Corporation (parastatal).

Table 5.8b Selected indicators of sample firms, by number of employees (engineering)

Name of firm	*Product category*[1]	*Ownership*	*Year founded*	*Employment 1994*	*Employment growth rate (%)*[2]	*Sales 1994 (US$ m)*	*Sales growth rate (%)*[2]	*Performance indicator*	*Export ratio (%)*[3]	*Technology index*	*Production system*	*Import liberal challenge*	*Response/ strategy*	*Details of strategy*
Deven Engineering	1	IDC[4]	1949/ 89[5]	450	20.7	6.1	24.5	1	—	0.6	—	2	Offensive	Locally appropriate products
Relmo	3	holding company	1968	300	—	3.66	−0.9	3	5	1.0	In process	2	Offensive	Agency, new products, exports
South Wales Electric	3	foreign	1956	300	−6.9	6.46	−3.9	4	10	0.6	In process	2	Wait and see	—
Sepe Metal	4	domestic group	c. 1952	180	—	1.59	1.1	3		0.4	—	0	Wait and see	—
Tinto Industries	5	domestic group	1972	150	3.6	14.63	−19.1	5	10	0.9	In place	2	Offensive	Agency, reorganization, exports
Modcraft	2	family/ LNA	1976	105	3.9	1.71	−2.6	3	30	0.7	—	1	Offensive	Joint ventures
Bain Farm Equip.	5	IDC and LNA[4]	1912	90	—	1.83		4	10	0.9	In process	2	Offensive	Increase exports
Copper Wares	2	domestic group	1959	84	−3.0	0.43	−1.6	4	10	0.5	In place	1	Offensive	New products, exports

Lane	1	foreign	1964	57	−10.0	0.74	−15.5	5	—	0.6	—	1	Wait and see	—
Stainless Steel Products	2	LA	1973/94[5]	50	5.7	1.22	−10.4	4	—	0.5	—	1	Offensive	Improve quality, exports
KSK	1	LNA	1982	50	2.7	0.37	−5.3	3	—	0.6	—	0	Wait and see	—
Modarc	4	family/LNA	1970	45	3.0	0.85	−2.6	3	—	0.5	—	0	Offensive	New products
Tromps	2	family/LNA	1971	44	—	0.24	21.0	2	—	0.4	—	1	Offensive	New products
Arthur Garden	2	foreign	1950	30	—	0.91	−3.6	3	25	0.6	In place	2	Offensive	Reorganization and export
Allan Cameron	2	LA	1982	19	—	0.17	−2.6	4	—	0.4	—	0	Wait and see	—
Megatronics	3	LA	1993	13	n.a.	0.07		2	—	0.1	—	1	Offensive	Joint venture, export
Las Vregas	2	LNA	1989	3	31.6	0.03	41.6	2	—	0.3	—	0	Wait and see	—

Notes:
[1] Motor, engine, gears; general engineering, consumer goods; electrical/electronic; construction; agricultural.
[2] Average annual growth rate 1989/90 1994 (where applicable or available).
[3] Percentage of sales generated through exports; number in brackets refers to 1989 where different.
[4] Industrial development corporation (parastatal).
[5] Dates of original founding and refounding after period of closure.

one of those with post-secondary education are in the engineering sector. Only one entrepreneur in the sample is a university-trained engineer. Some have had a modicum of secondary education plus an apprenticeship, although this was restricted to the engineering sector.

The great majority of firms (21 out of 33) are owner-managed, of which seven are family firms, and there is a strong emphasis on continuity of ownership. These firms are in the garments sector and include some of the oldest firms in the sample. They are mostly white-owned.

Outside the group of traditional family enterprises are the large number of local African firms founded after independence, usually as part of the government drive to indigenize the economy. This involved promotion by means of concessional loans, and most of the African enterprises in the sample were assisted in this way. The firms interviewed are mostly small- to medium-sized, founded and owned by entrepreneurs with fairly high levels of education (8–13 years of schooling, that is, secondary education up to 'A' levels). In these firms the entrepreneur is the pivotal figure and usually performs all the major business functions, including that of production manager. Functions such as product design and adaptation are also carried out by the entrepreneur. Many have worked in retailing. Their knowledge of technologies and production methods comes more from experience than from formal training.

The engineering firms are mostly owned and run either by holding companies, by the parastatal Industrial Development Corporation (IDC), or by local non-African entrepreneurs. This reflects the origin of the sector as a largely import-substituting activity during the UDI regime, when local Africans faced great obstacles to founding businesses. Three companies are owned and run by local African entrepreneurs: two of these have fewer than twenty employees, and the third had only just been reopened under African management at the time of the survey. Most of the local African engineering activity in Zimbabwe is in the small-scale and informal sectors not covered by this survey.

Local Africans have entered production largely through the clothing sector, which has the lowest technological and skill requirements. Local African firms that are expanding in size are mostly in the clothing sector, whereas the vast majority of formal engineering activities are dominated by local non-African entrepreneurs.

Most of the managers of the firms owned by holding companies and multinationals have a background in accounting and administration

Table 5.9 Background of entrepreneurs

Name of firm	*Education*	*Experience (general)*	*Experience (present firm)*	*Skill index*
Engineering				
Lane Engineering	1	1	0	0.7
South Wales Electric	1	1	1	1.0
Allan Cameron	0	0	0	0.0
Radar Metal	1	1	1	1.0
Tinto Industries	1	0	0	0.3
Megatronics	1	0	0	0.3
Sepe Metal	1	1	0	0.7
Modarc	0	1	1	0.7
Arthur Garden	1	1	0	0.7
Stainless Steel Products	0	1	0	0.3
Modcraft	0	1	1	0.7
Tromps	0	0	1	0.3
Las Vregas	0	1	0	0.3
Relmo El. Motors	1	0	1	0.7
Bain Farm Equipment	0	1	1	0.7
KSK	0	0	0	0.0
Deven Engineering	0	0	0	0.0
Mean				0.5
Clothing				
Universal Garments	1	0	1	0.7
Doma Enterprises	0	1	0	0.3
Chiratidzo	0	1	0	0.3
Cactus Clothing	0	0	0	0.0
Fashion Enterprises	0	0	0	0.0
City Clothing	n.a.	n.a.	n.a.	n.a.
Milford Clothing	0	1	0	0.3
Concorde	0	1	1	0.7
Playtime	0	1	1	0.7
Boss Fashion	0	0	0	0.0
Delswa	n.a.	n.a.	n.a.	n.a.
Paramount	0	0	0	0.0
Sprogz	0	0	0	0.0
Continental	0	1	1	0.7
Escapades	0	0	0	0.0
Bernstein	n.a.	n.a.	n.a.	n.a.
Mean				0.3

Notes: Education: 0 = secondary schooling and below, 1 = above secondary schooling. Experience: 0 = below sample mean, 1 = above sample mean (26.6 years).

and have been with the companies for a very long time. Many are of foreign origin (usually British) but have been resident in the country for many years.

In sum, all forms of ownership are represented in the sample. Larger companies, the technologically more sophisticated ones and exporting companies are usually managed by non-Africans. Companies that were founded after ESAP began are managed by Africans and tend to be smaller. Foreign-owned firms play a limited role in the country and are restricted to the engineering sector. There are no foreign affiliates in clothing (another contrast to most Asian exporters, where firms from the developed countries and the 'Tigers' are leading producers for the export market).

5.2.2 Characteristics of Plant and Technology

5.2.2.1 Capital Equipment

The production technologies in the clothing sector are fairly standardized, with differences according to market orientation and size. The firms produce either fashion (catering for either the local market or exports) or non-fashion items such as protective clothing/workwear or uniforms. They differ in the degree of specialization of their equipment: many of the smaller or even medium-sized firms work almost exclusively with general-purpose sewing machines and have very little specialized equipment, such as buttonholers, overlockers, or pocketers. The larger firms, or the more fashion-oriented medium-sized firms, operate more specialized equipment, and some at the very top end (the three largest firms) have CAD/CAM equipment, computerized pattern making and vertically integrated specialized divisions such as screen printing, embroidery or dry cleaning. An important distinction is between CMT activities (cut, make and trim – essentially an assembly operation subcontracted from other firms) and 'own' manufacturing in which the firm itself develops the designs and patterns.

The engineering sector encompasses a wide range of activities. The sample includes construction-related engineering (such as trusses or handrails), electrical and electronic engineering, assembly operations, machining and repair activities as well as general engineering (such as the manufacture of spare parts). All these differ in technological requirements, and in the degree of sophistication of the production process. Some are purely domestic activities that specialize in production and services of an 'appropriate' kind, closely geared to local requirements; others are subject to greater competition from the increasing influx of imported goods (or from overseas companies tendering for contracts) and a few may even have an export potential of sorts, even if this is limited to regional (Southern African) markets and is presently a negligible proportion of total sales. Table 5.8 shows the export orientation, import competition and product types for all the sample firms.

In the clothing sector, the sophistication (or complexity) of equipment is mostly determined by its export orientation, particularly export destination. In the engineering sector, the sophistication of the equipment is more related to the type of product made than to export orientation. The engineering firms export less than the clothing firms, and exclusively to a regional market (export orientation is around 30 per cent at most, whereas it is over 90 per cent for the most export-oriented clothing firm in the sample): the technology varies widely, with the more specialized companies (electricals, electronics) having the most sophisticated equipment. The smaller, or 'general', engineering companies mostly have all-purpose equipment (such as lathes and turntables) that can be used for a variety of products. What is characteristic of Zimbabwe is the wide variety of activities oriented towards a rather small domestic market. The bulk of the engineering firms in the country specialize in providing spare parts and repair services for a foreign-exchange-constrained, or sanctions-hit, economy: with the increasing liberalization many of these firms may disappear.

Almost all the firms report skill constraints in the operation of sophisticated equipment (Section 5.2.3). Smaller firms cannot afford specialized skills, even when the required ones are available, and many of the larger firms are currently static in outlook: unlike the clothing firms they have not yet experienced much import liberalization and many have no specific plans or strategies.

5.2.2.2 Age of Equipment

The average age of equipment is quite high: 12 years for clothing firms and just over 13 years for engineering firms (Table 5.10). This average masks a wide variation. Many of the firms operate 30-year old equipment, or older. Deteriorating capital stock is seen as a major constraint on Zimbabwean manufacturing: firms in most sectors operate machinery that on average is between 15 and 20 years old. Machine downtime is very high in such cases, and the problem is often compounded by the lack of proper preventive maintenance activities, particularly in engineering.

In the sample firms a great deal of (evidently successful) effort has gone into keeping old equipment alive and 'stretching' its functions. The exact extent of this is, of course, impossible to assess. In engineering, about half the companies have an 'established maintenance routine', but some do not have full-time maintenance personnel (even in the case of the larger and more sophisticated companies). The smaller companies (fewer than 20 employees) tend to undertake repairs as the need arises rather than conducting regular preventive maintenance. In the clothing sector, only one third of the companies carry out regular maintenance and the incidence of preventive maintenance is even lower. In general, the main exceptions being some of the large companies, maintenance tends to be rather *ad hoc*; however the age of the equipment means that a lot of it has to be done.

5.2.2.3 Investment

The sample companies came out of the UDI period in much the same shape as they entered it, at least with regard to their machinery and

Table 5.10 Machinery and equipment

Name of firm	*Average age of equipment*	*Additions since liberalization*	*Date of most recent addition*	*Production system*
Engineering				
Lane Engineering	20	1	1992	0
South Wales Electric	12	1	1992	ISO 9000*
Allan Cameron	10	1	1992	0
Radar Metal	20	0	1990	KPS
Tinto Industries	8	1	1993	KPS
Megatronics	3	1	1993	0
Sepe Metal	15	0	1990	0
Modarc	20	1	1993	0
Arthur Garden	15	0	1992	ISO 9000
Stainless Steel Products	15	1	1986	0
Modcraft	8	1	1992	0
Tromps	15	1	1992	0
Las Vregas	10	1	1994	0
Relmo El. Motors	10	1	1993	ISO 9000*
Bain Farm Equipment	15	1	1993	ISO 9000*
KSK	10	1	1992	0
Deven Engineering	20	1	1992	0
Mean	13.3			

Table 5.10 (*Continued*)

Name of firm	*Average age of equipment*	*Additions since liberalization*	*Date of most recent addition*	*Production system*
Clothing				
Universal Garments	15	1	1981	0
Doma Enterprises	10	1	1994	0
Chiratidzo	15	0	1989	0
Cactus Clothing	10	1	1992	0
Fashion Enterprises	8	1	1992	0
City Clothing	8	1	1992	0
Milford Clothing	15	0	1989	0
Concorde	8	1	1993	Considering
Playtime	12	1	1992	0
Boss Fashion	10	0	1989	0
Delswa	20	1	1993	0
Paramount	15	1	1991	0
Sprogz	10	1	1994	0
Continental	15	0	1989	ISO 9000*
Escapades	4	1	1993	0
Bernstein	15	1	1992	TQM
Mean	11.9			

Notes: * = in the process of implementation; TQM = total quality management system; KPS = Kawasaki production system.

equipment (though most of it was in need of replacement by then). Fourteen of the 33 firms in the sample were operating before UDI, and in many cases their equipment is older than 30 years. Another eight were founded during UDI and their investment in equipment was more or less restricted to what was in the country already, that is, redundant machinery from other firms or machinery auctioned off after bankruptcies. But although the type of equipment and machinery may not have changed much, there was been a considerable accumulation of idiosyncratic (that is, highly firm-specific) skills during the UDI period. Much of this was related to increasing and maintaining efficiency with the 'given' facilities, and companies developed capabilities that they still possess, particularly in relation to 'stretching' and improvization. The UDI period was an intensive learning period for many companies as they deepened and widened their capabilities far behind the technological frontier. What is at issue today is the degree to which the firms can build on these capabilities and become competitive in the present environment, or whether these peculiar (static) capabilities have 'locked' the firms into inefficient technological paths or organizational modes. This is a question that can only be answered over a longer period.

Between independence in 1980 and the launch of ESAP in 1990–91 other forms of control and constraint were in operation. The importation of equipment was controlled by licensing, and equipment was often purchased in 'tied aid' contracts or through barter trade. The firms were not free to choose, and there was very little search activity or 'shopping around'. A limited number of agents imported equipment; in the clothing industry this basically reduced the choice of machinery to one brand represented by the major agent. The firms were not even aware of alternatives in many cases. Occasional exceptions were the large exporting firms, or companies owned directly or indirectly by the state: these were able to acquire the equipment they needed because of their importance to the economy. The large clothing companies acquired their computerized equipment in this fashion. It was a period of technological 'satisficing'.

There was an initial positive response to liberalization. Most of the companies bought new equipment at the beginning of ESAP, mainly in 1991 and 1992. This was almost entirely due to the availability of capital goods imports (there was a strong emphasis on replacing worn-out equipment rather than upgrading) rather than the need to face up to new competition in product markets, which was seen as a relatively distant threat. However the arrival and installation of much of the equipment coincided with the severe drought in 1992 and, in the case of clothing, a large increase in inflows of second-hand items. This was reinforced by a general ESAP-related recession as real incomes dropped due to accelerating inflation, and a large increase in interest rates that made many of the previous purchases less viable. Devaluations made the importation of necessary inputs more expensive, and taxes were increased.

As a result, most of the companies were unable to utilize their new investments fully. The large exporting firms invested in new and sophisticated equipment just before the export incentive was abolished in early 1994: they partly turned to the domestic market again, crowding out many smaller producers. Many of these were uncompetitive without subsidies: a lack of export commitment (particularly viewing exports as a means of acquiring foreign exchange) meant that many firms had been exporting at a loss, and had not addressed the underlying problems of long-term competitiveness.

Almost all the firms acknowledge the opportunities offered by liberalization, most emphasize the difficulties of facing a much wider choice of technology, pointing particularly to a lack of information about and inexperience in search, evaluation and acquisition. Some companies have a head start through foreign buyers and parents, although this has to be pursued actively and never comes effortlessly or costlessly: the advantages of being foreign-owned are limited. For almost all the firms these options have remained hypothetical, since uncertainties mean that investments are being postponed.

Very few of the firms perceive technology and plant as their binding constraint under the present conditions, though most are aware of the limitations imposed by the obsolescence of their equipment. However they find their equipment appropriate for their (traditional) products and markets and are not concerned about penetrating new export markets. It is acknowledged that increasing exports will not be possible without technological upgrading, but the overall economic situation (especially recession and drought), the inflow of second-hand clothing, the reduction of export incentives and the uncertainty generated by ESAP are seen as more important current issues. The initial favourable response to opening up has been aborted by this combination of exogenous and policy-induced shocks.

5.2.2.4 The Organization of Production

Production organization refers to process or industrial engineering: plant layout, process optimization, quality control, scheduling of work flows and coordination of shopfloor activities. The organizational dimension is particularly difficult to capture. When studying the success of Japanese manufacturing, the focus has been on the description and interpretation of these organizational factors, which are contrasted with the traditional mass production paradigm. Recently these 'Japanese' management and production techniques have been diffusing to other countries.[14] Kaplinsky (1994) describes the application of Japanese management techniques in India, Latin America and, interestingly, Zimbabwe, and believes that there are benefits to be had from adopting these techniques, even in seemingly unsuitable environments. He focuses on the individual firm or factory, whereas other writers (for example Best, 1990, and Nelson, 1993) emphasize the systemic aspects of these new techniques, stressing the overall cultural and economic context of adoption.

As with equipment purchase, there was an early positive response to liberalization in Zimbabwe in terms of a 'jump' in the adoption of quality control and production systems from the late 1980s. Three firms in the sample have adopted production or quality management systems, and a further four are in the process of implementing them (Table 5.10); the results are mixed, and Kaplinsky's case studies underline the difficulty of implementing such procedures. Apart from these firms, only two others have made major changes to their production process in the wake of major equipment purchase. Many say they have made minor modifications, but this is difficult to evaluate and they do not appear to be related to the liberalization process.

The firms displayed three sets of arrangements for quality control and production systems:

- One group of firms (four in engineering, two in clothing) describe their quality control procedures as 'informal' or 'relaxed'. Almost all these firms have some form of quality control, but it is often carried out by the manager (in the case of small firms) or supervisors. Many note that quality is not really an issue that needs to be addressed – with one exception, these are all medium-sized or large engineering firms.
- The second group, the majority, employ full-time quality controllers (seven in engineering, 13 in clothing). This includes almost all clothing firms, since in-line and end-of-line checks are part of any clothing manufacturing system. The largest clothing companies in the sample have separate quality control departments, as do some of the large engineering companies. This has not been affected by liberalization.
- The third group of firms have introduced, or are in the process of implementing, more advanced quality control or production systems (six in engineering, one in clothing). These tend to be the larger firms as the relevant consultancy fees are very high, forbiddingly so for small firms. The smallest firm in the sample to use a production system employed 30 people at the time of the survey, but this firm is foreign-owned – all the engineering firms in this category are either foreign- or group-owned. The experiences and results are mixed: most have not fully implemented the systems and many are concerned about their ability to operate them.

In sum, quality control procedures are quite good in many firms and have improved since liberalization. However the lack of formal quality control in several engineering firms may indicate scant concern about quality and the largely sheltered nature of the domestic market. Not all improvements in quality control are traceable to liberalization: many sophisticated quality control systems predate ESAP, as do many purchases of sophisticated equipment, especially in the case of exporters. All the firms with formal production systems in place (or in the process of implementation) are fairly large (more than 80 employees), and all are exporters. The clothing firms are more consistently concerned with quality than the engineering firms. Process changes are implemented when new equipment or technology is purchased; there is widespread minor improvement activity with existing plants of the type found in more advanced NIEs. Thus size and export orientation seem to be important determinants of process engineering activity.

5.2.3 Technical Skills and Training

5.2.3.1 Skills

We distinguish two skill categories among workers: university-educated engineers and technicians (including all non-university degrees). The skill level of shopfloor workers depends on in-house training. This is practically the only path to skill acquisition, since industrial training institutions are lacking in Zimbabwe. Internal training is provided through apprenticeships or other formalized training programmes; external training through courses at training institutions or a training internship in other firms (Table 5.11).

In the clothing firms there are almost no employees with engineering degrees, which is one possible explanation of the difficulties faced in upgrading quality for export markets (in contrast, large garment exporters in East Asian countries employ significant numbers of formally trained engineers). The only exception in this respect is the largest firm in the sample, with over 1000 employees. Technicians of any description are not widely employed either. All firms rely heavily on internally generated skills and internal training, and feel that hiring skilled labour trained elsewhere is too expensive or inadequate. Even the companies that employ such personnel stress that the training had to 'start again from scratch'. This suggests that the education and training system is not addressing the skill needs of garment firms, or that the sample firms are incapable of absorbing higher levels of skill, or both.

In most of the small firms the entrepreneur plays the central role in organizing production, deciding on products and running the business from an accounting point of view; there are few specialized formal skills.

Table 5.11 Skills and training

Name of firm	*Employees (no.)*	*Engineers (no.)*	*Engineers (ratio)*	*Technicians (no.)*	*Technicians (ratio)*	*Employees (no.)*	*Apprentices (no.)*	*Internal training*	*Apprentice ratio*
Engineering									
Lane Engineering	57	4	7.02	4	7.02	5	2	1	10.53
South Wales Electric	300	5	1.67	2	0.67	0	10	1	3.33
Allan Cameron	19	0	0.00	3	15.79	0	2	1	10.53
Radar Metal	84	0	0.00	1	1.19	0	0	1	0.00
Tinto Industries	150	2	1.33	6	4.00	3	12	1	8.00
Megatronics	13	0	0.00	3	23.08	2	2	1	15.38
Sepe Metal	180	0	0.00	0	0.00	0	2	1	1.11
Modarc	45	0	0.00	1	2.22	1	0	0	0.00
Arthur Garden	30	2	6.67	4	13.33	0	0	0	0.00
Stainless Steel Products	50	0	0.00	7	14.00	0	0	0	0.00
Modcraft	105	2	1.90	0	0.00	0	2	1	1.90
Tromps	44	0	0.00	0	0.00	0	2	1	4.55
Las Vregas	3	0	0.00	0	0.00	0	0	1	0.00
Relmo El. Motors	300	3	1.00	20	6.67	60	5	1	1.67
Bain Farm Equipment	90	4	4.44	10	11.11	5	0	1	0.00
KSK	50	0	0.00	3	6.00	0	4	1	8.00
Deven Engineering	425	1	0.24	0	0.00	2	8	1	1.88
Mean	114.4	1.4	1.40	3.8	6.20	4.5	3.2		

Clothing									
Universal Garments	200	0	0.00	1	0.50	0	0	1	0.00
Doma Enterprises	5	0	0.00	2	40.00	3	0	1	0.00
Chiratidzo	117	0	0.00	0	0.00	1	0	1	0.00
Cactus Clothing	16	0	0.00	0	0.00	3	0	0	0.00
Fashion Enterprises	1100	0	0.00	0	0.00	3	0	1	0.00
City Clothing	300	0	0.00	0	0.00	2	0	1	0.00
Milford Clothing	69	0	0.00	0	0.00	0	0	0	0.00
Concorde	500	0	0.00	0	0.00	0	0	1	0.00
Playtime	360	0	0.00	2	0.56	5	5	1	1.39
Boss Fashion	150	0	0.00	0	0.00	0	0	1	0.00
Delswa	202	0	0.00	0	0.00	3	10	1	4.95
Paramount	1000	0	0.00	0	0.00	0	0	0	0.00
Sprogz	18	0	0.00	0	0.00	0	0	1	0.00
Continental	1100	2	0.18	8	0.73	3	30	1	2.73
Escapades	85	0	0.00	0	0.00	0	0	1	0.00
Bernstein	400	0	0.00	0	0.00	0	8	1	2.00
Mean	351.4	0.1	0.01	0.8	2.60	1.4	3.3		

One of the most widespread methods of skill acquisition is 'poaching' experienced workers from other companies, again suggesting the inadequacy of the formal training system.

5.2.3.2 Apprenticeship and Training

The Zimbabwean government sponsors apprenticeship programmes, and firms have to pay an apprenticeship levy of 1 per cent of the wage bill, which acts as an incentive to take on apprentices. However only five firms in the sample operate formal apprenticeship programmes. The large firms, which often act as 'training schools', rarely retain apprentices after the programme has concluded. All the sample firms provide some 'on-the-job training', but it is difficult to assess its effectiveness. Seven firms provide 'formalized training' (all are either foreign-owned or large firms) but this is not certified. Several of the large firms have training managers, but only two have separate training budgets. In clothing there is no recognized apprenticeship programme.

Two firms actively cooperate with training institutions and have programmes that involve internships, exchanges and stints at a university or technical college (these are both established, medium-sized engineering firms). External training is very rare, and usually *ad hoc*. Some companies offer to pay for evening courses if completed successfully, although employees are free to choose the type of course and it is usually unrelated to the firm's activities. Others send selected workers on administrative or supervisory courses, or short technical courses (usually related to equipment maintenance). The cost of these courses is trivial even for very small firms. None of them rate the results very highly. Occasionally the large companies will send an employee abroad for specialized (usually equipment-related) instruction. A number of companies exchange workers with other firms, or take interns from a university or polytechnic.

The only external training provided by the clothing industry is the occasional short design or dressmaking course. A new clothing industry training institute is currently being set up: many of the firms have heard of it, and there are high expectations. The absence of standardized qualifications in the industry is seen by many as an obstacle to increased exports. Liberalization has had no discernible impact on training in this industry.

Many of the firms in the engineering sector regard educational institutions as 'too passive'. Technical college and polytechnic degrees are preferred to university degrees, which are described as 'irrelevant'.

One of the companies closely involved in designing national training schemes pointed to the general decline in the quality of engineering degrees in Zimbabwe. This, as well as the disappointing cooperation between industry and educational institutions, is frequently contrasted with the situation during UDI, when there were very close links that resulted in much cross-fertilization, and syllabuses were closely coordinated with, and tailored to, industry requirements.

In sum, the provision of training has been little affected by liberalization. Indeed some medium-sized engineering firms have discontinued their previous training programmes. Larger firms pay more systematic attention to skill development, and tend to have full-time training managers (though many also have informal training procedures). The quality of local engineering education appears to be deteriorating, and there is a general lack of interest in increasing investment in human capital. However there is also a clearly felt need for better training facilities, as revealed by the response to the new clothing institute.

5.2.4 Products, Designs and Markets

Many of the clothing firms export their products, and four of the larger companies were producing under licensed brand names prior to liberalization. These companies have a number of designers (the firms label as 'designer' anyone concerned full-time with product development, including pattern makers, dressmakers and designers proper). The large exporters have the most sophisticated design-related equipment, and those producing sophisticated clothing such as men's formal wear or specialized items such as swimwear have the largest numbers of designers. For others, almost all products are either copied from catalogues or are variations of standard items. Only two companies are really fashion oriented (producing for boutiques); the vast majority produce staple items such as T-shirts, which are facing the direct impact of second-hand clothing competition. The uniform and workwear producers make standardized and (to a degree) naturally protected items that face little import competition; as noted, this less exposed segment is becoming increasingly attractive to vulnerable domestic manufacturers.

There has been little change in this area since liberalization began. Most of the large exporters have reduced their export activities. Only a handful of small and new companies appear to be addressing more specialized markets, for example children's fashion. In general, design capabilities in established firms are advanced by regional standards, but recent shocks have held back their upgrading. In addition, better designs require better equipment and higher productivity to reach higher-quality market segments. In this respect, Zimbabwe faces a considerable challenge.

The engineering sector is more difficult to evaluate because of the enormous variation in products, many of which are not finished products but inputs into other industries.

In the agricultural implements sector, products have been developed, produced and refined for many generations in close cooperation with farmers (mostly the owners of large commercial farms – the well-established, large-scale agricultural implements firms are all run by local non-Africans), and targeting a highly specialized market. In spite of being sheltered either through trade policy, high transport costs or knowledge of local circumstances, these companies have been experiencing difficult times. This is attributable to the drought-related drop in demand for agricultural machinery in Zimbabwe, and also to slowly increasing (but still weak) competition from imported items. Local companies have several advantages: they are able to respond quickly to local needs and have large service networks; interaction with customers generates new design ideas (mostly adaptations and minor changes to basic implements); and after-sales feedback is stronger. The two companies surveyed in this subsector are the only ones producing power-drawn equipment, so their design capabilities are more sophisticated than those of producers of mechanical equipment. Both are large companies that used to be foreign owned and have strong design capabilities, undertaking a lot of modification to their products.

Construction-related companies are currently facing no competition since the foreign presence in the building-equipment sector is negligible. They do not need independent design capabilities as the designs are provided by consulting engineering firms. The general engineering and machining firms mostly produce spare parts for other industries, and are strongly customer-related (they used to be the backbone of import substitution) and manufacture to specifications provided by buyers or copied from imported originals.

The specialized and sophisticated engineering firms (established in niches that are relatively protected from import competition) have the strongest design capabilities. The vehicle assemblers and producers in our sample are experiencing competition from second-hand imports, but are moving into 'appropriate' products (which are generally of lower technical sophistication).

5.2.5 Perceptions of Competition and Company Strategy

The competitive landscape in Zimbabwe was largely static prior to the start of ESAP, and at the time of the survey the companies noted that more had changed for them in the last three or four years than in the previous ten. The Confederation of Zimbabwe Industries commissioned a study of the level of competition in manufacturing subsectors in 1995.[15] Its evaluation of domestic competition was based on industrial concentration as measured by the Herfindahl index. Clothing and footwear ranked fairly low, indicating a fairly high level of concentration. As clothing imports were on the negative import list this sector was exposed to little foreign competition, in fact the lowest in the country. Overall competition was therefore judged to be low in the clothing and footwear industries. The opposite was reported for the two other sectors represented in our sample, particularly metals and metal products (and, to a lesser degree, transport equipment). Domestic competition was ranked an overall second, that is there were a large number of competing firms. Foreign competition was high in the metal products sector, and had increased since the inception of ESAP – overall competition was ranked as high.

These findings are not supported by our analysis, for a variety of reasons: Herfindahl indices identify high concentration with low competition, but the reality depends on individual circumstances. The duopolists engaged in the production of power-drawn agricultural implements are in strong competition, as are the handful of textile manufacturers. Many of the more 'atomistic' firms, though, are operating in narrow niches and do not perceive themselves as being in strong competition. The sectoral aggregations are too broad to say anything meaningful about the nature of competition facing individual firms. All the firms pointed out that the competitive landscape had been shifting strongly in recent years, with many entries, but also many exits. It appears that, although the number of firms counted in each sector is similar in consecutive years, the firms are not the same. Especially in engineering, part of the reluctance to give certificates to operatives firms wanted to keep was because they were more likely to leave and set up in competition, although most of these ventures appear to be short-lived.

For the clothing industry, the CZI study indicated that import competition was very low, since clothing imports were on the negative list. At the time of the interviews there was widespread speculation regarding the timing of the 'opening up' of Zimbabwean markets, but companies did not know what to expect, or when. Meanwhile, as noted, large quantities of second-hand clothing were flooding the market at around 10–20 per cent of the price of domestically produced items (shirts in particular). Another source of competition was the (illegal) sale of aid-related clothing. These clothes were very attractive to domestic consumers, hit by the recession and drought.

The abolition of the export incentive in early 1994 and the withdrawal of export privileges in South African markets constituted the other major challenge to garments producers. Many of the sample firms were pessimistic, and some did not expect to be in business for more than another year or two. Exporters were reconsidering their export strategy, and even committed exporters were planning to reduce their export orientation since profitability was seen to be dropping. Many were turning to the domestic market, much to the alarm of the smaller manufacturers, who were already being squeezed by illegal imports. Three companies were diversifying into unrelated business: fast food franchises, real estate, vehicle spares (all, importantly, goods perceived as non-tradable, reducing exposure to import competition). They were tentatively holding on to their core business, waiting to see whether more stable circumstances would emerge. Others were moving into non-tradable products in their core business, such as uniforms and protective clothing. However, later data suggest that the export pessimism was not entirely borne out: garment exports revived and the South African access was restored. This probably helped the larger established exporters, but others are still not in export markets and their situation continues to be precarious.

The engineering firms have been less affected by imports. The construction-related companies are almost entirely unaffected, and do not expect this to change in the near future. The general engineering companies, particularly the smaller ones, are highly customer oriented and are still performing import-substituting functions fairly successfully. The specialized engineering firms see themselves as vulnerable if import competition comes in the form of foreign companies tendering for large projects in Zimbabwe, as is the case in electricity generation, transformation and distribution. Concern seems to be focused more generally on the economic conditions under ESAP, and uncertainty about future developments.

To obtain a clearer idea of the impact of import liberalization we devised the following scale: 0 means 'no import competition', 1 means 'some import competition' and 2 means 'substantial or strong import competition' (Table 5.8). The categorization is rough, but it takes perceptions into account and is therefore better than purely quantitative import statistics. It can be seen from the table that half of the clothing companies are not affected by imports or illegal inflows at all. This is because they are either exporters, or producers of workwear and uniforms, or of specialized items such as children's clothing or fashion wear. The structure of the Zimbabwean clothing and textiles sectors is such that textile rather than clothing companies are being hit by second-hand clothing imports as these displace micro- and home production of garments from domestically produced fabrics. Those most strongly affected mainly produce staple clothing, which is directly competing with second-hand inflows. Firms in the intermediate category (1) are either exporters that also sell on the domestic market, or companies producing a mix of workwear, uniforms and casual clothing, mostly targeting the lower end of the market.

Of the engineering firms, those most strongly affected are vehicle producers and producers of electrical equipment. The latter are facing direct competition as well as 'indirect' competition from overseas companies tendering for contracts in electricity generation and distribution. One of the producers of agricultural equipment is also in direct competition with imports, particularly from Brazil. Those moderately affected produce either simple electronic equipment or spare parts, which are increasingly being imported. These companies appear to lie between the higher-technology large firms and firms that are protected due to the appropriateness of their products and strong customer links. Unaffected firms are either in the construction-related sector or in strongly 'localized' activities.

We also defined three types of strategic response to liberalization: defensive, no response (or wait and see), and offensive (Table 5.8). Defensive responses are as follows: attempting to minimize costs for a given product and market (especially shedding labour, or cutting wages in cases where the minimum wage is not yet binding),[16] moving into a non-tradable sector (such as real estate, construction, or services), and moving into a non-tradable segment of one's own sector. No response (or wait and see) strategies are making only marginal adjustments or waiting for a more decision-friendly environment to materialize; firms may also hope for policy action by the government, such as the reintroduction of the export incentive or a renewed commitment to some level of protection. Finally offensive strategies are a commitment to exports or an 'aggressive' marketing or technological response, that is, seeking new markets, improving product quality, technological upgrading, diversifying or specializing.

Clothing companies turn out to be the mostly defensively oriented, or are adopting a wait and see attitude: changes in the incentive regime (especially export incentives) have been affecting them more adversely, as have second-hand clothing inflows. Most see few generic niches, lack the capability to develop a higher-quality, fashion-oriented strategy, and suffer from 'export pessimism'. The three 'offensive' firms are focusing on exports (one of them is not yet an exporter, another wants to recapture its former export markets) and product quality. Strategic outlook does not seem to be correlated with technological sophistication, size, ownership or the degree of exposure to import competition.

Most of the engineering firms in the sample (11 out of 17) have an offensive strategy; the rest have adopted a 'wait and see' attitude. Import liberalization has been relatively mild and many firms produce appropriate products utilizing accumulated local knowledge. Many are thinking about entering export markets (regionally) or expanding their export operations. Offensive strategies do not appear to be related to performance, technological sophistication or ownership.

5.2.6 Linkages between Firms

This study is more concerned with technological (qualitative) linkages between firms, where information and skills are exchanged between firms, than with purely quantitative ones where only market transactions are involved. A study was recently conducted on interfirm linkages in Zimbabwe by Mead and Kunjeku (1993). The authors look at a number of subsectors, among them garments and textiles, as well as metals. They assume that increased linkages are beneficial since they encourage specialization, and are particularly interested in the links between the two constituent parts of Zimbabwe's 'dual economy': the 'large and relatively sophisticated' enterprises on the one hand, and the 'large number of very small traders' on the other.

In the clothing sector, Mead and Kunjeku mention export-related linkages, mainly by large, formal-sector, white-owned enterprises. They also point to the advantages and disadvantages of the cut, make and trim (CMT) system of subcontracting: it provides potential channels of skill and technology transfer, but this potential is mostly not realized. CMT links appear to be volatile, and are usually seen as second-best compared with greater vertical integration. There is a monitoring problem regarding CMT firms, especially with respect to quality control, and most larger enterprises do not seem willing to undertake coaching and training in order to make their business links more formal and more conducive to interaction.

Clothing firms have broadly two types of linkage: backward to textiles and fabrics producers, and forward to either CMT subcontractors or directly to customers. CMT is basically a capacity overflow, and has been reduced since the beginning of ESAP as demand has fallen and the firms that usually contract out are themselves producing below capacity. Most of the companies surveyed produce in isolation, purchasing some specialized inputs (embroidery, screen printing) but not cooperating with any other companies. Occasionally firms will lend each other a hand to overcome material bottlenecks, and the smaller ones cooperate to economize on maintenance personnel and expenditure. Other links include the purchase of used equipment, usually by smaller firms from bigger ones.

A greater degree of cooperation may help spread scarce and essential knowledge (that may not necessarily be competitively crucial to any one company but could benefit the entire industry) over a larger number of producers. To some degree these informational constraints are being addressed by export promotion bodies, but industry associations in Zimbabwe act more as lobbying groups *vis-à-vis* the government than as a forum for the exchange of information and knowledge, or even the coordination of strategy.

In engineering, Mead and Kunjeku point to the 'endless intertwining' of firms, and the 'almost cobweb activity' of firms in the metals sector (which is larger than our definition of the engineering sector). Linkages seem weaker in our sample: only six firms have qualitative links (Table 5.12), the same firms that have close links with institutions. No other companies report interfirm cooperation.

In sum, engineering firms are more likely to have qualitative links with their suppliers and subcontractors, although even these are weak by international standards. In the case of local non-African firms, very few of these links are directed towards upgrading their African counterparts and are mostly between established companies. Only two clothing firms have set up qualitative links with other firms. In one case this is a link with the shirt company for whom the firm produces under license, and in the other case these links are intended to coach and assist indigenous small businesses. There have been no changes in the linkage structure since liberalization began.

Table 5.12 Linkages

Name of firm	*Interfirm qualitative linkages*	*Institutional linkages (non-training)*
Engineering		
Lane Engineering	1	1
South Wales Electric	0	1
Allan Cameron	0	1
Radar Metal	0	1
Tinto Industries	1	0
Megatronics	1	1
Sepe Metal	0	0
Modarc	0	0
Arthur Garden	1	1
Stainless Steel Products	0	0
Modcraft	0	1
Tromps	0	0
Las Vregas	0	0
Relmo El. Motors	1	1
Bain Farm Equipment	0	0
KSK	0	0
Deven Engineering	1	0
Clothing		
Universal Garments	0	0
Doma Enterprises	0	0
Chiratidzo	0	0
Cactus Clothing	0	0
Fashion Enterprises	0	0
City Clothing	0	0
Milford Clothing	0	0
Concorde	0	0
Playtime	0	0
Boss Fashion	1	0
Delswa	0	0
Paramount	0	1
Sporgz	0	0
Continental	0	0
Escapades	0	0
Bernstein	1	0

Note: 0 = no linkages; 1 = one or more linkages.

5.2.7 Linkages with Institutions

Institutional linkages are particularly weak in Zimbabwean manufacturing. The importance of strong links between industry and the technology infrastructure (standards institutions, research institutes, extension services, universities, polytechnics and so on) is suggested by the experience of other countries. Lately there has been increased interest in 'national innovation systems', and the example of some East Asian countries suggests that a strongly coordinated effort by industry and technology institutions can help overcome problems of market failure in the area of research, development and innovation. The importance of this can be traced through many countries and periods, including other successful 'later' industrializers such as Germany and the United States.

The Zimbabwean science and technology infrastructure is very weak. This is acknowledged by the government, which is currently planning a large scientific and industrial research centre along the lines of similar institutions in East Asia (which a fact-finding team from Zimbabwe has visited). Figures on the public funding of R&D are not available, which in itself highlights past attitudes towards science and technology, but a stocktaking and evaluation exercise is currently under way.

The vast majority of companies in the sample (24 in all) have no links with research institutions or science and technology institutions. The most often mentioned institution is the Standards Association of Zimbabwe (SAZ), which is generally not even rated as 'satisfactory'. One entrepreneur pointed out that the problem of the SAZ is that it is 'too passive', and that firms are able to benefit only if they can specify precisely what type of assistance they want. Most firms have no use for the facilities offered, although most do not know exactly what the SAZ does. The most important services offered are the calibration of equipment and hallmarking of precious metals. Of the firms in the sample, very few have equipment that requires such regular servicing, and only one firm requires a hallmark. Another important potential area is assistance with the implementation of ISO standards, but the SAZ is frequently criticized for being too passive. Just seven firms in the sample have links with the SAZ (and only one of these is a clothing firm, one of the largest in the sample with 1000 employees) and these are probably only maintained because they have to pay a compulsory fee.

Very few firms collaborate with educational institutions such as the University of Zimbabwe, other colleges or the polytechnic. Only two companies (both engineering firms) work closely with the university and the polytechnic to devise training programmes and internships for students, but these are not technological linkages. These two firms, and one other engineering firm, also have technical connections with the university, but for metallurgical and chemical testing rather than for technological upgrading or research. Three firms have occasionally sent people on training courses at these institutions (again, only fairly large engineering firms). In general the university is regarded as too far removed from the needs and requirements of industry. The clothing firms tend to have no links with any institutions, except the occasional training link with a technical college (usually, as mentioned before, for supervisory or technical/maintenance training).

In sum, institutional linkages are negligible in Zimbabwe. Technology institutions are very passive; firms regard their abilities poorly and expect little from them. There is no contracting of industrial research to technology institutions. The few companies that do have links mostly use the testing facilities, and are either foreign-owned, well-established or have entrepreneurs with engineering degrees. This seems to reflect both the lack of initiative within the institutions (and possibly their lack of suitable equipment and skill) and weaknesses in the technological capability of the firms themselves. Experience elsewhere suggests that some research capability is generally required before firms can make good use of technology institutions, and this is certainly lacking in Zimbabwe.

5.3 DETERMINANTS OF PERFORMANCE AND TECHNOLOGY

This section looks at the sample firms' performance and technology, and the impact of import liberalization. While the small sample size has precluded attempts to use regression analysis to obtain quantitative estimates of the relationships, rank correlations are used in both sectors (Tables 5.13 and 5.14). The data also allow qualitative analysis of the key issues.

Sales growth figures are the average growth figures for the years between 1989–90 and 1994, with Zimbabwe dollar figures converted into US dollars at the average exchange rate for that year. This may not be an accurate reflection of the revenue actually generated by the firm (for example in 1991 the Zimbabwe dollar started out at around 2.6 to the US dollar but ended the year at 5.04 to the US dollar), and

Table 5.13 Rank correlation measures[17]

	Performance	*Technology*	*Size*
Clothing			
Technology	*0.1118*		
	−0.2382		
Size	*0.0147*	***0.8853****	
	−0.3676	**0.8147*****	
Import challenge	*−0.4029*	*0.5000***	*0.3647*
	−0.3118	0.3412	0.1147
Engineering			
Technology	*−0.2304*		
	−0.1691		
Size	*−0.0074*	***0.7770****	
	−0.2426	**0.5882****	
Import challenge	*−0.0294*	***0.8260****	*0.7672****
	−0.0980	**0.5466****	**0.4461***

Notes: Spearman rank correlation coefficients: ***significant at the 1 per cent level (two-tailed); **significant at the 5 per cent level; *significant at the 10 per cent level. The pairs of results in bold print appear to be robust to changes in intragroup rankings. See Table 5.15 for the ranking used in the first set of correlation results (printed in italics).

the average growth rate conceals fluctuations that may be important. Apart from that, the interviewees often gave an estimated figure and many firms were reluctant to divulge any performance figures. All the firms were asked for their impression of the business climate and firm performance, in addition to sales figures.

Using direct and the indirect information, we developed a performance indicator in which a firm is scored on scale from 1 to 5, where 3 means no or very little change since the inception of ESAP, 1 means a substantial improvement in performance, 5 means a substantial deterioration and 2 and 4 are intermediate scores meaning, respectively, improvement (of a 'satisfactory' nature to the person interviewed) and deterioration. The average performance in the clothing firms was 3.43, compared with 3.23 in the engineering firms: this indicates that, on average, firms have been experiencing stagnation or even a slight decline in performance.

Table 5.14 Comparative rankings of sample firms*

	Performance	*Technology*	*Size*	*Import challenge*
Clothing				
Paramount	1	2	3	7
Sprogz	2	11	15	16
Escapades	3	10	12	3
Bernstein	4	7	5	11
Universal Garments	5	9	9	12
Milford Clothing	6	16	13	14
Doma Enterprises	7	13	14	15
Fashion Enterprises	8	1	1	5
Continental	9	3	2	6
Concorde	10	6	4	10
City Clothing	11	5	7	8
Boss Fashion	12	15	10	13
Cactus Clothing	13	14	16	4
Playtime	14	4	6	1
Delswa	15	8	8	2
Chiratidzo	16	12	11	9
Engineering				
Deven Engineering	1	5	1	1
Tromps	2	14	13	11
Megatronics	3	17	16	12
Las Vregas	4	16	17	17
Relmo	5	1	2	2
Sepe Metal	6	13	4	13
Modcraft	7	4	6	7
KSK	8	8	11	14
Modarc	9	12	12	15
Arthur Garden	10	9	14	6
South Wales Electric	11	6	3	3
Bain Farm Equipment	12	3	7	5
Copper Wares	13	10	8	8
Stainless Steel Products	14	11	10	10
Allan Cameron	15	15	15	16
Tinto Industries	16	2	5	4
Lane	17	7	9	9

*This table shows the rankings used in the first set of correlation tests in Table 5.13.

In accordance with the methodology introduced and described in Chapter 2, we constructed a technology index (TI), in which the sample firms were assigned scores on a number of activities or investments (as in Table 5.8 above). Relating technology to other aspects of firm performance is problematic in Zimbabwe because of the turbulence in the economic environment. It is particularly difficult to separate the effects of recession and general economic uncertainty from those of technology. For instance some firms in the sample have purchased computerized equipment that they are not using: we cannot tell whether this is due to a fall in demand or to a lack of skills in the companies concerned. For the same reason, it is also very difficult to relate technological activity to market performance, especially in declining markets or where long learning periods are involved in mastering new technologies. The impact of import liberalization, given the limited extent that this had taken place by the time of this study, is also difficult to determine. This is to be expected *a fortiori* in the case of an adjusting economy in which the productive system and the macroeconomic framework are unstable and in transition.[18]

The index, as constructed here, tends to reward large and discrete investments and changes. While minor changes are included, they are grouped together and so may not have given their due weight in assessing technological performance. The tacit nature of many relevant skills (in the case of an individual) or capabilities (in the case of an organization) means that they cannot be measured directly. We have attempted to capture the more easily measurable elements here, but judgements involving more tacit capabilities have not been fully incorporated. However the other country studies suggest that there is a high correlation between the more easily measurable indices and those that (as in the Kenya case study) incorporate more qualitative measures: thus the present index is not expected to be too misleading.

It was not entirely clear to us how to describe or define a 'capable' firm, and as the evaluation was intuitive we decided to leave it out of our index. There were two main reasons for this:

- Capable firms appear to be characterized by entrepreneurial initiative and a 'plausible' (or 'well thought-out') 'offensive' business strategy, and by the presence of motivational factors or 'common purpose'. These are not included in the technological index since they are more entrepreneurial or managerial capabilities.[19]
- It was not possible for us to judge the presence of, or the nature of, a 'gap' between capacity and capability. A much longer time

Table 5.15a Breakdown of technology index (clothing)

Name of firm	*Computerized equipment*	*Additions since liberalization*	*Systematic quality control*	*Full-time QC personnal*	*Full-time maintenance personnal*	*Shopfloor layout changes*	*Inventory control system*	*Computerized inventory control system*	*Products since liberalization*	*Design activity (designers)*	*Technology index*
Fashion Enterprises	1	1	1	1	1	1	1	1	1	1	1
Paramount	1	1	1	1	1	1	1	1	1	1	1
City Clothing	1	1	1	1	1	1	1	1	0	1	0.9
Playtime	1	1	1	1	1	0	1	1	1	1	0.9
Continental	1	0	1	1	1	1	1	1	1	1	0.9
Concorde	0	1	1	1	1	0	1	1	1	1	0.8
Delswa	0	1	1	1	1	1	1	1	0	1	0.8
Bernstein	1	1	1	0	1	1	1	1	1	0	0.8
Universal Garments	0	1	1	1	1	0	1	1	0	1	0.7
Escapades	0	1	1	1	1	0	1	0	1	1	0.7
Sprogz	0	1	0	1	1	0	0	0	1	1	0.5
Doma Enterprises	0	1	0	1	1	0	1	0	0	0	0.4
Chiratidzo	0	0	0	1	1	0	1	0	0	1	0.4
Cactus Clothing	0	1	0	1	1	0	1	0	0	0	0.4
Boss Fashion	0	0	0	0	1	1	0	0	0	1	0.3
Milford Clothing	0	0	0	0	1	0	1	0	0	0	0.2

Table 5.15b Breakdown of technology index (engineering)

Name of firm	*Computerized equipment*	*Additions since liberalization*	*Systematic quality control*	*Full-time QC personnal*	*Full-time maintenance personnal*	*Shopfloor layout changes*	*Inventory control system*	*Computerized inventory control system*	*Products since liberalization*	*Design activity (designers)*	*Technology index*
Relmo EL. Motors	1	1	1	1	1	1	1	1	1	1	1
Tinto Industries	1	1	1	0	1	1	1	1	1	1	0.9
Bain Farm Equipment	1	1	1	1	1	0	1	1	1	1	0.9
Modcraft	0	1	1	1	1	0	1	1	1	0	0.7
Lane Engineering	1	1	0	0	1	0	1	1	1	0	0.6
South Wales Electric	0	1	1	1	0	0	1	0	1	1	0.6
Arthur Garden	0	0	0	0	1	1	1	1	1	1	0.6
KSK	0	1	0	1	1	0	1	0	1	1	0.6
Deven Engineering	0	1	1	0	1	0	1	1	0	1	0.6
Radar Metal	0	0	1	0	1	1	0	1	1	0	0.5
Modarc	0	1	0	0	1	0	1	0	1	1	0.5
Stainless Steel Products	0	1	0	1	1	0	1	0	0	1	0.5
Allan Cameron	1	1	0	0	0	1	0	0	1	0	0.4
Sepe Metal	0	0	0	0	1	0	1	1	0	1	0.4
Tromps	0	1	0	1	1	0	0	0	1	0	0.4
Las Vregas	0	1	0	0	0	0	0	1	1	0	0.3
Megatronics	0	0	0	0	0	0	0	0	1	0	0.1

period would have been required, a far greater familiarity with the technologies involved, and a more stable environment.

5.3.1 Determinants of Performance

5.3.1.1 Clothing

In the clothing industry, only three of the firms report an improvement in performance since 1991, the beginning of liberalization. All the other companies report either static business or a decline in performance (in three cases a substantial worsening). There is no clear relationship between performance and firm size. No firm has increased its exports since ESAP began. Of the exporters, half of the companies have reduced their exports, mostly, it is claimed, in response to reduced incentives. For many of the large firms (between 400 and 1000 employees) the reduction in exports has been substantial (between one third and one half of the 1991 values) and has been accompanied by job losses. Exporting firms are mostly in the 'deteriorating performance' category.

Because of the general malaise in the clothing industry and the impact of import competition, the sample shows no clear relationship between performance and TI (if anything, the correlation is negative, but this is not statistically significant).[20] All the 'improving' firms have a TI score of more than 0.5 but some of the highest-scoring companies are among the worst market performers, including some of the large and technologically sophisticated exporters. Some have also been affected by managerial and liquidity problems. The detailed composition of the TI (Table 5.15) shows no particular ingredient related to performance during the liberalization period. The use of computerized equipment may serve as an example: only the largest companies operate this type of equipment, and they are among the worst performers. Two of the best-performing companies do not operate computerized equipment. The only two companies considering (or actually using) a production or quality control system are quite low on the performance table. All the firms carry out regular maintenance, and almost all have some type of systematic quality control, or at least a person who is available and qualified for this task.

Nor does the sample show a clear relationship between performance and other variables. There appears to be no link between ownership and performance: the local African (LA) companies in the sample are represented in all performance categories.

In terms of strategic orientation, it can be seen that the top performers have an offensive strategic orientation, reflected in plans to increase exports, improve quality or target different and higher-income market segments. These are what we term the 'capable' firms. It is not clear whether offensive strategies have been developed because improved performance provided the 'breathing space' to do this, or whether a more dynamic and strategic outlook has been causal to their performance. Two of the three 'offensive' companies have been founded since liberalization began, and the other firm is planning a turnaround after a disappointing export performance, basing its strategy on licensed production. Almost all the other enterprises are either 'waiting to see' or planning to retreat in some way: this is expressed through a desire to reduce exports, to diversify outside the sector or simply to 'consolidate'.

Regarding entrepreneurial skill and experience, the top performers are not close to the top of the entrepreneurial skill table. The only exception is the one company to boast an entrepreneur with post-secondary education, that is, a diploma or university degree. Very few companies in the clothing sector rely on formal skills, and firms employing people with formal skills do not outperform the rest. Training does not discriminate between good and bad performers. Institutional linkages are not significant; this is due to the fact that, especially in the clothing industry, there are no institutions to link up with.

5.3.1.2 Engineering

Only one enterprise in the sample claims to be performing 'very well'. A further three firms claim to have performed 'well' during that same period. Two other companies – a small and young electrical/electronics firm run by a local African entrepreneur with a German engineering apprenticeship, and a family enterprise that is well established in a completely different activity (general mechanical engineering, spares and vehicle accessories) – claim to have been affected only mildly by import liberalization.

Seven firms report deteriorating performance, two having experienced severely declining sales. For the majority of firms, business has been static or slightly deteriorating, with scores of 3 or 4. The enterprises reporting slightly negative growth rates mostly have a score of 3, indicating a basically static business performance, including the two construction-related companies. Large firms do not perform better than smaller ones. This also holds for the age of the firm: the oldest firm, an agricultural engineering company, has not been performing well for reasons specific to its business. In engineering, the high-TI firms also tend to be exporters, though some top performers do not export at all, largely due to the nature of their products. With one exception, exports do not represent an explicit business strategy for the firms in this sector, which may be explained by the fact that exporting (even at a loss) was essential to the acquisition of foreign exchange prior to ESAP.

In engineering the top firm only scores 0.6, with the three runners-up sometimes well below 0.5. High scorers on the technology index report are either static or deteriorating (in one case, heavily deteriorating) business; these observations are reinforced by the insignificant correlation between the two variables. Engineering firms are more heavily represented in the middle-ranking technology scores (0.4–0.7), with clothing having six firms in this segment and engineering 12, whereas clothing firms are more represented in the high-scoring segment (8, compared with 3 in engineering). This may be explained by their greater export orientation, which in clothing requires more technological activity.

The six firms that have adopted, or are in the process of adopting, formalized production or quality systems such as ISO 9000 or KPS have suffered a deteriorating market performance. However almost all of these firms have either adopted these techniques recently or have not yet completed the process. The operation of computerized equipment does not contribute to performance (although these firms might have been expected to be the most competitive and best prepared for liberalization), with four of the five firms in this category recording a deteriorating performance.

The top performers are (parastatal) group-owned, family/local non-African and local African owned. The two runners-up are private group-owned and foreign-owned firms, respectively. This means that all ownership categories are represented at the top of the table. Hence foreign ownership is not correlated with performance.

The relationship between strategic orientation and performance is not clear-cut, since most firms entered ESAP with business plans that could not be realized. On the whole, strategic orientation is therefore more likely to reveal a firm's capability to formulate plans than its technological or managerial capability: this is more likely to be a matter for the longer term.

The engineering firms have pursued either an offensive or a wait-and-see strategy, while the clothing firms have displayed mainly defensive behaviour, for the reasons given above. The top performers are all pursuing offensive strategies: one firm wants to focus on locally appropriate products, while improving the service and customer-orientation of its business; another plans to develop new products and to diversify; whereas a third is looking for a foreign joint-venture partner in order to develop its exports, including exports to Europe. The development of exports is a much more widespread strategy in engineering than in clothing (seven firms compared with two respectively), where the experience of exporting is much more widespread.

Seven firms are pursuing wait-and-see strategies, and these are mostly static and deteriorating performers. The development of an offensive strategy is one indication of a potentially dynamic firm, although the relationship between strategy, capability and performance is a complex one: offensive firms are found among the worst performers as well as the best ones, and among firms with high as well as low technology scores.

While entrepreneurial skill (measured by combining scores on entrepreneurial schooling, work experience and years spent with the company) is not correlated with performance, the opposite seems to be true when it comes to the *type* of education received (for example technical or administrative): of the top four firms, three have technically skilled entrepreneurs or managers. Formal employee skills are not as important to performance as might be expected. The top performers employ almost no engineers; even the largest firm in the sample only employs one engineer in its drawing office. Internal training is more widespread than external, and seems to be related to performance: the top performers all train apprentices, although this seems to be taken more seriously by small companies than large ones. The largest of the engineering firms in the sample has a reputation for being the best training site in the industry, and is also the top performer.

5.3.2 The Effects of Import Liberalization

Most analysts assume a beneficial response to the process of liberalization: resource misallocation will have taken place under a controlled economic and trade regime, and 'opening up' will lead to resource reallocation in accordance with principles of relative costs and comparative advantage. But economic theory says very little about the process itself, the dynamics of transition. The literature on the sequencing of liberalization is mostly about stabilization, not structural adjustment. Some adjustment, some reallocation and the loss of a number of activities are to be expected and are probably unavoidable. But how firms actually improve their productivity, enter into new activities and deepen their capabilities is rarely examined. Since these processes are far from automatic and can face numerous market failures, the link between import liberalization and improved performance is tenuous, contingent on the fulfilment of several other conditions (Chapter 2).

Liberalization has two effects: direct and indirect. The direct effect relates to firms facing greater competition and having easier access to imported equipment and inputs. The indirect effect refers to a general perception of 'opening up' and enhanced business opportunities, which leads producers that may not (yet) be directly affected to formulate a new strategy they would not otherwise have followed. Linking the two is the credibility of the liberalization process, and the perceptions of firms.

It has proved particularly difficult to disentangle the effects of import liberalization in Zimbabwe from that of other factors. Some firms did take the opportunity to invest in better technologies during the initial stages of liberalization, mainly due to the increased availability of imported equipment. However this was soon offset by competition from imports, at least in clothing, and by macroeconomic turbulence. The changing policy environment (switches in the incentive regime, increased questioning of the sustainability of ESAP given the high budget deficits, public debt) and the drought have added general uncertainty to the specific competitive uncertainty that firms have faced in their respective markets. As a result, most normal technological upgrading seems to have been shelved for the time being, though some firms in engineering have continued to upgrade their capabilities. There is certainly a great deal of accumulated capability in Zimbabwean industry, and many sample firms display markedly higher levels of technological knowledge and expertise than their counterparts in Kenya or Tanzania. However it would seem (at least in the clothing industry) that many of these capabilities are not equal to the challenge of facing up to full import competition.

Engineering firms either do not regard import competition as particularly threatening, or they are confident of being able to carve out market niches for themselves, based on the appropriateness of their products and local links and knowledge. Many of the engineering firms in our sample were beginning to prepare for this. The firms in this sector that are being challenged most strongly are the large and technologically sophisticated firms: these are also exporters and therefore make the most tradable and 'competitive' products. The translation of capabilities accumulated under import-substitution conditions to an open economy is not easy: the entrepreneurial and managerial capabilities required are very different. At this stage, random factors, strategic orientation and entrepreneurial initiative appear to dominate technological factors as determinants of short-term performance.

Clothing firms are severely threatened by second-hand garments, an unintended but particularly extreme form of import liberalization (legal garment imports are still banned). Exporters are better placed to cope in that that they can expand into overseas markets; however they are not technologically well placed to move into the higher-quality segments that this would require. Since such upgrading would be expensive and difficult, they are now rethinking their strategy and reducing their exports, and may not be able to withstand competition without protection or subsidy. Competitiveness will require organizational change, greater attention to human resource development and almost certainly a phased period of protection and export promotion. A long-term liberalization strategy for this sector has yet to be worked out.

5.4 CONCLUDING REMARKS

Zimbabwe's industrial structure and performance are strongly determined by its economic and industrial past. The structure reflects a peculiar mix of well-established white firms (often family owned), a small number of relatively autonomous foreign, local group-owned or publicly owned companies, and some new (mostly local African-owned) firms promoted by the government. There is a strong base of inherited capabilities by SubSaharan African standards, which should provide a good springboard for technological upgrading in response to liberalization. However the design of liberalization has not taken account of the learning periods, costs and support needed; and its effects have been heavily overlaid by other unfavourable events.

After 25 years of protection and relatively stable economic conditions, manufacturers have had to contend with high inflation, rises in interest rates, precipitous declines in domestic demand, volatility in agricultural production and a limited and variable opening up to foreign competition. Although the government launched a structural adjustment programme it has been inconsistent in implementing it: first promoting and then withdrawing promotion from manufactured exports; attempting to stimulate industry by exposure to competition while burdening it with high interest rates; creating enormous uncertainty regarding the timing and scope of import liberalization; liberalizing some parts of the economy (for instance the foreign exchange regime) while maintaining a firm grip on others by procrastinating on deregulation and privatization; attempting to attract foreign investment while using the rhetoric of 'self-reliance'.

This has created contradictory and misleading signals for firms. There has also been concern about the political process, with the politicization of many economic issues, such as improved opportunities for local Africans in enterprise. Although the manufacturing sector has contracted since 1990, there is considerable resilience in industry (though the opening up has so far been limited). How far this will translate into industrial growth in a competitive setting remains to be seen.

Unless this is known, however, it is difficult to assess whether the liberalization programme is efficient or not. If some activities involve long and costly learning, the liberalization process should ideally be adjusted accordingly. But simply slowing down parts of the liberalization process is not enough. Factor markets also have to be improved. Of these, one of the most important is human capital; while putting considerable resources into expanding access to basic education, Zimbabwe has been weak in developing the specific skills needed for industrial development. The average level of formal skills in the sample is low; the former training practices of the firms may have been appropriate for their activities at the time, but a more competitive industrial structure cannot be sustained with this strategy.

There are other inconsistencies in the liberalization process, such as fluctuating incentives to export and the sequencing and implementation of import liberalization measures. The earlier reluctance of the government to place crucial inputs on general import licence is particularly relevant for our firms. The lack of transparency (and perceived lack of commitment) of the government's import liberalization plans, particularly regarding the liberalization of garments, which were still on the negative list at the time of our survey, is also important. Firms do not know what to prepare for. The toleration of widespread smuggling of second-hand clothing gives a signal to clothing firms that the government is not committed to the development of the industry, or even its continued existence.

Although many of the firms have adopted 'offensive' strategies for coping with liberalization, there has been only modest increase in technological activity that is attributable to liberalization. Managerial capabilities and, in many cases, technological capabilities do not often appear to be competitive. Adaptations and adjustments have been mostly minor, although there was considerable replacement investment between 1990 and 1995. But much of the equipment now in place, except in the leading and large firms and exporters, is over-aged. The implementation of new business strategies has been affected by considerable uncertainty, and also by the low level of formal skills. The present (perhaps surprisingly good) situation of many firms is probably due mostly to the protected and diversified industrialization of the past and is probably an imperfect indicator of future performance.

The absence of any coherent industrialization strategy or 'vision' to support firm-level investment and upgrading plans is often mentioned by companies. Such a strategy would ideally include institutional support and a coherent and well-sequenced liberalization of imports, as well as a credible and committed export-promotion package to promote learning and widespread improvements to factor markets. Whether this is fact a realistic option depends on the government's competence and capacity to pursue such a policy – many analysts in Zimbabwe appear sanguine in this respect. It appears that the reform agenda is now being pursued with less speed and intensity. A detailed assessment of government capacity is beyond the scope of this study, but the conclusions in Chapter 7 point strongly to the need for capacity building.

Notes

1. From the 'Unilateral Declaration of Independence' by Southern Rhodesia in 1965. The UDI period lasted from 1965 to Zimbabwe's independence in 1980.
2. Jansen (1983).
3. World Bank (1987c).
4. For an account of the political process leading up to liberalization, see Skålnes (1995).
5. An export incentive of 9 per cent of f.o.b. value (net) was introduced in 1993, partly to counteract a loss of competitiveness due to an overvalued exchange rate.
6. Robinson (1993).
7. Standard Chartered Bank, *Business Trends Zimbabwe*, June 1996. It is important to sound a note of caution regarding the GDP figures. A revised set of for the ESAP period was given a restricted release, but these were the subject of such controversy that the official figures have not been released to date (January 1997).
8. See Economist Intelligence Unit, *Country Report Zimbabwe*, 1/1996. The Standard Chartered Bank of Zimbabwe's *Africa Quarterly Review* (April 1996) estimates a decline in GDP of around 3 per cent for 1995.
9. Standard Chartered Bank of Zimbabwe, *Business Trends*, December 1995.
10. See Economist Intelligence Unit, *Country Report Zimbabwe*, 3/1996.

11. For an overview of the political economy of economic reform, see Skålnes 1995.
12. The tariff structure is currently (January 1997) about to change in a more protectionist direction after considerable and sustained lobbying by manufacturers.
13. Knight (1995), p. 16.
14. In essence, 'total quality management', 'total quality control' and 'just in time' all refer to the same idea: a commitment to constant quality and the upgrading of production. To implement techniques a firm uses a package that generally includes training, consultancy and engineering. The best-known packages are the Kawasaki Production System (KPS) and the International Standard Organisation's ISO 9000 series of process and organizational procedures for quality management.
15. Braunerhjelm and Fors (1995).
16. It is important to remember that the level of the real minimum industrial wage has actually *fallen* since 1982, by between 20 per cent and 30 per cent depending on the source of information. Many firms were wary of the fact that cutting wages, even when the minimum wage was not binding, would seriously affect basic living standards.
17. In order to avoid ties within groups of firms (grouped according to technology index, firm size and import challenge), which would have reduced the reliability of the Spearman measure, firms have been given unique rankings. This table shows correlation measures for two different intragroup rankings, in order to indicate whether correlations are robust.
18. For an excellent survey of theoretical and empirical issues surrounding the trade policy and industrial policy reform complex, see Rodrik (1995b). The large number of possible influences on firm-level performance (including country-specific effects that are rarely controlled for) and the indeterminacies of non-competitive modelling make the evidence highly vulnerable to contradictory interpretation. This leads Rodrik to be *a priori* sceptical of both neoliberal and pro-intervention (or 'neostatist') conclusions.
19. See Lall (1990), p. 20.
20. Contrast this with the situation in Ghana, where 'technologically capable' firms reported significantly better performance under structural adjustment (Lall *et al*., 1994, p. 41). The index used in the Ghana study was more comprehensive and included more qualitative elements, but a more comprehensive index is very highly correlated (0.96) with a technology index such as ours in the case of Kenya.

6 Comparative and Pooled Analysis of the Three Countries

Sonali Deraniyagala

6.1 INTRODUCTION

This chapter presents a comparative analysis of technology upgrading and firm performance in the three countries as a group, using a pooled sample of 130 firms for which relevant data are available. It seeks to identify common factors that determine technological dynamism in the three countries, and examines whether the positive relationship between technology and firm performance obtains across all the countries when country-specific effects are controlled for. It compares the extent to which manufacturing firms in the three countries have responded to trade liberalization by upgrading technology and technological skills and capabilities, and looks at micro-level supply-side factors that determine the capacity of firms to upgrade their technology and skills. The behaviour of firms with respect to export orientation and employment growth is also examined.

6.2 FIRM CHARACTERISTICS

Table 6.1 provides details of the sample firms.

Engineering firms in Zimbabwe are, on average, larger and have a higher degree of foreign ownership than those in Kenya and Tanzania. Firm size is smallest in Kenya and the extent of foreign ownership lowest in the Tanzanian sample. There is little difference in the average age of firms in the three countries, most firms having been established prior to the period of trade liberalization. While entry into this industry since liberalization has been low across all the countries, the number of new entrants is highest in Tanzania. In Kenya there have been no new entrants in the post-liberalization period.

Table 6.1 Characteristics of the sample firms

	No.	*Average size**	*Average age (years)*	*% Foreign*	*% Exporters*
Engineering					
Tanzania	46	75	21	8	15
Zimbabwe	17	114	27	24	41
Kenya	21	65	23	19	42
Clothing					
Tanzania	15	46	25	7	13
Zimbabwe	16	386	29	–	50
Kenya	20	128	18	5	21

* Size is measured as the number of employees in 1994.

Export orientation is lowest in Tanzania, with only 15 per cent of firms undertaking any degree of export activity; the comparative figure is just over 40 per cent for Kenya and Zimbabwe. In Kenya and Zimbabwe there were no new exporters in the engineering industry as a result of liberalization; the Tanzanian sample contained three new exporters. However some firms that exported prior to trade liberalization increased their export orientation afterwards: 75 per cent of exporters in Kenya and nearly 50 per cent in Tanzania, have increased the export proportion of their output since 1989. None of the Zimbabwean firms have increased their export orientation in this period.

In clothing, firm size by employment is markedly higher in Zimbabwe than in Kenya and Tanzania, with Tanzanian firms being, on average, less than one fifth the size of those in Zimbabwe while Kenyan firms are about one third. The size distribution of the country samples appears to be broadly representative of the clothing industry more generally in each country. The Zimbabwean firms are also somewhat older than those in Kenya and Tanzania. As with engineering, entry into this industry since liberalization has been limited: only one firm in Tanzania, two in Zimbabwe and two in Kenya. In Zimbabwe and Kenya the new entrants were small firms, while in Tanzania the new entrant was a large foreign affiliate producing for export markets.

Zimbabwean clothing firms are notably more export-oriented than their counterparts in the other countries: 50 per cent of firms in Zimbabwe export some proportion of their output. This is only true of 21 per cent of firms in Kenya and 13 per cent of those in Tanzania.

Overall, therefore, the sample firms in Zimbabwe are larger, more export oriented and have a higher degree of foreign ownership than firms in Kenya and Tanzania. While engineering firms in Tanzania are slightly larger than those in Kenya, they are marked by a lower degree of foreign ownership and export orientation. Tanzanian clothing firms are smaller and also have a lower degree of foreign ownership and export orientation than Kenyan ones.

6.3 TECHNOLOGY AND SKILLS IN THE POST-LIBERALIZATION PERIOD

6.3.1 Technology Index (TI)

In this section we compare the technological 'response' of firms in the three countries to trade liberalization by examining the extent to which they differ in the extent of technological activity and upgrading undertaken. In order to do this, we use a variant of the technology index (TI) discussed in previous chapters. The present index captures technological improvements since liberalization. As in the earlier chapters, this index is computed by observing specific types of technological improvement since liberalization (listed below). This information provides a set of dichotomous (0, 1) variables that are aggregated and normalized to provide a firm-specific technology index.

- Equipment upgrading involving computer-aided design.
- Replacement investment since liberalization.
- Improvements in inventory control since liberalization.
- Improvements in maintenance since liberalization.
- Improvements in quality control since liberalization.
- Changes to existing products since liberalization.
- Introduction of new products since liberalization.
- Adaptive process changes since liberalization.

The country analyses suggest that different measures of the index tend to give very similar results (that is, firms that are 'good' in certain forms of technological activity tend to be good in other aspects, though this does not hold in all cases). Thus while the composition of the present TI has been determined by the availability in comparable data across countries, it is likely that the results would not be very different if its composition were slightly different.

Summary indicators of the TI scores for each country are given by industry in Table 6.2. It should be reiterated that these measures are *not* indicators of how well the sample firms perform with reference to world 'best practice' frontiers; we did not try to assess this, though our observations suggest that the overall technological level is relatively low. Thus even the best sample firms are below international levels of technological activity (say, the level achieved by the dynamic exporting firms in East Asia).

Bearing these qualifications in mind, the TI scores show a broader and more advanced range of technological activity in Zimbabwe, followed by Kenya and then Tanzania. This is intuitively plausible. It accords with what may be expected (noted at the start of Chapter 1) from the relative levels of industrial development in the three countries. Given the relative experience, size, export activity and diversification of Zimbabwean firms, it is not surprising that they are the most sophisticated in terms of production processes, products and organizational systems. The index also suggests that the technological response of Zimbabwean firms to trade liberalization has been greater than in

Table 6.2(a) Technology index (TI) scores (means)

	Engineering	*Clothing*
Kenya	0.40	0.32
Tanzania	0.34	0.28
Zimbabwe	0.56	0.66

Table 6.2(b)

	Distribution of firms in high, low and medium TI groups (%)		
	High	*Medium*	*Low*
Engineering			
Kenya	25	30	39
Tanzania	16	25	49
Zimbabwe	57	45	12
Clothing			
Kenya	26	29	33
Tanzania	67	20	55
Zimbabwe	67	51	11

the other countries. For instance the proportion of sample firms that have responded by investing in advanced machinery and equipment (such as CAD and CNC) is higher in Zimbabwe than in the other countries; a larger proportion of Zimbabwean firms have also introduced advanced process engineering procedures such as formal quality control systems.

However, exogenous and policy-induced shocks appear to have largely offset the initial positive response of Zimbabwean firms; after the first two years there was some technological 'regression' as many firms had suffered rising excess capacity, high interest costs, growing uncertainty and a drought-hit domestic market. These factors, combined with the removal of export incentives have also led Zimbabwean firms to reduce rather than increase their export activities; the initial positive response to liberalization has not led to a sustained increase in competitiveness that would cause firms to compensate for falling domestic demand by looking overseas.

The firms in the three country sample can be separated into three categories: high TI, medium TI and low TI, grouped by TI scores (Table 6.2).[1] The distribution of sample firms over the three TI categories confirms the overall technological strength of Zimbabwean firms. A substantially higher proportion of Zimbabwean firms fall into the high and medium TI categories than in Kenya or Tanzania. In engineering, the proportion of Zimbabwean firms in the low TI category is only 12 per cent, compared with 39 per cent and 39 per cent in Kenya and Tanzania respectively. Tanzania has the smallest proportion of firms in the high TI group, 16 per cent; the corresponding figures for Zimbabwe and Kenya are 49 per cent and 25 per cent respectively. The lead of Zimbabwean firms is also evident in clothing; 67 per cent of firms in the high technology group are Zimbabwean, compared with 26 per cent in Kenya and 6.7 per cent in Tanzania.

6.3.2 Technical Skills in Engineering Firms

The availability of trained technical manpower is an important determinant of the ability to improve technological capabilities, and this section presents some comparative data on two measures: the proportion of the workforce accounted for by engineers and the percentage of entrepreneurs who have engineering qualifications. Both these indicators differ between the three countries.

Table 6.3 shows the two summary indicators of engineering skills in the sample engineering firms. The average proportion of graduate

Table 6.3 Engineering skills in engineering firms

	% of engineers in workforce	*% of entrepreneurs with engineering qualifications*
Kenya	1.8	45
Tanzania	2.0	56
Zimbabwe	3.5	42

engineers in the workforce is highest in Zimbabwe, and Tanzania has a slightly higher figure than Kenya. The proportion of entrepreneurs with engineering degrees is highest in Tanzania and lowest in Zimbabwe. The high level of engineer-entrepreneurs in Tanzania is a reflection of a special SME promotion programme there rather than a widespread tendency for entrepreneurs to have engineering backgrounds. It is important to note, however, that these are averages across all firms. It is not expected that the availability of engineers *per se* will cause higher levels of technological activity – much depends on the nature of the engineering qualifications, the use to which the engineers are put and the technical skills of the other employees.

In terms of training (not shown in Table 6.3), Zimbabwe performs better than the other countries. Some 70 per cent of Zimbabwean engineering firms conduct regular in-house training programmes, compared with around 25 per cent in Kenya and Tanzania. The extent to which firms provide training at external institutions is also markedly higher in Zimbabwe, as is the proportion of engineering firms with a formal training budget. Tanzania has the lowest proportion of firms that explicitly devote resources to training.

6.4 DETERMINANTS OF TECHNOLOGY AND SKILLS IN THE ENGINEERING INDUSTRY

6.4.1 Determinants of Technological Activity

This section presents the results of econometric analysis of the determinants of the technology index for the pooled sample of engineering firms. It must be noted that all the models estimated below have to make the restrictive assumption that the relationship between the independent variables and the dependent variable is of similar dimensions in all three countries. This limitation must be borne in mind when interpreting the econometric results. Despite this, the gains to be achieved from pooling the sample are seen as justifying this methodology. Four models are estimated, two relating to the determinants of technology upgrading and two to the determinants of skills.

Table 6.4 shows the results of estimation of the two models relating to the TI. Model 1 uses ordinary least squares to estimate the determinants of TI. Firm characteristics such as firm size and age, as well as variables relating to skills are included as independent variables in this model. While this model posits that technology upgrading is determined by skills, in reality there is likely to be a two-way causality between the skill variables and the dependent variable TI.

The independent variables are as follows:

- SIZE: number of employees in 1989.[2]
- AGE: age of firm.
- ENGPROP: graduate engineers as a proportion of the total workforce in 1994.
- FOREIGN: a dummy variable taking the value 1 if more than 25 per cent of the equity is foreign-owned.
- ENTRE: a dummy variable taking the value 1 if the entrepreneur is a graduate engineer.
- INTRAIN: a dummy variable taking the value 1 if the firm provides regular in-house training.
- ZDUM, TDUM: country dummies for Zimbabwe and Tanzania.

Model 2 is an ordered probit model that examines the characteristics of high, medium and low technology firms, as defined above. Both models include country dummies, with Kenya being treated as the base country.

The results of Model 1 show SIZE and AGE to be positive and significant: thus large firms display a greater capacity to respond to trade liberalization by upgrading technology than smaller ones in the three countries. This may reflect both greater access to finance as well as technological advantages such as access to skills and information, both internally and externally. The significance of SIZE could also be partly due to the fact the technology index captures many aspects of technology that are more easily obtained by larger firms, such as CAD and CNC machinery.

The significance of AGE may indicate learning-by-doing effects. Firms with greater production experience may have acquired the skills required to introduce new technology. In addition, this result may

Table 6.4 Determinants of technological activity in engineering firms

	Model 1 (OLS) *Dependent variable: TI*		*Model 2 (Ordered Probit)* *Dependent variable: TECH*	
	Coefficient	*T-value*	*Coefficient*	*T-value*
SIZE	0.0004	(2.30)**	0.003	(1.99)*
AGE	0.003	(2.00)**	0.014	(1.40)
ENGPROP	0.008	(1.40)	0.005	(0.20)
FOREIGN	0.05	(0.78)	1.24	(1.80)*
ENTRE	−0.03	(−0.51)	−0.18	(−0.34)
INTRAIN	0.15	(2.70)**	0.57	(1.19)
ZDUM	0.04	(0.73)	0.13	(0.24)
TDUM	−0.06	(−1.62)	−0.54	(−1.25)
Constant	0.255	(3.40)	−0.07	(−0.13)
Adjusted $R^2=0.39$ ($F=7.6$)			Chi squared = 30.6	

*Significant at the 10 per cent level.
**Significant at the 5 per cent level.

partly reflect a positive correlation between firm size and age. As noted above, the positive relation between age and technological dynamism is most notable in the case of Kenya and Zimbabwe. In both these countries, older firms tend to be better established, larger and have the capacity to invest in new technology.

The variable INTRAIN is also positive and significant, indicating that firms with regular in-house training programmes are likely to have higher levels of technological dynamism than those that do not provide this type of training. This result partly confirms the hypothesis that the accumulation of requisite technological skills and capabilities is a precondition for technological dynamism. It may also indicate an element of simultaneity between training and investment in new technology, with firms providing special in-house training programmes when new technology is introduced. Unfortunately data limitations do not allow us to differentiate between these two effects.

The country dummies TDUM and ZDUM are not significant in the estimation. Thus despite the differences in the technological dynamism of the three countries discussed above, country effects do not appear to exert an independent influence on technology once other firm-specific variables are controlled for.

6.4.2 Differentiating between High, Medium and Low TI Firms

The determinants of technological activity can also be analysed by identifying factors that discriminate between high, medium and low technology engineering firms. This is done here using an ordered probit model (Model 2). The dependent variable is TECH and takes the values 0, 1, 2 for low, medium and high technology firms respectively. As noted above, these categories were derived using the TI scores for the sample firms. The values on the TI index of the thirty-third and sixty-sixth percentiles were used as cut-off points when deriving the three groups. The results are shown in Table 6.4.

The categorization of firms into broad groupings means that the explanatory power of this model is fairly weak. Two variables are significant, but only at the 10 per cent level. SIZE is positive and significant, indicating that high technology firms are likely to be larger than medium and low technology ones. In addition, FOREIGN is also positive and significant, indicating that foreign firms have higher levels of technological competence that domestic ones. The technological advantage of foreign firms may arise from better access to finance as well as other 'intangible assets' such as technology, skills, training and R&D facilities. Again the country dummies are not significant: once other factors are controlled for, country characteristics are not important determinants of technological capabilities.

6.4.3 Determinants of Technological Skills

The above analysis treated technological skills as a determinant of technological capabilities. Some skill-related variables such as in-house training emerged as important determinants of technology development. Here we analyse factors that determine skill and skill development at the firm level in the engineering industry. While acknowledging that there is likely to be reverse causality running from technology upgrading to skill acquisition, this analysis does not treat technology as an independent variable. Instead the focus is only on several firm characteristics that could influence skill.

Model 3 examines the determinants of technological skill intensity at the firm level. Technological skill intensity is measured narrowly in this model. The dependent variable is ENGPROP, the proportion of graduate engineers in the workforce, and an OLS estimation is used (Table 6.5). The definitions of the independent variables are as above.

Table 6.5 Determinants of skills and training in engineering firms

	Model 3 (OLS) Dependent variable: ENGPROP		*Model 4 (Probit) Dependent variable: INTRAIN*	
	Coefficient	*T-value*	*Coefficient*	*T-value*
SIZE	−0.001	(−0.91)	0.005	(2.9)**
AGE	−0.001	(−0.03)	−0.008	(−0.07)
ENTRE	2.27	(3.50)**	0.49	(1.8)*
FOREIGN	1.48	(1.03)	0.8	(2.1)**
TDUM	1.6	(1.50)	1.3	(1.4)
ZDUM	3.82	(2.34)**	2.9	(2.2)**
Constant	−3.6	(−1.6)	−2.6	(−2.4)**
	Adjusted $R^2=0.14$, $F=3.3$**		Chi squared = 40.8	

*Significant at the 10 per cent level.
**Significant at the 5 per cent level.

The variable ENTRE is positive and significant in the estimation. Thus firms in which the entrepreneur or chief executive is a graduate engineer are likely to employ a larger proportion of graduate engineers. This may indicate that entrepreneurs with formal qualifications are more likely to be aware of the usefulness of such qualifications. This result could also indicate that the variables ENGPROP and ENTRE are related to a third unobserved factor. For instance firms engaged in advanced engineering activities may be more likely to employ a larger proportion of graduate engineers. Such firms may also be more likely to be run by entrepreneurs with formal engineering qualifications.

The country dummy ZDUM is positive and significant, indicating that firms in Zimbabwe are likely to employ a higher proportion of engineers than those in Kenya or Tanzania (due to the non-significance of the country dummy TDUM). This may reflect the fact that Zimbabwean firms undertake more advanced engineering activities and have a better ability to use engineering skills than those in Kenya and Tanzania.

6.4.4 Determinants of Training Efforts

We also examine factors that determine firm-level training efforts in the pooled sample of engineering firms. The focus here is on in-house training, defined as regular, sustained training (excluding occasional training undertaken for the specific purpose of introducing new technology), which is a reasonable indicator of a firm's commitment to skill development. Model 4 is a probit model and estimates factors that determine the likelihood of a firm having an in-house training programme. The dependent variable is INTRAIN, a dummy variable taking the value 1 if the firm provides regular in-house training, and 0 otherwise.

The results of the estimation are presented in Table 6.5. The estimation of the probit model shows the variables SIZE, FOREIGN and ZDUM to be positive and significant at the 5 per cent level and ENTRE to be positive and significant at the 10 per cent level.

The estimation indicates that large firms are more likely to provide in-house training than smaller ones. This suggests that larger firms have more demanding activities and greater access to the resources required for training, or are more conscious of the need for skill upgrading. It may also reflect their ability to retain more of their trained workers than smaller firms.

The fact that foreign-owned firms are more likely to have in-house training programmes is also a reflection of greater access to resources and personnel. Foreign firms generally have access to skilled personnel from parent firms or other subsidiaries. The individual country studies showed that foreign firms often draw on such personnel to conduct in-house training programmes. In many cases, in-house training programmes accompany new investments in technology.

The estimation also suggests that entrepreneurs who are graduate engineers are likely to be both aware of the need for in-house training and have the capability to organize and undertake such training. This result, together with the positive influence of entrepreneurial skill on the technical skill intensity of firm (previous estimation), suggests that entrepreneurs play a pivotal role in the development of technological capability. This is even more plausible when we consider that in most firms in the three countries decision-making power tends to be highly centralized and concentrated in a single entrepreneur.

The significance of the country dummy ZDUM indicates that firms in Zimbabwe are more likely to have in-house training programmes that those in Kenya and Tanzania. The comparison of training efforts in the three countries shows that this is clearly the case.

6.5 DETERMINANTS OF TECHNOLOGICAL DYNAMISM IN CLOTHING

This section attempts to identify the determinants of the technological activity of clothing firms in the three countries. Here again we use two models to estimate factors that determine technological activity for the pooled three-country sample.[3] Model 5 uses OLS regression to examine factors that influence technological activity; the dependent variable here is TI, the firm-specific technology index for the clothing industry. Model 6 is an ordered probit model that attempts to identify the characteristics of high, medium and low technology firms. The dependent variable TECH takes the values 0, 1 and 2 for low, medium and high technology groups respectively.[4] All the variables included are defined as in Models 1 and 2. The results of both estimations are given in Table 6.6.

Both models produce only one firm-level factor with a significant influence on the TI: firm size. The general reasons for the higher technological dynamism of large firms were discussed earlier. In the garment industry, it is likely that larger firms have greater access to financial resources as well as the in-house and external skills required for investing in advanced technologies such as computer-aided drawing, marker making and operator programmable sewing machines. Larger firms are also more likely to introduce formal quality control systems.

The only other significant variable is the country dummy for Zimbabwe, ZDUM, which is significant in the estimation of Model 6. As discussed above, the mean score of the clothing technology index for Zimbabwe is markedly higher than for the other two countries: 0.66 compared with 0.32 for Kenya and 0.24 for Tanzania.[5]

Table 6.6 Determinants of technological activity in clothing firms

	Model 5 (OLS) *Dependent variable: TI*		*Model 6 (ordered probit)* *Dependent variable: TECH*	
	Coefficient	*T-value*	*Coefficient*	*T-value*
SIZE	0.002	(2.7)**	0.0056	(2.2)**
AGE	0.003	(1.4)	0.9	(0.2)
ENTRE	0.09	(1.4)	0.54	(0.9)
INTRAIN	0.10	(1.5)		
TDUM	−0.2	(−0.22)	0.4	(0.6)
ZDUM	0.19	(2.47)**	0.2	(2.3)**
Constant	0.14	(2.2)**	−0.5	(−0.9)
	Adjusted $R^2 = 0.59$		Chi squared = 35.7	

**Significant at the 5 per cent level.

6.6 TECHNOLOGICAL DYNAMISM AND EXPORT PERFORMANCE

Technological dynamism is not wanted for itself, but for the effect it has on firm performance. In this section we examine the relationship between the TI and one measure of firm performance: the propensity to export. Due to data limitations we use a narrow measure of export performance: EXDUM, a dummy variable that takes the value 1 if the firm exports any of its output and 0 otherwise (given the small number of exporters in all three country samples, it was not possible to estimate an alternative export model with a continuous variable such as the proportion of output exported as the dependent variable). Thus Models 7 and 8 are probit models that examine differences in the level of technological capability and dynamism between exporters and non-exporters. The independent variables in these models have been defined in relation to Models 1 and 2. The results are shown in Table 6.7.

In engineering, two variables are positive and significant determinants of whether firms export: TI and ENTRE. The significance of the technology index suggests that production for export markets generally requires higher standards of quality and efficiency than production for domestic markets. Investing in new technology and improving the organization of production is generally a necessary precondition for exporting. While the estimation indicates that technological dynamism determines export capability, it is also necessary to allow for the causality running from exports to technology.

Thus firms producing for export markets may have better access to the technological skills and information that promote technological development. In addition, during a period of trade liberalization exporters may face less uncertainty than firms in import-competing sectors. This low uncertainty, together with the greater availability of imported capital goods and technology following trade liberalization, is likely to generate higher levels of technology upgrading among exporters.

The variable ENTRE is only significant at the 10 per cent level, indicating a weak relationship between the education of entrepreneurs and the decision to export. Thus entrepreneurs with higher levels of education may be better able to achieve the higher product quality and efficiency levels required for exporting. They may also be better placed to obtain information, that is central to the decision to export, for instance information on potential markets and products.

In clothing, as in the case of the engineering industry TI is positive and significant in Model 8, indicating that exporters have a higher level

Table 6.7 Determinants of exporting, dependent variable: EXDUM

	Model 7 (probit) Engineering		*Model 8 (probit) Clothing*	
	Coefficient	*T-value*	*Coefficient*	*T-value*
SIZE	0.001	(0.49)	0.004	(1.7)*
AGE	0.01	(1.14)	−0.008	(−0.2)
FOREIGN	−0.6	(−1.19)		
TI	5.3	(3.8)**	3.6	(2.2)**
ENTRE	1.2	(1.6)*		
TDUM	−0.6	(−1.2)	−0.12	(−1.56)
ZDUM	−0.2	(−0.2)	−0.27	(0.34)
Constant	−4.0	(−3.8)**		
	Chi squared = 41.7		Chi squared = 30.8	

* Significant at the 10 per cent level. **Significant at the 5 per cent level.

of technological dynamism than non-exporters. Again the general reasons for this and the possibility of reverse causality in the technology–export link discussed above remain valid. With specific reference to the clothing industry, we can recall from the individual country chapters that certain forms of technology upgrading such as investment in computer-aided marker making and formal quality checks are largely undertaken by exporters. Such factors would appear to underlie the positive technology–export relationship.

The variable SIZE is also positive and significant in the estimation, although only at the 10 per cent level. Large firms may benefit from economies of scale that enable them to achieve the efficiency levels required for exporting and may have better access to skills and capabilities that promote productive efficiency. The positive relationship between size and exporting may also partly reflect the positive association between technology and size discussed earlier.

6.7 TECHNOLOGY UPGRADING AND EMPLOYMENT GROWTH

6.7.1 Engineering

This section examines the relationship between technology upgrading and employment growth in the engineering industry in the post-liberalization period. Let us start with some background data.

Table 6.8 Employment growth in engineering by size of firm, 1989–95

	Median growth	*Micro* (<*10 employees*)	*Small* (*11–30*)	*Medium* (*31–99*)	*Large* (>*100*)
Tanzania	−2.2	−6.0	2.10	−4.8	−2.9
Zimbabwe	1.4	40.0	0.55	0.0	1.4
Kenya	10.0	19.1	23.60	8.5	9.2

Post-liberalization employment growth in the engineering industry (measured as the median annual average growth of employment during 1989–94) was fastest in Kenya (10 per cent) and lowest in Tanzania (2.2 per cent), with Zimbabwe showing modest growth of 1.4 per cent (Table 6.10). Table 6.10 also presents data on employment growth rates by size of firm. Micro and small engineering enterprises experienced the fastest rates of growth in Kenya; in Tanzania, small firms recorded positive growth rates, but all other size classes contracted, most markedly micro enterprises. However in Zimbabwe micro enterprises had the most rapid rates of growth, with large enterprises following and small and medium enterprises stagnating. While there is no strong pattern in these data, in broad terms small and micro firms fare better overall than medium and large firms.

In order to examine the relationship between firm growth and technology upgrading we undertook an econometric analysis of the determinants of firm growth. Existing analyses of firm growth have largely focused on the relationship between firm size, firm age and growth, and have indicated a tendency for growth to be inversely related both to the size and to the age of firms. In this study, Model 9 includes the size and age variables as well as variables relating to technology upgrading in order to estimate the impact of technology on firm growth when controlling for the effects of size and age.

Following earlier studies, for the purpose of this estimation firm growth is measured as follows: growth = [ln(employment in 1994) − ln(employment in 1989)]/firm age. The independent variables included in the model are:

- LNSIZE: number of employees in 1989 in logarithmic form.
- LNAGE: age of the firm in logarithmic form.
- TI: technology index.
- CZDUM, CTDUM: country dummies for Zimbabwe and Tanzania.

Table 6.9 Determinants of employment growth, dependent variable: growth

	Model 9 (OLS) Engineering		*Model 10 (OLS) Clothing*	
	Coefficient	*T-value*	*Coefficient*	*T-value*
LNSIZE	−0.092	(−4.0)**	−0.012	(−2.5)**
LNAGE	−0.094	(−4.3)**	0.02	(1.7)*
LNSIZESQ	0.005	(1.70)*		
LNAGESQ	0.009	(1.9)*		
LNSIZEAGE	0.01	(1.5)		
TI	0.20	(2.1)**	0.02	(2.8)**
TDUM	−0.009	(−.79)	−0.18	(−1.4)
ZDUM	−0.006	(−.60)	−0.06	(−.52)
Constant	0.35	(8.4)***	0.01	(.31)
	Adjusted $R^2=0.58$, $F=15.3$***		Adjusted $R^2=0.19$, $F=2.9$**	

*Significant at the 10 per cent level.
**Significant at the 5 per cent level.
***Significant at the 1 per cent level.

The squared and interaction terms of the size and age variables (LNSIZESQ, LNAGESQ and LNSIZEAGE) are also included.

The estimation shows LNSIZE and LNAGE to be significant with the expected signs (Table 6.9). In addition the variable that is of primary concern, TI, is also positive and significant at the 5 per cent level. Thus technological upgrading appears to have exerted a positive influence on firm growth in the post-liberalization period, when controlling for the effects of firm size and age.

6.7.2 Clothing

The employment growth rates in clothing are lower than in engineering in all three countries (Table 6.10). However they show a similar pattern to the engineering industry, with firms in Kenya exhibiting the fastest rates of growth and those in Tanzania the most rapid rates of contraction.

Growth rates by size class in the clothing industry show a different pattern from engineering. There appears to be a tendency for smaller firms to contract and larger ones to expand, especially in Kenya and Zimbabwe. The country chapters indicate that the contraction of small

Table 6.10 Employment growth in clothing, 1989–95

		Growth by size			
	Average growth rates	*Micro*	*Small*	*Medium*	*Large*
Tanzania	−26.0	−33	−14	−40	–
Kenya	0.31	−19	0	−24	42
Zimbabwe	−1.2	–	−40	11	5

firm reflects 'defensive' moves by firms in the form of shedding labour or moving out of garment production altogether, largely prompted by competition from imports, in particular of second-hand clothing. Note that the clothing industry in all three countries has faced far more sudden and intense import competition than engineering, more as the result of illegal (or semilegal) imports than of deliberate policy measures. Since a large part of its output is more tradable than that of engineering, it probably provides a better indication of the impact of import liberalization.

The relative expansion of larger firms in Kenya and Zimbabwe suggests that they are less affected by import competition, or are better able to gear themselves to face it. Closer examination reveals that the fastest rates of expansion are by large firms that export; thus larger firms have been able to respond to import competition by moving into export markets. Smaller firms, on the other hand, lack the capacity to upgrade technology sufficiently to meet international standards and have contracted. Thus employment growth in the clothing industry in the post-liberalization period is negatively related to production for import-competing sectors and positively related to production for export sectors, with only a few firms able to mount the technological effort needed to enter the world market.

Let us examine how technology upgrading relates to these firm dynamics. For the engineering industry we examine the relationship between technology upgrading and firm growth in a multivariate context. Model 10 in Table 6.9 above shows the determinants of employment growth for the clothing industry. Growth is measured using the same definition as for the engineering industry. The independent variables are also defined as for the engineering industry model (Model 9).[6]

TI again shows up as positive and significant; technologically capable and dynamic firms grow faster in the face of severe competition, when controlling for the usual effects of firm size and age. As shown by the earlier econometric analysis, TI and exporting are positively related in the clothing industry – thus technological dynamism benefits growth and export activity.

6.8 CONCLUSION

The comparative analysis of technology upgrading and firm performance in Kenya, Tanzania and Zimbabwe suggests that factors such as firm size, firm age and training efforts are significant common determinants of technology upgrading at the firm level, as well as significant factors in discriminating between high, low and medium TI firms. Factors such as firm size and entrepreneurial education also determine skill development at the firm level.

The analysis in this chapter shows that, for the pooled three-country sample, technology upgrading is positively related to the decision to export, after controlling for country-specific effects. Technology upgrading was also found to be positively related to firm growth upgrading in both industries, when controlling for the usual effects of firm size and age. Thus firm performance in the post-liberalization period in all three countries appears to be positively related to technological dynamism.

Notes

1. The values on the TI index of the thirty-third and sixty-sixth percentiles were used as cut-off points when deriving the three groups.
2. Size at the beginning of the period for which technology upgrading was observed is used to avoid problems of two-way causality between technology and size.
3. Unlike the engineering industry, skill and capability determinants are not estimated for the clothing industry due to data limitations.
4. As in the case of engineering, these categories are derived using the TI index; the values of the thirty-third and sixty-sixth percentile are used as cut-off points when deriving the three groups.
5. In the case of the clothing industry, the variable ENTRE is defined as a dummy variable taking the value 1 if the entrepreneur received post-secondary education, 0 otherwise.
6. The squared and interaction terms were included initially, but were dropped from the final estimation as they were not significant.

7 Opening Up – and Shutting Down? Synthesis, Policies and Conclusions

Sanjaya Lall

7.1 INTRODUCTION

This study has produced a wealth of findings on liberalization, technology development and manufacturing performance in Kenya, Tanzania and Zimbabwe. However the interpretation of these findings is not straightforward. All three countries are opening up at a difficult and uncertain period in their economic life – not an ideal setting for studying technological development, which thrives in a growing and stable environment. The impact of liberalization is (as usual in these studies) difficult to disentangle from that of other factors affecting enterprise behaviour. The degree and nature of liberalization itself differs between countries, making cross-country comparisons difficult; moreover the two activities studied, garments and engineering, face differing exposure to import competition. Then there are the inevitable difficulties in generalizing from the experience of individual firms to a broader industrial setting or to different countries.

These problems are inherent to all such studies. Macroeconomic studies of adjustment cannot avoid these difficulties – they too have to pose realistic counterfactuals and to account for the effect of exogenous factors. Much lies in the interpretation of the data, and the soundness of the interpretation depends on the validity, realism and relevance of the theoretical apparatus being used. Here, at least, we believe that this study has an edge. While the problems noted above cannot be fully resolved, the analysis of micro-level data, based on micro-level theories of learning and capability development, does add significantly to the understanding of what happens in the 'front line' of adjustment in Africa.

Bearing these caveats in mind, let us draw out the general lessons of the three country studies. We start with a brief look back at what import liberalization was expected to do in technological terms, the general data on industrial performance and the status of liberalization in the three countries. We then summarize our main findings on technology in the sample clothing and engineering firms, placing the experience of the three countries in the wider context of liberalization in other regions. We conclude with some policy implications: for this we draw upon the policy experience of the East Asian 'Tigers' in supporting technological development in their industrial enterprises.

7.2 THE GENERAL BACKGROUND

7.2.1 Expectations of Liberalization: Reprise and Critique

The three countries liberalized imports as part of broader policy reform to achieve faster, more sustained growth in which manufacturing was to play a leading role. Their expectations were based on the advice and theory that accompanies and underlies structural adjustment, an integral part of the body of analysis that has led its main proponent, the World Bank, to advocate 'market friendly' policies and the removal of selective government interventions. As far as import liberalization was concerned, this approach envisaged two essential benefits.

The first was to improve incentives for existing exports. In concert with devaluation and other measures to liberalize domestic prices and controls, import liberalization would reverse the bias towards the domestic market and improve access to imported inputs and equipment (at world market prices). This would lead to the realization of comparative advantages that the existing policies were suppressing, in particular with respect to exports of local primary products. This aspect of reform is relatively uncontroversial and its efficacy is taken for granted here.

The second component was the resource allocation and technological benefits of liberalization. While the exact nature and sequence of these effects were not clearly spelled out, exposure to competition was regarded as generally 'good' for technical efficiency. It was expected, in line with standard economic theory and assuming efficient markets, to lead to a reallocation of resources within and across firms and industries: this would raise efficiency in existing activities and induce their restructuring, and would lead to the launching of new (efficient) activities. Static optimization was assumed to lead automatically to dynamic growth; indeed no distinction was drawn between the two.

Underlying this reasoning were implicit assumptions about how technology was absorbed, used and mastered by industrial firms. There were three elements to the technological argument:

- Import liberalization would shut down activities that were costly and economically unjustified, the result of distortions created by protection. This would raise industrial efficiency, releasing scarce resources for other uses. Only economically efficient activities would survive.
- Liberalization would induce surviving firms to use technologies in line with 'correct' prices (given by efficient markets after the removal of government-induced distortions) and improve their operational efficiency. This would be a largely costless process of moving to the optimal position on a known production function.
- Free markets would signal new investment opportunities in areas of 'true' comparative advantage, with no problems of coordination or other market failures; new activities would be set up with the requisite technological capabilities generated by efficient factor markets.

There was thus an implicit unidirectional and universal causal chain, running from liberalization via improved resource allocation to growth and diversification of output, employment and exports. This reasoning applied regardless of the level of development, and it provided a case for rapid and across-the-board liberalization. Thus it was as relevant to Africa as to other regions: indeed in the early days of adjustment it was expected that African economies would emulate the Asian 'Tiger' economies (whose growth was traced at that time to wholly liberal policy regimes) simply by liberalizing their economic policies. The links between liberalization, static optimization and dynamic growth were taken to be seamless and universal. The case has been analysed in Chapter 2; here we reiterate the main points.

The first step in the liberalization argument is incontrovertible: activities exposed to liberalization that cannot compete will certainly die out. However it is not clear that activities that are presently uncompetitive are *inherently* uneconomic, hence not worth saving. This assumes that there are no learning processes, and that activities cannot be in the process of becoming more efficient. If there are, exposed activities would include both those that are inherently inefficient as well as those that are potentially economic after they undergo a learning process. The second and third steps are even more debatable: it is not clear, given the nature of the capability development process and the market failures involved, that fully liberal policies are necessary or sufficient to stimulate the development of industrial capabilities. The liberalization case rests again on a particular, oversimplified view of the learning process – essentially that it is automatic, costless and similar across technologies. If, on the other hand, industrial development involves a costly, risky and differentiated technological learning process, with diffuse externalities and strong linkages, the outcome of liberalization may be very different. There need be no necessary and automatic transition from static optimization (even assuming that this is possible) to dynamic growth since the process of technological development is likely to face market failures: in product markets (because of unpredictable and expensive learning processes and coordination problems) and factor markets (because of incomplete or asymmetric information, risk, missing markets and coordination failures).[1]

Given such market failures, there may therefore be a role for government interventions to stimulate industrial growth. These interventions need not be entirely 'functional' or what the World Bank calls 'market friendly' – they could often involve selectivity between activities according to the nature of the technology involved, the externalities generated and the coordination required between vertically linked activities. The empirical case adduced by the advocates of liberalization, the Asian Tigers, can also be shown to support the argument for intervention rather than for free markets, and there is a large body of literature on this that we need not recount here.

It follows that the optimal design of import liberalization would also differ under the capability approach. This approach accepts that policy reform is needed in typical import substituting economies, since wholesale protection and inefficient interventions in factor markets have not constituted rational interventions to overcome market failures in the learning process. The interventions have largely attempted to bypass markets rather than improve them, and have not aimed at technical efficiency or competitiveness: as such they could not create a dynamic base for industrial learning. A new incentive regime is clearly needed, but it would, if it were to overcome market failures, retain a significant role for government interventions. The new regime has to give clear and credible signals for industry to invest in new technologies and capabilities, allowing for the 'learning' or 'relearning' periods involved, the coordination of linked activities and the creation or improvement of factor markets. The outcome of liberalization may thus be mixed, by the economy and the sector: positive, static or negative, depending on the starting base of capabilities, the speed of liberalization and the design of the policy package.

To simplify a complex picture, the outcome of liberalization in any given economy can be seen to depend on the interaction of three elements:

- The *credibility and pace of the liberalization*, which determines, first, whether the signals are clear and strong enough for enterprises to make the requisite investment in new technologies and learning, and, second, whether enterprises are given the time they need to learn or relearn.
- The *status of existing capabilities* in relation to world 'frontiers', which defines the distance that firms have to travel in order to survive liberalization.
- The *efficacy of related interventions* to coordinate linked activities, improve factor markets (labour, skills, finance, information and marketing) and develop the support institutions needed to provide firms with the wherewithal to become competitive. This includes both existing activities and new ones that could become competitive.

In the light of these considerations, it is useful to divide industrial activities into four groups in order to analyse the impact of liberalization:

- *Activities that benefit from immediate liberalization.* These can include two very different sorts of product: (1) those with well-developed capabilities or a strong natural resource base that are already competitive in world markets; and (2) those that are non-traded (though they may be potentially tradable) and thus not directly exposed to import competition. The first would benefit from full liberalization in terms of commencing or expanding export activity; this benefit would be especially large if the previous, import-substituting, regime had suppressed export activity. The second are manufactured products that have 'natural protection' because they are heavy and expensive to transport, specifically geared to very local markets, receive special government preferences in procurement or require close producer–buyer interaction. Among our sample firms, examples in the clothing sector include army and school uniforms and custom-made garments, and in the engineering sector tanks and vessels, simple agricultural implements and construction products. These benefit from liberalization because of easier access to imported inputs and rising incomes (say, from greater aid inflows or better performance in the primary sectors from the lifting of export restrictions).

- Activities a *short distance from the world technological 'frontier'*, that is, with a base of capabilities sufficient to reach competitive levels relatively quickly and with little cost and risk. These can be liberalized relatively quickly and their response left to the markets. If factor markets are inadequate, however, the pace of liberalization has to be geared to the rate at which these can be improved. These policies may be largely 'functional' (not aimed at supporting particular activities over others).
- Activities that have developed capabilities and are *potentially viable*, but can only reach competitive levels if given time to undergo learning and relearning, coordinated with linked activities essential to their own learning and operation, and provided, on the supply side, with specific technological, skill and financial inputs. These activities have to be exposed more gradually and in a differentiated way, with activities with difficult and costly learning periods being given more time and support than others. Factor market improvements may have to be specifically targeted to meet their specific needs. Thus a large element of selectivity is implicit in the policies needed here.
- Finally, activities that are *economically unviable 'white elephants'* and should be allowed to die out. These have such a small base of capabilities, or are so unsuited to local resources and markets, that they cannot become competitive despite reasonable levels of support and shelter, bearing in mind the ability of the government to provide relevant support measures.

This distribution can be laid out in a matrix (Figure 7.1). The spread of enterprises over the matrix will differ by country and period. At any given time, however, the distribution of enterprises will determine the overall response of a country's industrial sector to liberalization.

In our sample countries, for instance, category 3 is likely to be the largest single category. However it is likely that in the least industrially developed country (Tanzania), the majority of firms will lie in categories 3 and 4, while in the most developed (Zimbabwe) there will be more firms in categories 1 and 2. Where liberalization is rapid and indiscriminate, opening up is likely to ravage enterprises concentrated in 3 and 4, and – if factor markets are deficient – even those in 2. Our findings, reviewed below, support these general presumptions.

	No interventions needed	Interventions needed
Strong base of capabilities before liberalization	1. Competitive activities	2. Nearly competitive activities needing functional support
Deficient capabilities before liberalization	4. 'White elephants' that do not deserve support and should be left to respond to markets	3. Potentially competitive activities needing functional and selective support

Figure 7.1 Illustrative matrix of industrial capabilities and liberalization

To conclude, our reasoning suggests that the best adjustment policy is the one that takes learning processes and needs into account and incorporates measures to overcome market failures into the liberalization package. This approach seeks to build upon on the existing stock of human capital (arguably the most valuable legacy of past investments) and attempts to save enterprises whose restructuring is viable and economically worthwhile. It involves a positive role for governments but one that is very different from that in earlier import substitution regimes. In several important respects, therefore, it differs from the 'ideal' form liberalization, and from the form of liberalization being conducted in the countries under study.

7.2.2 The Extent of Liberalization

At the time of our study (1995) all three countries had removed practically all quantitative restrictions on non-strategic imports (with some exceptions, for example garments in Zimbabwe, though this was bypassed by semilegal imports) and had rationalized and lowered tariffs. The trend was to approach a range of nominal tariffs of 10–25 per cent, with lower rates on equipment and components and higher rates on finished products. The exchange rate and other arrangements (for imported inputs) affecting exporters were also improved, though in Zimbabwe some of the effect was diluted by the removal of some incentives. While effective tariff rate calculations are not available for the most recent year, it seems that Tanzania was the most advanced in terms of effective import liberalization. The Tanzanian government had also shown the strongest and most consistent commitment to liberalization over time. Kenya had vacillated the most, and its liberalization programme may have had the least credibility. However by late 1996 the Kenyan government was moving more strongly towards a moderately low tariff structure. Zimbabwe, which had started opening up the most recently, also seemed firmly launched on the liberalization path, though the government was coming under strong industry pressure to raise tariffs in some threatened activities.

The garment and textile industry was more exposed to import competition than engineering, a result of the surge of 'second hand' (including unused, end-of-run or slightly defective) clothing imports. These had started in a small way in many African countries in the late 1980s, but by 1995 had captured large shares of the low-price, low-quality end of the market. Their impact was exacerbated by stagnant or declining incomes that made them more attractive to consumers and dissuaded governments from undertaking serious countervailing measures. The most threatened producers were those of standard items of mass-produced clothing, especially those without access to imported low-cost fabrics.

In the engineering sector there were naturally few such unintentional problems of liberalization, since the products were large, heavy and difficult to smuggle, and there were no end-of-run leftovers that could be disposed of very cheaply. The extent of exposure was generally more gradual, though by the time of the survey some effects were being clearly felt. Since the engineering industry is very diverse, the impact of liberalization varied according to the nature of the product. The part of production that concentrated on 'non-tradable' items – metal products made to order, simple tools, repair services, implements and spares adapted to local conditions, and some more advanced capital goods with strong and well-established linkages with customers – was relatively less threatened (at least in the short term) by the liberalization of imports. Other engineering products were more directly exposed to competition. In general the weight of relatively simple engineering activities geared to very localized markets meant that the industry as a whole was less exposed than garments.

7.2.3 Industry Performance

7.2.3.1 Growth Rates

Table 7.1 shows the growth rates of manufacturing value added (taken from Chapter 1). Kenya and Zimbabwe did worse after liberalization, while Tanzania did better. For the former two, exogenous reasons contributed to the deterioration of performance (drought, power cuts, aid freeze, stabilization, uncertainty and macroeconomic difficulties),

Table 7.1 Growth of MVA (per cent)

	Period	*Kenya*	*Tanzania*	*Zimbabwe*
Pre-liberalization	1980–85	3.8	−5.0	2.4
	1985–90	5.7	2.4	4.4
Post-liberalization	1990–94	2.2	4.6	−2.5

though these did not account for the whole of the decline. The drought ended some two years ago, and the agricultural sector has revived; but this has not led to a surge in manufacturing production. Data from Zimbabwe show sharp fluctuations: a revival in growth in 1994 after declines in the previous two years, followed by another sharp decline in 1995 (−8.6 per cent) and then a revival in 1996 (8.5 per cent).[2] Manufacturing typically took two to three years to recover from the reductions in purchasing power brought about by the drought, while agriculture recovered as soon as the climate improved; thus Zimbabwe, with its large manufacturing sector dependent on local markets, tends to be relatively more vulnerable to climatic shocks than the other two countries. This makes a strategic response all the more difficult for industrial firms. In Kenya, aid has been restored but the growth rate of MVA continues to languish. Tanzania is not doing much better.

The causes of poor industrial performance thus do not lie entirely in exogenous shocks – the liberalization process is also a contributor. There is ample anecdotal evidence to show that liberalization is forcing many manufacturing firms to shut down or move to products that do not face direct import competition: much of the growth seen in recent years, especially in small enterprises, is in activities that have 'natural protection' against imports. With the exception of resource-based activities, these activities tend to be simple and low-productivity, aimed at local low-income consumers. Their growth, while desirable, does not presage well for longer-term industrial or export development.

We should remember that for Tanzania the first part of the 1980s was a long period of industrial decline, and the resumption of growth in the 1990s was largely driven by the availability of imported inputs for utilizing existing capacity. In the light of this, however, the rate of expansion was rather low, and the previous peak in industrial production still had not been reached by 1994. Moreover most of the growth came in a spurt in 1991–92, with a substantial slowdown in subsequent years. A similar 'petering out' of growth occurred in the other major adjusting country in SubSaharan Africa, Ghana,[3] suggesting that the initial growth momentum was based on the use of existing capacity, but did not translate into significant industrial restructuring, capability acquisition and gains in competitiveness. With the growth of import competition, therefore, the spurt could not be sustained.

7.2.3.2 Manufactured Export Performance

Manufactured export performance improved in each country in the 1990s, a result of the improved environment for export activity: better primary production, stronger incentives for exports and easier access to imported inputs and equipment. These comprise the first set of benefits of trade policy reform – the realization of existing comparative advantages – and are relatively non-controversial. They reflect the fuller exploitation of existing comparative advantages, not improved efficiency and resource reallocation in response to import competition. However there are differences across countries in intensity of export response that reflect their relative capabilities.

The largest improvement in manufactured exports took place in Tanzania, though the values involved were very small ($63 million in 1993) and the growth was from a tiny base. Moreover the growth was a manifestation, as with industrial production, of the reversal of a long decline (the 1993 export value, in current dollars, was lower than in 1980). Most of the growth came from processed local natural resources and from established firms, rather than from new manufacturing activities or entrants. It did not denote significant technological upgrading or diversification. Exports by the two sample industries were negligible, and in textiles there was a downgrading of export quality. In Kenya, manufactured exports also declined over the 1980s, then grew at 4 per cent per annum after 1989 (but by 1993 had not reached their nominal 1980 dollar value). While there was a higher 'value added' content here than in Tanzania (Kenya was the dominant industrial power in the East African Economic Community), practically all growth was in established activities. There was a more vigorous export response outside manufacturing (led by horticulture), based more on resource endowments than on improved technology in response to import competition. However there was certainly some technological response on the part of Kenyan exporters of manufactured products; our study shows efforts to raise quality and enter new products and markets, largely by activities with a well-established domestic base.

Zimbabwe's manufactured exports were growing strongly before liberalization (13 per cent per annum during 1980–89), reflecting the relative strength of its industrial sector after the ending of UDI, its long experience of export activity and its special access to the South African market. During 1989–91, there was a decline in exports, a result of the removal of export incentives and the general recession and macroeconomic uncertainty. In 1992–95 there was a surge in manufactured export growth (to 18 per cent), mainly to regional markets. In this period, exports of resource-based products such as processed foods, wood products and ferrochrome grew rapidly, as did 'value added' products such as machinery, metal products and the products of printing and publishing. Garments and textiles, the highest manufactured exports after ferrochrome and processed foods, showed more modest rises (of 6.2 per cent and 2.0 per cent respectively), despite the fact that similar exports from other developing regions were growing rapidly (note that Zimbabwe is still a tiny exporter of clothing, with some 3–4 per cent of the value of similar exports from newcomers such as Mauritius, Sri Lanka and Bangladesh). To some extent this growth may have been driven by domestic recession since production continued to decline; however it also reflected the superior competitive base of Zimbabwean industry. Again it seems that the efforts were based largely on existing export capabilities, including new and old firms using the existing base of skills and know-how.

The evidence does not suggest, therefore, that import liberalization has sparked off a process of sustained industrial growth in these countries. Manufacturing production is growing very slowly or stagnating, and some of the growth that has occurred may simply be a result of the utilization of existing capacities and making up for long periods of decline. Many of the firms that are exposed to direct import competition are dying out. Where there has been a more positive response, as with exports in Zimbabwe, it is based on capabilities built up during import substitution: it is not clear that these capabilities will continue to grow once the existing comparative advantages have been fully exploited, regional markets have opened up to full international competition, and the special privileges for exporting to regional and European markets are eroded.[4]

Let us now consider the growth performance of the two sample industries, as a whole and for the sample firms (Table 7.2). We draw upon different sources of information. The first part of the table uses UNIDO data, which gives consistent data across the countries for 1980–90 but in the post-liberalization period only go up to 1993. Data from the countries themselves vary in coverage and perhaps in definition (for example of engineering), but they go up to the end of 1994

Table 7.2 Growth of garment and engineering industries and firms (per cent)

	Value added growth rates				*Sales growth of sample firms*
	Pre-lib.	*Post-liberalization*			
Country/industry	*1980–90*	*1990–93*	*1990–94*	*1989–94*	*1989/90–1994*
Kenya					
Garments	−0.55	−3.28	−13.5		−1.0[1]
Engineering[2]	2.09	−3.74	3.8		−3.20
Tanzania					
Garments	−18.89	n.a.		−22.30	−6.00
Engineering[2]	−13.34	−4.46		5.30	−3.00
Zimbabwe					
Garments	3.48	−8.02	−6.04[3]		Negative[+]
Engineering[2]	1.95	−7.71	−3.44[3]		−1.5[1]

Notes:
[1] Excluding one outlier with an extraordinarily high growth rate.
[2] 'Engineering' includes metal products, electrical and non-electrical equipment.
[3] Including January–May, 1995.
[+] Estimate. Data for half the firms were not available, in particular those with falling sales.
Sources: UNIDO, *Industry and Development, Global Report*, 1995, 1993/94; country sources.

or early 1995. There are some minor inconsistencies between these sources but there is little we can do about this.

The garment industry has done distinctly worse since liberalization than before. In Zimbabwe, it went into decline after a decade of modest rates of growth. In Kenya and Tanzania, liberalization accelerated a decline that had started in the 1980s, most probably under the impact of 'second hand' imports (which had started in that period but accelerated in the 1990s). In Kenya, the decline was particularly sharp in 1994; in Zimbabwe, there was a large fall in 1991–92, followed by modest rises and then a massive fall in 1994–95. In contrast the Tanzanian garment industry seems, according to UNIDO data, to have declined significantly in the 1980s, and the recent deterioration represents a relatively minor worsening of the earlier performance.

Engineering has also performed worse than garments in Kenya and Zimbabwe since liberalization according to UNIDO data; in contrast engineering in Tanzania has done better than garments since liberalization. In the former two countries the reason for the decline appears to lie in a combination of import competition and a fall in domestic demand. The export growth that has taken place is insufficient to compensate.

Turning now to the sample firms, these have suffered declining sales in the past five years (although some data are patchy). Their decline is slightly lower than that recorded by the respective industries, except for engineering in Tanzania and Kenya. This is probably due to the fact that the samples are small and not random. Nevertheless their experience confirms that liberalization has been harsh on industry. How much of this has actually been caused by the 'opening up', and how much by the other unfavourable circumstances mentioned, cannot be assessed from the data – both are likely to share the responsibility. However a more detailed understanding of the technological forces at work can cast some light on this issue.

7.3 THE TECHNOLOGICAL STATUS OF THE SAMPLE FIRMS

Before reviewing the response to liberalization it will be useful to consider the technological level of the two industries, as revealed by the sample firms. This is essential to establish some sort of 'base line' from which changes take place, and to allow the assessment of two vital issues:

- Whether liberalization has led to an improvement in technological capabilities, and the nature and incidence of such improvements (this section).
- Whether the improvement that has taken place is enough to allow firms to compete in their domestic markets with liberalized imports or in export markets, at least in the near future (Section 7.4).

Let us start with an overview of the status of technological capabilities in the sample.

The *Zimbabwean sample firms have the best developed technological capabilities, followed by the Kenyan and then the Tanzanian firms.* Within the sample, this shows up as a positive correlation of capabilities with size, age and international exposure, with the Zimbabwean firms scoring best on these features. The technological base today is largely the product of the import substituting period in each country, but this period has left very different legacies, reflecting differences in the initial base of human capital and entrepreneurship and the nature of the industrialization strategy pursued by each government. In many instances, especially in smaller firms, there has been little effective technological learning, and even many of the larger firms show little technological development in Tanzania. In fact Zimbabwe stands out as something of an exception in the generally gloomy picture of industrial progress under import substitution in SubSaharan Africa (Lall, 1992).

Second, while there are clear exceptions, *the general level of technological capabilities in the sample is relatively low.* While it is difficult directly to compare technological capabilities across regions, the available qualitative evidence suggests that the African sample lags well behind comparators in other developing regions in many aspects of technological performance.[5] Moreover their upgrading in reaction to liberalization is relatively slow, and in most cases inadequate (next section). There is also a *wide dispersion of capabilities*: a relatively small number of firms in each sample are able to cope with import competition (where they are directly exposed, which not all firms are), the proportion being highest in Zimbabwe and lowest in Tanzania. Other firms, the majority in the sample, are reacting passively or withdrawing from the exposed parts of their manufacturing activity, or from manufacturing entirely. The garment industry is doing worse than engineering because its exposure has been more drastic; practically all garment firms making standard, low-price products are failing to compete with imports, and are surviving by making non-traded products such as uniforms. The few that are doing well are established firms in higher-quality segments and in export markets. Engineering firms making more customized or 'heavier' products are less exposed and so have more time to adjust; the better firms are making an effort to upgrade their technologies. However most of those facing direct competition are finding it difficult to cope. Barring the relatively few 'good' firms, therefore, the manufacturing growth that is taking place is largely in the non-tradable segments of manufacturing – this may not provide a sound basis for longer-term development.

Third, the *technological specialization of most of the sample firms is relatively simple.* While in garments the technological range is inherently limited, the firms in our sample, with some exceptions in Zimbabwe and a couple in Kenya, specialized in low-quality segments where skill requirements are low, design needs minimal and technical inputs simple. The 'high-technology' end of the sample firms in clothing are the few export-oriented firms, but these are mainly engaged in simple cut-make-trim operations, which, while demanding in terms of organization and quality control, are at the low end of the international scale. These are nevertheless technologically far ahead of the small domestic market oriented firms, especially in Tanzania, which are basically large tailor shops. In engineering, most firms make basic metal products or, at the higher end, relatively straightforward machines with mature technologies and low precision and performance requirements. Even the ostensibly complex products made by some foreign affiliates are essentially assembly operations with a low local technological content. In contrast engineering industries in East Asia are engaged in a much broader range of sophisticated manufacturing operations with much greater local integration, often using state-of-the-art equipment and designing complex engineering goods.

Fourth, *no formal research and development is conducted by the sample firms*. There are few instances of major improvements to process technology or the introduction of new processes based on local efforts, in contrast to the situation in the newly industrializing countries. As far as product development goes, the almost complete absence of formal R&D is particularly noteworthy in the engineering sector, where complex manufacturing requires a separate design/development effort. In the NIEs, many machinery, component and electrical equipment manufacturers undertake formal R&D, even if this mainly involves 'reverse engineering' of foreign products. While this does occur in the better engineering firms in Africa, particularly in Zimbabwe, where locally 'appropriate' designs are sometimes developed (such as designs for buses or boilers), in general the focus of design work is relatively simple equipment. In the other countries, the level of design capabilities is much lower. The lack of local research and design capability is one factor keeping African producers at the bottom of the quality chain or, in complex product segments, making them exit altogether in response to rapid liberalization. In the clothing sector, formal R&D is uncommon for all but the most advanced producers; however entry into high-quality segments requires the development of independent design capabilities. Few firms in the African sample are building up such design capabilities, in contrast to the better export-oriented producers of East Asia. The exceptions that do exist (among the larger exporters in Zimbabwe and Kenya) cannot be rated highly by Asian standards. The lack of design capabilities may prevent firms from moving up the quality ladder and broadening their range of foreign buyers.

Fifth, the lack of in-house technological activity is *not sufficiently counteracted by a significant transfer of new technologies from abroad*, via direct investment or licensing, in any of the countries.[6] This may seem surprising, given that both industries have extremely active technology transfer and FDI in other regions. Of the licensing activity that does take place in our sample firms, most is confined to foreign affiliates; local firms have relatively few licensing agreements. New foreign direct investment is sparse; most foreign affiliates have been established for a long time. Moreover their technology upgrading is limited by their small capability base: foreign firms tend to use the lowest end of the range of technologies their companies deploy, and generally at productivity levels that are lower than in most other regions. The low level of licensing by local firms to offset low FDI inflows reflects the same weaknesses in technology capability, since to find, import, use and adapt new foreign technologies requires a relatively good knowledge and technical skills base. This weakness is particularly worrying for longer-term manufacturing development and competitiveness.

Sixth, the *'embodied' technology (capital equipment) used by the sample firms is generally old, and there is widespread use of second-hand machines.* In several activities this makes it very difficult, or impossible, to upgrade quality and precision to international levels with the given plant. In others, old equipment may be operated at 'best practice' levels of efficiency and quality, but this requires highly skilled manpower and close technical supervision, which is not available in most of the sample firms.

Seventh, there is a *large variation between firms in their ability to manage process technologies*. In general the larger firms, especially those that are export-oriented or have foreign management, tend to be better at quality control, maintenance, adapting technologies and improving the embodied technologies. The smaller firms, especially those serving localized markets and using traditional techniques, tend to have a low level of process know-how. Zimbabwean firms have the best general process capabilities, followed by the larger Kenyan firms. In garments, the best firms are the leading exporters from these two countries; in engineering, the long-established equipment manufacturers in Zimbabwe. However even the technologically 'good' firms (the top seven to ten firms in the sample in Zimbabwe and Kenya with formal quality management systems and specialized process engineering capabilities) show no sign of the sustained and systematic search for improved productivity and quality that mark the more successful firms in the NIEs, nor of efforts to increase the capacities of equipment, substitute materials and processes and improve worker skills. This may have been exacerbated by the uncertainties facing the African firms, though this does not fully account for their technological weaknesses. As far as the smaller, more traditional enterprises are concerned, it is difficult to see how they could improve their process capabilities to competitive levels; on the present evidence they are likely to stay in their non-tradable niches, at least until competition from imports or larger firms finally reaches them.

Eighth, *the employment of technically qualified personnel (managers, supervisors and workers) in the three countries is low by international standards.*[7] While this is to be expected in the garment industry, it may be a competitive handicap even in this activity where export production is involved. In the engineering industry it is far more important, especially if firms are to move beyond the simplest products and processes. In addition there are doubts about the quality and relevance of the engineering education provided by universities and by vocational training and other centres. Nevertheless some firms have a better appreciation of the need for improved technical manpower: an econometric analysis of the propensity to employ engineers suggests that the educational background of the entrepreneur is important, and that those with formal engineering qualifications tend to employ more engineers. In line with their higher capabilities by other measures, Zimbabwean firms have a greater propensity to employ engineers than those in Kenya and Tanzania.

Ninth, the sample firms have a *relatively low awareness of and expenditure on employee training.* While the current skill levels may have been adequate for the technological demands and quality levels of protected regimes, they are likely to constrain attempts to cope with full import competition or enter export markets. Again there are differences: the larger firms in Zimbabwe are more aware of skill shortages – and train more people – than firms in the other two countries. The smaller and technologically weaker firms in all three countries tend not to feel skill constraints, and invest little in human resources. While on-the-job training is provided by many firms (as in enterprises the world over), this tends to be the minimum needed to transmit basic operational skills from existing to new operatives. More formal in-house training to raise the capabilities and productivity of employees is carried out by relatively few enterprises. This is not compensated for by external technical training, which tends to be modest,[8] exacerbated by a lack of local institutions that can provide training that is relevant to industrial needs. While government programmes exist to promote training, as in Zimbabwe (a 1 per cent training levy on payrolls), they are limited and not widely or effectively used. The most common form of external training is that provided by foreign capital goods suppliers, but this only helps large firms that have invested in new foreign technologies; in any case, such training only provides once-and-for-all skill transmission. Our econometric analysis of training efforts in the sample suggests that size is a significant positive influence, as well as the education of the entrepreneur and foreign ownership.

Tenth, the sample firms that are *good at one form of technological effort are also good at others* – it is the same (few) firms that invest in most aspects of technological activity, since they tend to be aware of the various ramifications of their technical needs. This has made it possible for us to construct a technology index (TI), based on certain critical and identifiable features of technology in the sample firms that capture their overall capabilities. What are the characteristics of the 'best' sample firms? Econometric analysis of the determinants of TI suggests the following: in engineering, technologically dynamic firms are *larger* and *older* than others, and *invest more in training*. In garments, only *firm size* shows up as significant. There are no specific country effects in the engineering sample, once size, age and training are accounted for. In garments, Zimbabwean firms have a technological edge after other factors have been accounted for.

Eleventh, *export activity by the sample firms is positively correlated to their technological capabilities*. As expected, the export response is strongest in the Zimbabwean firms, which not only have a stronger technological base but also considerable experience of international markets over decades of export activity. The initial boost to their exports from devaluation and liberalized access to imported inputs has been diluted by and domestic policy uncertainty, the removal of export incentives and the temporary withdrawal of special access to the South African market. This now seems to have been overcome and manufactured exports are growing strongly in Zimbabwe, at rates exceeding those in the preliberalization period. However the main contribution of liberalization has not been to stimulate resource reallocation and domestic restructuring, but to provide access to inputs and force firms to look for new markets in order to offset competition in a depressed domestic market. It is the large firms that are expanding their overseas sales in established and new export activities (for example furniture), by adding to or improving the utilization of existing capabilities. Whether or not this growth will be sustained once the initial impetus runs out will depend, however, on their ability to develop new capabilities: regional markets are liberalizing to global competition and

South Africa is gearing up for its own export thrust in similar products. The smaller Zimbabwean firms are finding it very difficult to cope with import competition, and do not have the capabilities needed to launch into exports.

The Kenyan sample firms have also increased their exports since liberalization, though with less, vigour than their Zimbabwean counterparts. A few clothing firms – some established, some new – have aimed at OECD markets, while engineering firms have targeted regional markets, selling simple, heavy metal products that enjoy transport cost advantages. Again, smaller firms are finding it very difficult to cope with import competition, and the overall ability of the local manufacturing sector to enter world markets with new products seems relatively limited. Much of the export growth in Kenya is coming from resource-based products (for example horticulture) rather than manufacturing. The Tanzanian sample firms (with one exception in garments) are the least active in exporting and show the weakest response to the reforms. Their low overall level of industrial capabilities means that the prospects for export growth in manufactures are dim. In all these cases, the entry of fresh FDI would seem to be essential to an export drive.

Twelfth, *linkages between the sample firms and other firms and technology institutions are very limited*. This is a further sign, and cause, of weak technological capabilities. Subcontracting is not widespread, and firms tend to rely on imports or the in-house production of components (Biggs *et al.*, 1995). Links with technology institutions are confined to necessary, rather basic, activities such as the mandatory certification of products or material testing. There is very little research contracting or use of institutions to search for and adapt new foreign technologies. In fact the sample firms are generally unaware of the technological services and capabilities available in government institutions, or regard them as irrelevant or inefficient. This view is not entirely unjustified: the institutions offer little as they suffer from similar technological weaknesses. They tend to be poorly equipped, staffed and motivated, and are unable to provide the services that industrial firms need. Thus there exists an exaggerated form of the isolation between the technology infrastructure and the productive sector that can be seen in many other countries (although some are overcoming this, as noted below). The adjustment process has reduced institutional funding and may have further isolated the institutions from the productive sector (Enos, 1995). The lack of institutional support for technology development is unfortunate, since firms face market failures in identifying their technological problems, obtaining relevant technical information and mounting the necessary technological effort.

Thirteenth, the *relationship between growth performance and technological capabilities is difficult to establish* for the sample firms because of the 'noise' created by shocks, macroeconomic problems and uncertainties. Statistical analysis of employment growth for the pooled sample (the only performance variable for which comparable data could be obtained) does, nevertheless, show a positive relationship between TI and growth in clothing; no significant effect is found in engineering. In Kenya, where growth has been stronger and sales data are available, it is interesting to note that TI emerges as the only significant influence on sales growth.

Finally, *foreign and non-African firms generally show stronger technological capabilities than African firms.*[9] In the Kenyan study, which investigates this at some length, non-African firms have significantly higher average values for the technology index than African firms. They also tend to grow faster, be larger or older, use more capital-intensive techniques, pay higher wages, have better educated entrepreneurs and a higher proportion of quality control and maintenance manpower than African firms. As a consequence, even the 'best' African-owned firms are finding it difficult to survive in the liberalizing environment. However, most of the recent entrants into industry in all three countries are African-owned firms, thus exacerbating the negative effects of liberalization. The weaker technological status of African firms may mean that liberalization will affect them more severely than others. However it is important to note that African ownership *per se* is not the cause of technological weakness, but the associated problems of size, age, technology and so on. Thus policy measures have to be aimed at remedying these problems.

To sum up, our study suggests that there are serious technological deficiencies in all three countries, but with significant differences between them and between firms within each country. These deficiencies will prevent the majority of enterprises from reaching a competitive level. Zimbabwe is the best placed to cope with the challenge of import competition, Tanzania the least. In each country there are a few firms that are technologically active and competent; the remainder, in particular the smaller firms, are not internationally competitive and will probably not be able to withstand direct competition. The better firms, while having a reasonable degree of competence in the technologies they operate, are still at the lower end of the technological spectrum in their respective activities, and need considerably to enhance their physical and human capital and technological effort in order to grow and diversify under liberalized trade.

Only a handful of firms seem to have the ability to use the liberal regime positively, to take on new competitive activities and enter the world market. The rest seem likely to retreat from directly exposed activities: the standard end of the clothing industry is withdrawing massively from direct import competition, and in the tradable sections only some of the largest and most capable firms are thriving. In engineering, firms are sheltered for the time being by the nature of their products. Some are using this grace period and open access to new technologies to restructure and upgrade, but most are not. It is not clear that even the best firms will become competitive in any but the simplest products, in which they presently specialize.

Does this matter? In our view it does, certainly for long-term industrial and export growth. There are certainly several 'protected' activities, based on local resources or other natural trade barriers, that can allow firms to flourish: food processing, wood working, mineral processing, simple metal products, cement and other building materials, ethnic garments and so on. However these are unlikely to be sufficient to carry the whole manufacturing sector forward at a significant rate, and their technological externalities and linkages are likely to be limited. Many of the 'easy' entry-level activities that provided the export impetus for the NIEs are precisely the ones where African countries are facing Asian competition today, and the more complex engineering activities that provided the NIEs with a fertile learning base (capital goods, electronics, transport equipment) seem largely out of reach for the foreseeable future. The future of manufacturing development in a liberalized setting thus seems rather bleak and constrained.

7.4 THE TECHNOLOGICAL RESPONSE TO LIBERALIZATION

The technological changes undertaken by firms in response to liberalization have been mixed. The weak firms have responded by moving out of manufacturing altogether, or by reducing their technological activities. They have tended not to recognize the extent or nature of their technological deficiencies, and so have ignored skill and technology upgrading. As a result, as well as reducing employment, they have reduced the quality of their products and used poorer materials in an attempt to cut costs. This is particularly the case with the majority of firms in Tanzania, but has also been true of smaller or less capable firms in the other two countries. Such responses are not conducive to competing with imports.

Among the minority of 'better' firms, the response to liberalization has been more positive. For instance, of the 41 sample enterprises in Kenya, four garment and seven engineering firms have responded by improving their technology and moving into exports. Their quality control has improved, reject rates cut, training provision increased and maintenance and inventory control improved; there has also been some increase in subcontracting. In Zimbabwe, the initial response to liberalization in 1991–92 was positive, with the larger firms starting to renovate equipment and improve their technical activity and training. Thereafter, recession and stringent stabilization measures and growing uncertainty largely forced them to put their efforts 'on hold'. This was especially so with garment firms; but there are signs that several engineering firms are continuing to make minor improvements to their technological practices. In the absence of the exogenous shocks, it is likely that the Zimbabwean firms would have taken their response further than the Kenyan ones. It is also possible that, since our fieldwork was conducted, there has been an increase in the technological activity of the exporting firms in Zimbabwe.

We have distinguished between firms with 'defensive' and 'offensive' technological strategies in response to liberalization. While our evaluation is subjective, we find that *the majority of firms in the sample have adopted defensive (retreat or passive) strategies*, cutting employment and costs without upgrading technologies, or withdrawing from direct competition altogether. There are, however, differences between the industries: *clothing firms are overwhelmingly defensive while engineering firms are mainly offensive*. Within the engineering industry, the Tanzanian firms have adopted the least offensive strategies – only 11 per cent of the firms there have tried to improve their competitiveness by buying new equipment and developing new skills. In Kenya, about half of the engineering firms have responded offensively by introducing new products and trying to enter export markets; in Zimbabwe, the corresponding figure is nearly two thirds.

The difference in response between the two industries appears to be due to the *differing intensity of competition faced*. In garments, the low-end producers (the majority) have found it almost impossible to compete with second-hand imports on the basis of price and lack the ability to move upmarket or into exports. Thus they have retreated from the exposed segments into non-tradable garments or out of garment production altogether. In engineering, the extent of direct competition has been much lower, giving a 'grace period' in which firms could restructure themselves.

It is interesting to contrast the reactions of our sample with those of industrial firms in Argentina, which has a long history of import substitution and has recently implemented a rapid – and much more sweeping – liberalization programme. The base of technological capabilities in Argentina is far in advance of that in Africa: Argentina has an old and complex industrial structure, with high levels of technical skills, a diversified capital goods industry, strong indigenous entrepreneurs as well as a considerable MNC presence, and predominantly large-scale operations using advanced modern technologies. A recent study examines the response of 2000 Argentine manufacturing enterprises to liberalization (Kosacoff, 1996). Of these enterprises, the largest 400, accounting for 40 per cent of manufacturing value added, are classified as having responded 'offensively' to liberalization (defined as raising their facilities and capabilities to world class levels).[10] The remaining 1600 firms reacted 'defensively', defined as being unable to face full import competition. However these firms did upgrade their capabilities, showing average productivity increases of *100 per cent* (on our criteria most of these firms would have been counted as 'offensive'). However their inability to achieve 'best practice' technology means that many are closing down or selling imported products.

As a result there has been a massive rise in manufacturing unemployment. The industrial growth that has taken place has been mainly in 'heavy' activities where capabilities were developed during the long period of import substitution (cars, chemicals or basic metals). Many of the heavy processing industries that have upgraded also have a local raw materials base. The general process of industrial restructuring has not, however, resulted in an overall rise in the technological sophistication of manufacturing (in terms of the technological content of production or export activity). Unlike East Asia, where export and industrial growth has been propelled by a steady rise in the technological and skill content of manufacturing activity, Argentina (and Latin America more generally) has seen a retrogression of the structure to resource-based activities under the impact of 'opening up'.[11] In other words, the relatively high technological capabilities built up earlier are now being exploited under liberalization, but they are not being expanded and diversified into high-tech activities. Part of this seems to be due to the lack of intervention to overcome inherent market failures.

There would appear to be important lessons from this for our countries. In Africa, the skill and capability levels built up under import substitution are generally much lower than in Argentina (though Zimbabwe is in advance of the others). The technological response to liberalization has thus been weaker, and there are fewer activities that are ready to react offensively. The Argentine response, even given its costs and shortcomings, is out of reach for most of our sample firms. The improvements achieved by even the 'defensive' firms in Argentina are unlikely to be achieved by most of our sample firms, where defensive strategies have meant doing little or nothing in technological terms. This means that the adjustment process in Africa is likely to be much more difficult: though the existing industrial structure is relatively small, its future growth is likely to be more severely constrained. The prospects of a dynamic and diverse manufacturing sector providing the engine of growth along Asian lines seems rather unrealistic in these countries.

The Latin American model of 'opening up', with rapid and sweeping liberalization, has its own high costs. Fortunately it is not the only way to adjust. East Asia has generally followed a different pattern of liberalization. Its opening up has been more gradual and controlled, leaving more discretion in the hands of the government during and after liberalization. Korea, for instance, followed a deliberate and slow process of structural adjustment. Its first adjustment programme was launched in 1980; by 1995 it was still not an 'open' economy and strong complaints were still being voiced about the difficulties of selling foreign products in Korea. The government announced its schedule of import liberalization years in advance, giving discretionary protection to activities with difficult learning requirements and mounting strong measures to support firms. Exports, which were growing strongly before the domestic markets were exposed, were further promoted. The government retained the power to guide credit, set up new infant industries and target technological activity. This meant that there was no damage to the existing industries or employment, growth was maintained at high levels and new areas of comparative advantage were built up while more mature activities were subjected to competition. The policy implications of this are taken up below.

These comparisons help illustrate the adjustment problems facing our three countries. Once the simplifying assumptions on learning that underlie structural adjustment are dropped, it is no longer evident that merely 'opening up' will act as a catalyst to industrial growth and competitiveness. Even in economies with relatively advanced levels of technological capability, rapid liberalization imposes severe costs if not accompanied by a strategy of upgrading and gearing liberalization to the learning requirements for different activities. However, when the pace of opening up and the support policies adopted to help firms upgrade are guided by a clear strategy, the results are far better. How do the three African economies fare in these respects?

The initial technological capability base in the three countries was weak, ranging from relatively deficient in the most advanced country to extremely poor in the least. The liberalization process has been rapid and not guided by a strategy. There has been little attempt to gear the opening up to the learning requirements for different activities. Support policies are virtually non-existent, and the institutions that could have assisted the adjustment process are weak and isolated from industry. This places the entire burden of adjustment on firms, which often lack the knowledge, resources and skills required to upgrade to international levels. To make matters worse, adjustment is being undertaken under very difficult and uncertain macroeconomic conditions, with stringent stabilization programmes saddling firms with high interest costs. The liberalization programme itself lacks credibility and is not properly communicated to firms, causing them to remain passive and wait for policies to revert to their old, less threatening patterns. What is surprising is that the disappointing reaction to liberalization was not anticipated – even a basic understanding of technological processes would have led to a differently designed liberalization programme. Enterprise-level reactions are still not fully appreciated by those who design and administer adjustment programmes, at least in their pronouncements on policy reform. They still argue that further liberalization is all that is needed.

Of course it could be argued that Africa is not really suited to industrialization, beyond elementary resource-based, low-technology activities that do not compete with imports. In this case full liberalization would lead to the 'efficient' outcome that very little industry survives, with growth proceeding from primary and service sector activities. This study takes the opposite view and proposes that industrial development and dynamism are as feasible in Africa as elsewhere, and as necessary for its structural transformation and development.

7.5 POLICY IMPLICATIONS: LEARNING FROM THE ASIAN 'TIGERS'

The analysis of the African response to liberalization suggests that there is a greater need for gradual liberalization and supply-side support, especially with respect to the indigenous private sector, in this region than in others because of its smaller industrial capability base. This is not to argue the case for a return to old strategies of wholesale, unselective and inefficient intervention for industrialization, which were not conducive to the development of a dynamic industrial base. Trade and industrial policies were long characterized by high levels of protection and intervention in domestic resource allocation, a dominant role for public enterprises and a general distrust of the private sector. Small and fragmented local markets led to the setting up of small-scale plants that could not compete internationally. Foreign direct investment was often deterred by hostile and unstable policies, and by the small and stagnant domestic market, while export-oriented investments gravitated to regions with better policies, skill bases and infrastructure. Indigenous industrial entrepreneurship was weak, dominated by small and micro enterprises that were mainly concentrated in traditional low-productivity activities serving very local markets. While the number of such enterprises has multiplied in recent years, this has often been a survival strategy in the face of the adverse economic climate – it has not led to the widespread graduation of small-scale enterprises to large-scale modem production or to export activity geared to world markets.

This study suggests that while reforms to the incentive structure (and greater market orientation) are essential to industrial progress, 'getting prices right' by itself cannot solve the existing problems. Trying to do so rapidly may even make matters worse. Part of the reforms must be to improve the macroeconomic management of the economy: no one disputes this objective. There is also no dispute about the need for adjustment in the sense of policy reform: what is in dispute is the nature, speed and scope of the liberalization process, and the role that governments should play in promoting efficient industrial development.

7.5.1 Incentive Reforms

'Incentive structure' as applied to industrial development, refers to the competitive situation that firms face in allocating resources, and to the general macroeconomic environment and the credibility of the reform process. Investment decisions in this case relate not only to the purchase of plant and equipment, but also to investment in technological effort. Industrial progress depends on firms finding the right plant and technology, developing the skills and knowledge to use that technology, forging the right supply and information links with other firms and support institutions, and finding and developing domestic and export markets. If the incentive structure is distorted by high and sustained protection and other barriers to competition, the process of mastering technology can be hampered or misdirected, leading to inefficiency and uncompetitiveness. The restoration of competition is necessary and desirable for healthy industrial development. Similarly, if the macroeconomic conditions are uncertain and the reform process lacks credibility, there is bound to be insufficient investment in upgrading technological capabilities; stability and credibility are clear requirements for adjustment.

The reform of the trade regime need not, however, mean rapid and sweeping exposure to international competition. To reiterate an argument made earlier, there are different ways of exposing industrial firms to a 'stimulating' environment. Helping industries to adjust to competition can be a slow and difficult process, calling for a range of external support measures, since learning within firms cannot make up for deficiencies in the supply of essential inputs such as education, training, technical information and supplier networks. The provision of these is generally a complex task, involving a great deal of active government intervention and guidance.[12]

In the three countries under study, we find that in the sector where exposure to imports has been most severe and rapid – the clothing industry – the results have been most devastating. The engineering industry generally has been less exposed and has done relatively better. Similarly, overall performance has been better in the economy that has liberalized the least, Kenya, if the effects of the exogenous shocks of the 1990s are taken into account. It was noted above that the East Asian 'model' of liberalization was very different from the sweeping and rapid liberalization being recommended to the sample countries, and may offer some lessons. Most Asian economies liberalized in a gradual manner, retaining considerable control over resource allocation during the process. They undertook a controlled process of 'opening up', accompanied by a strategy of industrial restructuring and upgrading, rather than rapid, indiscriminate and sweeping exposure to international market forces. The speed of liberalization was based on a realistic, detailed and differentiated assessment of which activities were internationally viable in the medium term, with the process geared to the learning and relearning required for various activities. At the same time, this model placed strong pressure on industries to invest in building up new capabilities that would enable them to compete with imports within a limited period. *It was designed to overcome market failures, not to ignore them.* It involved close monitoring of the progress of liberalization, and required the government to address the supply-side needs of industries (see below) during the phased liberalization process. The strategy was generally developed in collaboration with the industrial sector, and was announced in advance so that enterprises had time to adjust. Once announced, however, the government rigidly stuck to the programme in order to minimize backsliding and 'hijacking' by inefficient performers.

This is clearly a better adjustment strategy for our countries than the adjustment package they are presently promoting. To some extent, the avenues for slowing down liberalization may already have been closed by the governments themselves, but to the extent that there is still scope for independent action, it would seem advisable to adopt a more cautious and carefully considered approach. However, to recommend a more gradual and nuanced strategy of liberalization is not to suggest that these countries should simply abort the adjustment process. What is needed is not to delay the adjustment and then do little else, but to *prepare actively for it* in the grace period provided. Even with well-designed adjustment policies, the outcome here cannot be expected to be the same as that in East Asia, since the initial conditions, capabilities, market size, location and infrastructure are very different. An important factor to take into account is that government capabilities themselves have to be greatly improved (with information, training, better incentives and greater insulation from the political process) in order to make liberalization work effectively. In contrast to the neoclassical position that the removal of government intervention restores economic efficiency, it is a strengthening of government intervention that is needed to make markets work properly.[13]

7.5.2 Promoting Technological Development

The four main elements of technological development – importing technology, upgrading the capabilities of small and medium sized enterprises, improving the technological infrastructure and increasing the technological effort (including R&D) of larger enterprises – are taken in turn.

7.5.2.1 Importing Technology

The acquisition of technology can take several forms. At one extreme the process can be entirely *internalized* by the seller of technology, as with wholly foreign-owned direct investment. At the other it can be fully *externalized*, with the firm putting together its own package of equipment, know-how and other inputs, with no long-term contractual arrangement with a foreign supplier (an extreme example would be a firm buying machinery on the open market and 'reverse engineering' a product design with no explicit technology agreement). In between lie various equity or non-equity contractual relationships. The choice of mode of technology import depends on various factors, including the capabilities of domestic firms and the level of technology aimed at. In general, the more capable the local firms, the better it is to obtain externalized technology since this is cheaper than acquiring the same technology through direct investment and may generate more local linkages and externalities. The more complex the technology and the more direct investment is important for obtaining access to export markets, the better it is to obtain internalized technology imports.

In the three African countries discussed here, most technology transfer has been externalized and has, mainly involved capital goods (a substantial proportion of which have been secondhand), with relatively low reliance on licensing or FDI. This reflects not so much a high absorptive or imitative capability on the part of domestic firms as the relatively simple nature of the technologies being used. In fact, given their existing technological capabilities there are strong arguments for increasing internalized technology imports (via direct foreign investment) in order to upgrade the industrial structure. This does not mean that governments should not seek to develop the capabilities of indigenous enterprises. On the contrary, a strong local sector is needed to go into activities that foreign investors are unlikely to enter (products geared to very localized markets and resources), complement foreign investments (as suppliers) and absorb the beneficial spillovers from their operations (as competitors). However, for the foreseeable future the main strategy should be to attract FDI while supporting the development of local firms by upgrading their skills and capabilities. In the emerging international investment scene, the rapid growth of outward investment by companies in other developing countries (mainly East Asia) offers the prospect of attracting companies with the skill and ability to use local labour and resources in relatively simple activities aimed at the world market.

Given our general presumption in favour of attracting FDI, the experience of the East Asian NIEs suggests that there are strikingly different approaches to attracting and using FDI in the national interest (Lall, 1996). One is simply to adopt a *laissez faire* strategy and let market forces decide: the 'Hong Kong approach'. This works well when there is a strong indigenous base of industrial skills, with dynamic local enterprises and a strong infrastructure of financial services, trade and communications. Even with these conditions the Hong Kong strategy runs the risk that letting market forces entirely decide the pattern of technology imports in a free trade setting will lead to a shallow industrial base that is unable to sustain growth and competitiveness with rising wages. Hong Kong, for instance, is the only East Asian Tiger with declining industrial production and manufactured exports. The industrial sector continues to specialize in low-technology consumer products, with little deepening in the absence of government policy to encourage firms to go into heavy industry.

An alternative strategy, also in a free trade setting, is that adopted by Singapore. This has been an intensely interventionist strategy, with FDI being aggressively sought, targeted for particular activities and induced to upgrade over time. With a much smaller economy than Hong Kong, Singapore has managed to deepen its industrial structure far more and to maintain high manufacturing growth and export rates. It intervened selectively to move its industry from labour-intensive to capital-, skill- and technology-intensive activities. The public sector often played an important role in leading particular activities that the government wanted to promote, acting as a catalyst to private investment. Singapore's technology acquisition policy was directed at acquiring and subsequently upgrading the most modern technologies in selected sectors. This allowed it to engage and specialize in the emerging global system of production under the aegis of MNCs, focusing on particular stages of production while drawing upon the continuing flow of innovation of the parent company. In order to attract foreign investment while inducing technological upgrading, Singapore invested massively in human capital and infrastructure, these investments being targeted at the particular activities being promoted.

Yet another successful strategy from East Asia is that pursued by Taiwan. Taiwan started its industrialization process with a strong human capital base and a large number of small and medium sized enterprises (SMEs). It combined trade policy with intervention in technology transfer, the aim of which was to provide strong support for technology acquisition by and the deepening of local enterprises. It drew upon the whole gamut of technology imports, changing the balance over time. In the 1950s it sought to attract FDI within a liberal policy regime, with no discrimination by origin, destination (only services were protected from foreign entrants) or degree of ownership. Over time the regime became more discriminatory, with the government exercising case-by-case approval to ensure that the technology was in line with national priorities, that domestic technology would benefit and that certain performance requirements were met. In areas where domestic firms were strong, FDI was discouraged; where they were weak, foreign firms were made to transfer technology and contribute to the development of local capabilities. The attraction of high-technology FDI was also strongly promoted by setting up a science park, and the government sometimes played a direct role in attracting advanced technologies by entering into joint ventures with technological leaders. It sought to maximize the benefits of FDI for local firms by promoting local subcontracting. This was done by setting local content rules, insisting that foreign firms transfer their skills and technology to the subcontractors and raising the technological capabilities of local firms.

Finally, the case of Korea represents the strongest selective FDI strategy. In accessing foreign technology, Korea promoted externalized technology imports to the maximum possible extent. FDI was permitted when it was the only way of obtaining the desired technology or gaining access to the world market; and even then the government encouraged local control by promoting majority Korean-owned or equal joint ventures. In some cases the foreign investors were even induced to sell out after the technology had been absorbed locally. In recent years, under pressure from its trading partners, the Korean government has liberalized its foreign investment law. Nevertheless Korea remains a small recipient of industrial FDI, while its *chaebol* have become major MNCs in their own right. This policy has enabled a massive build-up of local R&D capabilities.

Korea relied primarily on capital goods imports, technology licensing and other technology transfer agreements to acquire technology. It encouraged 'reverse engineering', adaptation and R&D by importing firms to build upon technology imports and develop indigenous technological capabilities. In the field of plant and process engineering, the government required foreign contractors to transfer their design knowledge to local firms, and some processing industries quickly absorbed design technologies. The SME sector had to be helped to search for technologies overseas. As with Taiwan (and Japan), Korea compiled a data base on the sources and prices of technology. This was linked to similar data bases overseas and provided on-line in major industrial centres. There was also a programme to increase SMEs' technological linkages with large firms (see below), but unlike in Taiwan, this was directed mainly at large local firms rather than MNCs. It should be noted that the Korean strategy required firms to have a relatively strong absorptive capability, without which it would have been very costly and inefficient.

There are lessons for the three African countries in these experiences. Given their current technological capabilities, a *strong pro-active strategy to attract FDI* would seem to be the most desirable immediate strategy for technology imports. This strategy is unlikely to work unless certain economic conditions are created (needless to say, political and macroeconomic stability, good physical infrastructure and a conducive FDI regime are basic preconditions), such as skilled technical and managerial manpower and stronger local supply systems. The strengthening of local capabilities will still be necessary to attract FDI and upgrade its 'quality' over time, and this should focus on the technological development of SMEs (drawing on the Taiwan strategy, also see below). Only when local capabilities have reached much higher levels can externalized forms of technology imports be used extensively.

While the general policy environment for FDI inflows in the three countries has improved in recent years, much work remains to be done on creating an attractive investment environment. Poor infrastructure, political and economic uncertainty, lagging market growth and lack of skills and supply capabilities are all deterring the growth of investment in a period when flows to the developing world are booming. It is imperative for the governments to remedy these constraints if a significant upgrading of industrial technology is to take place in the region. There also needs to be a focused and targeted strategy to inform and attract potential investors and help them overcome the bureaucratic barriers to entry and establishment. It is very important to set up the organizational structure and procedures carefully, minimizing the number of rules and permits that affect investors.

7.5.2.2 *Upgrading Small and Medium Enterprises*

Perhaps the most important and difficult challenge to policy makers in the three countries is the technological upgrading of the myriad medium, small and micro enterprises that form the backbone of industry and provide the bulk of employment. This sector is the seedbed of modern industrial entrepreneurship, and has the potential to become the catalyst for the growth of new manufactured exports. The evidence of our studies suggests, however, that many SMEs are suffering particularly badly in the liberalization process. In Kenya, for instance, the 'best' African enterprises are regressing as a result of liberalization.

In all parts of the developing world, the technological upgrading of SMEs has proved to be a very difficult task. The sheer number and dispersal of small enterprises make extension and support difficult to organize. Many SMEs are unaware of their own technological problems, or are unable to articulate them sufficiently to take advantage of the services on offer. They are unable or unwilling to pay the cost of many services, even if these may yield larger profits in the longer-term. Small size prevents the enterprises themselves from undertaking the training, technical search and marketing investments needed for technical progress. Entrepreneurs from rural or traditional backgrounds, with low levels of education, are hostile to the use of modern technologies. Larger enterprises are reluctant to strike up supply or subcontracting linkages because of the costs inherent in raising SMEs to the requisite technical and reliability standards.

These problems are not unique to Africa – they are also prevalent in Asia, including the dynamic NIEs. However the governments of the NIEs have introduced policies to overcome some of these handicaps and bring the SMEs into modern industrial and export activities. Let us look at some examples.

Despite its *laissez faire* approach to industry, Hong Kong has provided strong technical support to SME exporters through the Hong Kong Productivity Council (HKPC). The HKPC, the first support institution of its kind in the region, was set up in 1967 to help firms progress from declining labour-intensive manufacturing to more advanced, high-value-added activities. It also acts as a major technology transfer and technology development agent, and over time has developed specialized technical services for all the main industrial sectors. It assists local firms in automation by designing and developing special purpose equipment and advanced machines to improve process efficiency. Because small firms experience difficulties when adopting new technologies and have problems with obtaining training and information support, even in an open and dynamic economy such as Hong Kong, the HKPC has always subsidized the cost of its services to SMEs. Despite the growth in the share of revenue-earning work and its withdrawal from activities in which private consultants have appeared, the government still contributes about half of its budget.

In Singapore, the government launched several schemes for financial and technical assistance to SMEs to help them modernize their equipment. Of these the most significant was the Small Industries Finance Scheme. A Small Enterprises Bureau was established in 1986 to act as a one-stop consultancy agency, helping SMEs with management and training, finance and grants, and coordinating assistance from other agencies. The Singapore Institute of Standards and Industrial Research undertook technology dissemination activities among SMEs, and helped their export efforts by providing information on foreign technical requirements and how to meet them. A Technology Development Centre was established to help firms identify their technological requirements, purchase technologies and design technology upgrading strategies. The government encouraged subcontracting to local firms through its Local Industries Upgrading Programme, under which MNCs were encouraged to source components locally by 'adopting' particular SMEs as subcontractors. In return for a commitment by the MNCs to provide on-the-job training and other assistance to subcontractors, the government provided a package of assistance to the latter, including cost sharing grants and loans for the purchase of equipment or consultancy and the provision of training. By the end of 1990, 27 MNCs and 116 SMEs had joined this programme.

Taiwan's support of its myriad SMEs perhaps ranks among the best anywhere, and is described here at slightly more length. There are around 700 000 SMEs in Taiwan, accounting for 70 per cent of employment, 55 per cent of GNP and 62 per cent of total manufactured exports. In 1981 the government set up the Medium and Small Business Administration to support SME development and coordinate the several agencies that provided financial, management, accounting, technological and marketing assistance to SMEs. Financial assistance was provided by several banks and financial agencies, while management and technological assistance was given by the China Productivity Centre, the Industrial Technology Research Institute (ITRI) and a number of industrial technology institutes. The ITRI conducted R&D for projects considered too risky for the private sector. The ITRI has spun off laboratories as private companies, including Taiwan's most successful integrated circuit makers. The Institute for the Information Industry (III) was set up to complement the ITRI's work on hardware by developing and introducing software technology.

There is a strong element of subsidy involved in these programmes. The government covers 50–70 per cent of the fees charged to SMEs for management and technical consultancy services. The 'Centre–Satellite Factory Promotion Programme' of the Ministry of Economic Affairs groups smaller factories with a principal one. This programme involves vendor assistance and productivity raising efforts, and a rational sharing of tasks between participating enterprises. By 1989 there were 60 networks with 1186 satellite factories in operation, mainly in the electronics industry. In addition the Programme for the Promotion of Technology Transfer maintains close contact with foreign corporations that have developed leading-edge technologies in order to facilitate the transfer of those technologies to Taiwan.

Among the technological support measures provided to SMEs, one of the most important is the transferral to firms of 'production-ready technology' that the government has imported and adapted. Another is to encourage industry to contract research to universities: half of the National Science Council's research grants of about $200 million per year funds such contracts, with enterprises providing matching funds. A number of institutions have been set up to provide credit, technology and marketing assistance to SMEs: the China Productivity Centre (CPC) is best known for its efforts to promote automation in industry in order to cope with rising wages and the increasing need for precision and quality. The CPC sends out teams of engineers to visit plants throughout the country and demonstrate the best means of automation and solve the relevant technical problems. In a period of two years the CPC visited more the 1000 plants and made over 4000 suggestions for improvement. It also carried out more than 500 research projects on improving production efficiency and linked enterprises to research centres to solve more complex technical problems.

In Korea, a number of laws were passed in the 1980s to promote SMEs, which previously had been relatively neglected because of Korea's strategy of promoting heavy industry, spearheaded by the giant *chaebol*. These laws led to a perceptible rise in the SME share of economic activity – between 1975 and 1986 the share of SMEs in employment, sales and value added rose by at least 25 per cent. A host of tax incentives was provided to firms participating in these programmes, as well as finance at subsidized rates for support services, plus credit guarantees, government procurement and the setting up of a specialized bank to finance SMEs. A number of other institutions were set up, such as the Small and Medium Industry Promotion Corporation to provide financial, technical and training assistance and the Industrial Development Bank to provide finance, and the government greatly increased its own budget contribution to the programme, though the SMEs had to pay part of the cost of most of the services provided to them.

To promote subcontracting by the *chaebol*, the government enacted a law designating parts and components that had to be procured through SMEs and not made in-house; by 1987 about 1200 items were so designated, involving 337 principal firms and some 2200 subcontractors, mainly in the machinery, electrical, electronic and ship-building fields. Generous financial and fiscal support was provided to subcontracting SMEs to assist in their day-to-day operations as well as process and product development. In addition, subcontracting SMEs were exempted from stamp tax and were granted tax deductions for a certain percentage of their investment in laboratory and inspection equipment and for the whole of their expenses for technical consultancy. Subcontracting promotion councils were set up for each industrial subsector and also within the Korea Federation of Small Business to help SMEs with the incontractual relationships, to arbitrate disputes and to monitor contract implementation.

What lessons do these policies and experiences have for our sample countries? Several suggest themselves, taking into account the differences in industrial structure and level of development:

- Without assiduous and comprehensive efforts to enhance the capabilities and competitiveness of SMEs, industrial development will remain stunted and shallow and import liberalization will confine SMEs to non-tradable, low technology activities.
- SMEs lack the knowledge, time and resources (material and human) to identify their technological needs and articulate them to government institutions. A passive support service such as exists in most African countries cannot hope to reach them effectively; far more aggressive efforts are needed whereby experts go into the enterprises, help them to understand their own problems and devise remedies. This is a skill-intensive task, involving a well-staffed, equipped and funded set of institutions, and it is imperative that industrial policymakers address their human and financial resource needs.
- The most effective approaches involve support services delivering comprehensive packages of assistance comprising technical know-how, finance, management skills, training and sales information. If the services provide only a few of these components, leaving it to firms to seek out other sources of information, finance or training, the upgrading of SMEs will be delayed or never completed. They will find it difficult to put the package together themselves – there are too many market failures in the relevant factor markets.
- 'Productivity centres' can be an effective way of organizing the delivery of technical upgrading services to industry. These centres

are charged with importing suitable technologies for local industry and adapting and disseminating those technologies. They provide good facilities for firms to conduct testing and other work, provide technical consultancy services and well stocked technical libraries, offer training and a range of other assistance. The NIEs have used such centres to very good effect.

- Support services need a significant subsidy element, since SMEs are either unable or unwilling to pay the full market costs for a considerable period of time. However the subsidy should cover only part of the cost, and should decline over time as the services become better established and the SMEs grow more aware of their benefits.
- A vital element of the SME upgrading process is to encourage linkages with large enterprises. This can be done by promoting subcontracting through various incentives and support measures, 'subcontracting exchanges' and local content provisions. At the same time, it is important to make sure that the principal firms are not handicapped by being forced to buy expensive components from the SMEs. The government may need to provide compensatory incentives to the principals while the SMEs undergo a 'learning' process, simultaneously working to improve their competence and attractiveness as suppliers.
- Finally, specific and targeted measures are needed to induce SMEs into export markets. The cost of entering these markets are high for small firms, and help is needed in terms of information support, market intelligence, contacts with foreign buyers, visits to trade fairs, design and packaging and so on. Even a modest injection of resources can help SMEs greatly, if used judiciously to overcome the main market deficiencies.

7.5.2.3 Improving the Technology Infrastructure

The technology infrastructure includes, apart from the services noted above, metrology, standards, testing and quality institutions, public research institutions and university-based industrial research. As industry liberalizes and restructures, the quality and spread of these services has to improve if firms are to solve their technological problems, upgrade quality, introduce new products and processes and enter export markets. Experience in other countries shows that effective institutions can provide invaluable inputs into enterprise technology development.

The three countries have infrastructural institutions, but they suffer from serious deficiencies. There are standards institutions to provide mandatory testing, calibration and certification services, but they do not play an active role in disseminating or improving technology. In particular, they lack an effective programme for encouraging firms to obtain ISO 9000 quality standards, which are now a major assest in world markets. Few firms in the sample have been accredited to this level; a large proportion are not even aware of the existence of the standard.

Research institutions, where they exist, tend to be poorly staffed and and funded and do little work that is relevant to industrial needs. They do not provide African firms with information on the costs and characteristics of foreign technologies, and do not import and adapt them for local users. Their structure and incentive systems tend to be bureaucratic, and there is little motivation to go out to industry and meet its needs. Universities and technical colleges have relatively little contact with industry, and industry in turn rarely goes to them for technical information and assistance. In addition, since the introduction of the stabilization and adjustment programmes the technological infrastructure has suffered along with other social sectors (Enos, 1995).

The experience of the Asian NIEs again bears out the importance of improved technological services. Take quality standards: each Asian NIE made a concerted effort to promote the ISO 9000 standards. In late 1993, for instance, the number of ISO 9000 certified companies were as follows: Hong Kong 10, Indonesia 8, Malaysia 224, Singapore 523, Taiwan 96, Korea 87 and Thailand 9. Two years later the numbers had risen to around 200 in Hong Kong, about 700 in Malaysia, more than 1000 in Singapore and 60 in Indonesia. The East Asian region is now the most advanced in the developing world in terms of ISO accreditation, and its standards bodies are playing an aggressive role in propagating advanced quality management and providing assistance and consultancy services. Asian governments give strong financial and technical support to industrial firms seeking to improve quality and achieve ISO 9000 accreditation. In the process, the standards institutions have had to be restructured and upgraded.

The Korean government's support for the technological infrastructure is one of the most impressive in the developing world and is worth describing here. In 1966 the government set up KIST (Korea Institute of Science and Technology) to conduct applied research of various kinds for industry. In the 1970s the government set up other specialized research institutes related to machinery, metals, electronics, nuclear energy, resources, chemicals, telecommunications, standards, shipbuilding, marine sciences, and so on. These were largely spun off from KIST, and by the end of the decade there were 16 public R&D institutions. In 1981 the government decided to reduce their number and rationalize their operations. The existing institutes were merged into nine under the supervision of the Ministry of Science and Technology. KIST was merged with KAIS (Korea Advanced Institute of Science) to become KAIST (Korea Advanced Institute of Science and Technology), but was separated again – as KIST – in 1989.

The government's strategic thrust in this sphere was mainly a series of National R&D projects launched in 1982. These were large-scale projects that were regarded as too risky for industry to tackle alone but were deemed as being in the country's industrial interest. The national projects were conducted jointly by industry, public research institutes and the government, and covered items such as semiconductors, computers, fine chemicals, machinery, material science and plant system engineering. 'Centres of excellence' were formed in these fields to boost Korea's long-term competitiveness. The national projects were a continuation of the strategy to identify and develop the country's dynamic comparative advantage, orchestrating the different actors involved, underwriting part of the risks, providing large financial grants and directly filling in gaps that the market could not remedy. The total expenditure on these projects was US$680 million between 1982 and 1989 and the sums involved increased steadily each year: from $25 million in 1982 to US$151 million in 1989. Strategic technological activities are still targeted and promoted, and national projects continue today.

Other policy measures to stimulate technological effort in Korea included the setting up of science research centres and engineering research centres at universities around the country to support R&D activities, the common utilization of advanced R&D facilities by smaller private firms, and the construction of science towns. Daeduk Science Town has been under construction since 1974, and a large number of research and educational institutions are already well established there. The construction of Kwangju Science Town has started; others are planned. Technology diffusion was advanced by the Korea Institute for Economics and Technology, which collected, processed and disseminated scientific and technical information to industry.

In sum, it will be important for the three African countries to improve their technology infrastructure to meet the demands of liberalization. The existing institutions should be strengthened in both physical and human terms, and reoriented to meet industrial needs. Research institutions should be made to earn a larger proportion of their keep from the sale of their services, and industry should be offered financial incentives to subcontract research to them. Quality awareness and the adoption of international norms of quality management should be promoted by public campaigns backed by financial assistance for firms. The relevant standards institutions should be greatly strengthened and motivated to 'reach out' to industry. The private sector should be encouraged to participate as much as possible by setting up laboratories and consultancy services. Considerable foreign resources are available for quality and standards bodies, which Asian countries have been able to tap (the European Union, for instance, offers funds for promoting ISO standards). These should be explored by African governments.

7.5.2.4 Promoting R&D by Industry

Our sample firms conduct no formal R&D; at most the 'good' firms engage in production engineering and quality control/testing rather than technological development. This may not matter in the short term, since the main task at present is to master and adapt the existing technologies rather than develop new ones. However there are no clear dividing lines between mastering, adapting, improving and adding to technologies, and as firms mature they progress from one kind of technological activity to another. As the technologies grow more complex it becomes necessary for firms to set up formal R&D facilities in order to absorb and adapt technologies, even though they are not 'innovating' in any real sense. Thus the NIEs have increased their R&D investments significantly in recent years: Korea spends 2.4 per cent of GDP on R&D, Taiwan around 1.8 per cent and Singapore around 1 per cent. The new NIEs such as Malaysia, Thailand and Indonesia spend less, around 0.2–0.4 per cent; but even this is much more than the amount spent in African industry.

It may be instructive to look at how Korea and Taiwan promoted R&D among their private firms (some 25 years ago these firms also conducted negligible amounts of research). Industrial R&D in Korea was promoted by a number of incentives and other forms of assistance. Incentive schemes included tax-exempt technology development reserve funds; tax credits for R&D expenditure, upgrading human capital related to research and setting up industry research institutes; accelerated depreciation for investments in R&D facilities and a tax exemption for 10 per cent of the cost of relevant equipment; reduced import duties for research equipment; and reduced excise tax on technology-intensive products. The Korea Technology Advancement Corporation helped firms to commercialize their research results; a 6 per cent tax credit or special accelerated depreciation provided further incentives. The importation of technology was promoted by tax incentives: the transfer costs of patent rights and technology import fees were tax deductible; income from technological consultations was tax-exempt; and foreign engineers were exempt from income tax. In addition the government provided grants and long-term, low-interest loans to participants in the National projects. Tax privileges and official funds were given to private and government R&D institutes to carry out these projects, and finance was also provided by the Korea Technology Development Corporation.

However the main stimulus to the tremendous upsurge of industrial R&D came less from the specific R&D incentives than from the overall incentive regime that created large firms, gave them a protected market in which to master complex technologies, minimized their reliance on FDI and forced them into export markets where competition ensured that they would have to invest in their own research capabilities. This is why, for instance, Korea has 35 times more R&D expenditure by industry as a proportion of GDP than Mexico (with roughly the same size of manufacturing value added), an economy that has remained highly dependent on technology imports (Najmabadi and Lall, 1995).

The history of Taiwanese R&D growth has some similarities to that of Korea, but there are also marked differences because of their different political economies and industrial structures: the Taiwanese government has always had a more distant relationship with industry and has not promoted large private conglomerates such as the *chaebol*. It started to address the development of local R&D capabilities fairly early, in the late 1950s, when its growing trade dependence reinforced the need to enhance the local innovative effort in order to upgrade and diversify its exports. A science and technology programme was started in 1979, whereby energy, production automation, information science and materials science technologies were targeted for development. In 1982, biotechnology, electro-optics, hepatitis control and food technology were added to this list. In 1986 the science and technology development plan (1986–95) was launched, continuing the targeting of strategic areas of technology.

Around half of R&D in Taiwan (a much higher proportion than in Korea) is financed by the government, though the contribution has reduced over time. Private sector R&D has been relatively weak because of the preponderance of small and medium enterprises, which cannot afford the large minimum investments involved in much of industrial reserach. However enterprise R&D has risen over time as some local firms have grown in size and become significant multinationals. Such R&D has been encouraged over the years by a variety of incentives: the provision of funds for venture capital; financing facilities for enterprises that develop 'strategic' industrial products (of which 151 were selected in 1982 and 214 in 1987); encouraging product development by private firms by providing matching interest-free loans and grants of up to 25 per cent for approved projects; full tax deductibility for R&D expenses, with accelerated depreciation for research equipment; special incentives for enterprises based in the Hsinchu Science Park (with government financial institutions able to invest up to 49 per cent of the capital); and requiring larger firms to invest 0.5–1.5 per cent of sales, depending on the activity in R&D. The government also launched large-scale research consortia, funded jointly with industry, to develop critical products such as a new-generation car engine, and 16M DRAM and 4M SRAM chips.

The Taiwanese example is of greater relevance to our sample countries than that of Korea. Not only do African countries have large numbers of small and medium enterprises, they also lack the political economy needed to create and discipline large private firms along Korean lines. The Taiwanese strategy involves less detailed direction of economic activity and resource allocation. The cost of this is that it entails much more pervasive and persistent R&D support for small enterprises that are unable to undertake it themselves. And underlying this is the need for a large investment to create the human capital that Africa lacks. This is reviewed next.

7.6 HUMAN RESOURCES FOR INDUSTRIALIZATION

Chapter 1 noted the low enrolment rate at practically all levels of schooling and higher education in the three African countries. For instance Korea alone had 730 000 students enrolled in science, mathematics, computers and engineering in 1993, compared with 17 000 in the three African countries combined. While the African countries' present stage of development does not require the level of technical education needed in Korea, the current supply of technical manpower is so low that even in existing industries there is an insufficient supply of skills to upgrade to world efficiency levels. Moreover these figures do not reveal the quality and relevance of the education provided: these may also be lacking in relation to other industrializing regions with which the African countries will have to compete in the new world order. The other main form of skill creation in the industrial workforce, in-house or external training, is also low by the standards of other industrializing countries.

Several kinds of skill development are relevant to industrial competitiveness in the three countries under study and need to be improved. Of these, the ones that need immediate attention are specific skills for industrial activities that can form the dynamic edge of industrial growth, in terms of competing with imports or entering export markets. While this study could not analyse these in detail, casual observation suggests that activities such as garment making and design, textiles, wood working, food processing, metal working and other light consumer goods should be assigned top priority. Needless to say, investment in education and vocational training is also necessary, but this can only be undertaken over the longer term.

The stimulation of in-firm training is another key area of policy intervention that could be undertaken in the short to medium term. This would require a concerted campaign to inform firms, especially smaller ones, of the benefits of and need for employee training to meet the rigours of import competition. But information and propaganda would not be enough: firms would have to be *shown* how to train, how much and in what areas; they would need teachers with industrial experience and financial support in order to provide appropriate training. Often training has to go together with the provision of new equipment, better layout, improved process know-how and more modern product technology. All these may need specific policies to address their informational, financial and other needs.

7.7 FINANCING INDUSTRIAL RESTRUCTURING

The financing of industrial restructuring in the face of policy reform and liberalization is an important issue in our sample countries, as in the rest of SubSaharan Africa. It is unfortunate that most adjustment programmes have been launched in the midst of economic crises, accompanied by stringent stabilization measures that sharply curtail the supply of financial resources to industry, raise interest rates and create uncertainty. The worst hit is probably the small and medium enterprise (SME) sector, which even in the best of circumstances faces a hostile credit market; but even large scale enterprises can find it difficult to finance new equipment, technologies and capability-building efforts:

This is more of a problem for locally owned than for multinational firms (which have better access to foreign resources), and there is a need to prepare a financial package that can help them to adjust rather than go under.

Apart from the financial crunch produced by stabilization and macro imbalances, the three African countries also have to look to the longer-term financing needs of industry. At low levels of industrialization, when firms are small and use 'easy' technologies with low capital requirements and limited possibility of improvement, the absence of designated technology finance is not a major handicap. Working capital may cover most technology development activities related to production engineering, quality improvement and productivity improvement. Even at this level, however, there is a risk that such financing will not be sufficient for training and other activities that are not strictly classifiable as working capital needs; in any case, small firms may not be able to offer commercial banks collateral even for working capital. As industrial development proceeds, the financing gap grows more serious. Increasingly risky investment in new technologies by new and established firms is required, but the financial system is generally not willing to finance such investments, except in the case of very large firms that can cross-subsidize their R&D activities.

The Asian experience in financing the technological needs of industry may thus be interesting in a long-term perspective. Korea's policies to encourage selected activities and firms, via credit allocation and subsidization, are well known. As far as the specific financing of technology development goes, in the early 1980s the government launched the Korea Technology Development Corporation (KTDC), in collaboration with the private sector and the World Bank. It had realized that small industrial firms found it extremely difficult to raise funds from the existing financial institutions for technological development, so the KTDC was designed to provide such financing, particularly for SMEs, and to fulfil several other functions. It provided information on technological trends and influenced and reinforced industry's attitude towards R&D. The finance provided acted as a catalyst for increased R&D spending by industry, and the KTDC assisted industry to identify international trends and areas in which it should focus its technological efforts. It induced better discipline into technology planning by private firms, and so increased the efficiency of industry's management and implementation of R&D activities. It promoted closer links between industry and research institutes, encouraging and financing projects sponsored by industry in these institutes. It brought together researchers and inventors with entrepreneurs in Korea and overseas. It was consultant and advisor to government agencies making technology policy.

About half of the KTDC's loans went to SMEs, whose activities were supported by promotional activities and technical and managerial advice. Over time the KTDC also introduced new financing instruments (such as leasing) and developed its capacity to appraise and supervise more complex and riskier projects. It set up a subsidiary, the KTIC (Korea Technology Investment Corporation), to invest in technology start-ups. The success of the KTDC led to the setting up of several private venture capital funds in Korea, and today Korea has the largest number (58) of venture capital companies in the developing world, with the largest outstanding loan portfolio to technology-based start-ups ($750 million).

Taiwan also encouraged the emergence of a venture capital industry by providing funds. By mid 1993 Taiwan had 23 venture capital companies, which had invested some NT$9 billion (US$ 340 million) in nearly 400 companies in high technology industries. The Taiwanese government also directly financed industrial restructuring. Take the textile industry, which is facing great difficulties in the African countries. Textiles are Taiwan's second largest export (US$12 billion in 1993). Though most of Taiwan's labour-intensive garment firms have relocated to lower-wage countries, there remain large sections of the industry that need upgrading. In the late 1980s the government launched a campaign to restructure the industry, raise exports to US$20 billion during the 1990s, help producers to improve the quality of their products and move the more labour-intensive processes overseas. The Industrial Development Bureau developed a US$95.4 million programme, of which 95 per cent was to be provided as grants to private firms. Over 250 textile plants were to receive financial and technical assistance under this programme, enabling them to import the latest automated equipment, and train their staff in the new technologies and develop new design skills. A number of other agencies, both public and private, were involved in this restructuring exercise. Banks provided low-interest loans to SMEs to move their facilities overseas and special credit lines (up to US$60 000 each) to import new equipment.

This example is particularly interesting in the present context, in that it illustrates strategic government intervention to target and support, not a new high technology activity (which Taiwan was also doing) but a mature industry facing market failure or expensive restructuring. This market failure did not involve, as in the African context, firms that were financially strapped, generally behind world 'best practice' frontiers and incapable of accessing and upgrading technology, but large, export-oriented firms that were already world-class exporters. The corresponding market failures facing African firms are much larger and more daunting. Given that the African governments have to pay particular attention to the needs of SMEs in the immediate future, their financial needs are even greater and more pressing.

7.8 CONCLUSIONS

The case studies presented in this book lead to mixed conclusions about the impact of import liberalization on technology development. While there clearly has been some positive response to increased import competition, it is weak and confined to a relatively small number of firms. In the majority of cases, the existing technological base is too underdeveloped, given the state of factor markets and institutions, to allow firms to face direct import competition or enter world markets. In the future, moreover, much manufacturing growth will have to be export-oriented, since domestic markets by themselves are too small to permit efficient operations. Successful export expansion requires an even stronger base of technological and other capabilities than surviving on a liberalizing domestic market. Given the current status and distribution of capabilities, therefore, liberalization seems unlikely to stimulate high rates of manufacturing growth.

Assuming favourable macroeconomic and exogenous conditions, there will certainly will be some manufacturing growth on the basis of the current technological capabilities: parts of manufacturing do not face direct import competition, and the more capable firms will be able to expand their exports using their existing capabilities. However, unless there is a massive rise in the inflow of foreign technology and a matching rise in the skills base (and, needless to say, an appropriate FDI regime and competitive physical infrastructure), this is unlikely to result in sustained growth and diversification. Without this, 'opening up' could lead to a widespread process of 'shutting down' and to a regression of the natural resource base – not what most analysts and governments would regard as the foundations for long-term development and structural transformation.

This is not to argue that the past policies (import substitution, heavy government intervention and a large public sector role) were more efficient. The way in which these strategies were managed, on a small human capital base and an even smaller industrial capability base, did not succeed in fostering the learning process that would lead to industrial competitiveness. They exacerbated the existing market failures and created new ones. The response to the present difficulties should not be to revert to the 'good old days'. Nor should it, however, be to emphasize more stringent and sweeping liberalization as an end in itself. Believing that whatever free markets throw up is by definition efficient and desirable has an element of ideology that rational analysts should eschew. The economic case for rapid and sweeping liberalization, with no strategy to help upgrading, is based on assumptions of market efficiency and costless learning that bear little relation to reality.

There do exist models of 'opening up' without 'shutting down', which involve a strong and positive role for the government. However this role has to be very different from the previous one, and will be very demanding of skills, information, honesty and public–private interaction. The policy initiatives undertaken in the Asian NIEs, examples of which were noted above, seem to offer useful lessons in this respect for African governments, but these lessons can only be implemented if the capabilities of the latter are themselves greatly improved. Thus perhaps the first and most important aspect of policy reform should be to improve those capabilities. Here again there may be lessons from Asia, where at some point the governments were also incompetent, inefficient or corrupt. What should be done in each particular case requires a separate study.

Finally, as has been noted many times, there are no 'quick fixes' to the industrial problems of these countries. Any process of building up industrial capabilities is bound to be slow, particularly when the human capital base is weak. However our analysis at least suggests that something *can* be done. In fact there seems to be an enormous amount to be done, and further work should concentrate on analysing in greater detail what, how, when and by whom.

Notes

1. See Lall (1996) and Stiglitz (1996) for a review of the arguments.
2. These data are from a special supplement on Zimbabwe in *The Observer* (London), 26 January 1997, p. 3.
3. Ghana started in the late 1980s with a burst of manufacturing growth as imported inputs were liberalized and existing capacity was used up;

as import competition intensified, however, growth slowed down, and in the past five years or so has hovered around 2–3 per cent per annum (Lall, 1995). In Ghana, unlike some of the sample countries, there were no exogenous shocks, the macro economy had been stabilized and there were substantial inflows of foreign aid. This suggests that the causes of the slowdown lay in the design and implementation of the liberalization programme.

4. For instance the Lomé convention, which gives African countries duty and quota free access to Europe will end soon and past concessions may not be renewed. See 'Wanted: some Asian tigers', *The Economist*, 30 November 1996, p. 77.
5. This conclusion is shared by the World Bank RPED project (Biggs *et al.*, 1995), which covered a larger sample of firms in Ghana, Kenya and Zimbabwe, and concludes after examining various forms of technological activity: 'The detailed "snapshot" of endowments of firm technological capabilities reveals levels that are significantly lower than international standards' (p. 3). This study also ranks the technological capabilities of Zimbabwean firms higher than those of others in its African sample.
6. The World Bank study (Biggs *et al.*, 1995) also notes a 'bleak picture' in the context of foreign technology transfer: 'With the exception of multinational companies and a few large exporters, most firms are technologically isolated from the rest of the world. As a consequence, connections with international private learning sources, such as foreign buyers and suppliers, are weak or non-existent' (p. 4).
7. This is more marked if the entrepreneur is excluded from the calculation: in Kenya and Tanzania, several SMEs were started by African engineers as part of special government programmes to promote African entrepreneurship.
8. The World Bank study (Biggs *et al.*, 1995) also notes the low levels of internal and external training efforts, and their limited scope and sporadic nature, among the African manufacturing firms in their samples. In Kenya it is only the 'best' garment exporting firm that has been able to draw upon its relationship with foreign buyers to improve training.
9. The World Bank study also remarks on the lower level of technological capabilities in African owned firms compared with foreign or local non-African firms in its sample. Biggs *et al.* (1995).
10. These offensive strategies are found most commonly in firms that 'matured' under import substitution – large producers of intermediates such as iron and steel, petrochemicals, cement and aluminium, which have now upgraded to set up world-class plants. They also include resource-based industries such as oil seed and fish processing, cars (which is restructuring under multinational aegis as part of a special plan) and light consumer goods industries that serve local tastes differentiated products. Kosacoff (1996), pp. 3–4.
11. See Benavente *et al.* (1996) and Guerrieri (1994). For the case of Chile, the country with the longest history of liberalization in the developing world, see Pietrobelli (1997), who shows that the manufacturing sector has still to reach the production levels achieved before liberalization (in 1973), technological dynamism has been narrowed by the non-interventionist

regime, and manufactured exports are small, based mainly on natural resources and low levels of technological sophistication. Chile is one of the best endowed countries in Latin America in terms of human capital, and has practised liberal trade and FDI policies for over two decades.

12. Interestingly, the case for infant industry protection is accepted in Biggs *et al.*'s (1995) study of technological capabilities, while the World Bank's 1994 report on adjustment does not mention this critical need.
13. For a good analysis of how government intervention was mounted effectively in East Asia, see World Bank (1993a).

Bibliography

African Development Bank (1995) *African Development Report 1995* (Abidjan).

Amsden, A. (1989) *Asia's Next Giant: South Korea and Late Industrialization* (New York: Oxford University Press).

Barba-Navaretti, G. (1994) 'The Acquisition of Technological Capabilities: Ghana, Kenya and Zimbabwe Compared', Regional Programme on Enterprise Development, Mimeo (Washington, DC: World Bank).

Barro, R. and X. Sala-i-Martin (1995) *Economic Growth* (London: McGraw-Hill).

Behrman, J. and T. N. Srinivasan (1995) *Handbook of Development Economics*, vol. IIIb (Amsterdam: North-Holland).

Bell, M. and K. Pavitt (1993) 'Technological Accumulation and Industrial Growth: Contrasts Between Developed and Developing Countries', *Industrial and Corporate Change*, vol. 2, pp. 157–210.

Bell, M., B. Ross-Larson and L. E. Westphal (1984) 'Assessing the Performance of Infant Industries', *Journal of Development Economics*, vol. 16, pp. 101–28.

Benavente, J. M., G. Crispi, J. Katz and G. Stumpo (1996) 'New Problems and Opportunities for Industrial Development in Latin America', draft (Santiago: Economic Commission for Latin America and the Caribbean).

Bennell, P. (1984) 'Indigenous Technological Capability in Africa: The Case of Textiles and Wood Products in Kenya', in M. Fransman and K. King (eds), *Technological Capability in the Third World* (London: Macmillan).

Best, M. (1990) *The New Competition: Institutions of Industrial Restructuring* (Cambridge: Polity).

Bhagwati, J. (1989) 'In Free Trade Passé after all?', *Weltwirtschaftlichen archiv*, vol. 125, pp. 17–44.

Biggs, T., M. Shah and P. Srivastava (1995) *Technological Capabilities and Learning in African Enterprises*, World Bank Technical Paper no. 288, (Washington, DC: World Bank).

Braunerhjelm, P. and G. Fors (1995) *The Zimbabwean Manufacturing Sector: Current Status and Future Development Potential* (Harare: Confederation of Zimbabwe Industries).

Bureau of Statistics (1994) *National Accounts of Tanzania 1976–1993* (Dar Es Salaam: Bureau of Statistics).

Cappelen, A. and J. Fagerberg (1995) 'East Asian Growth: A Critical Assessment', *Forum for Development Studies*, vol. 2, pp. 175–95.

Caves, R. and D. Barton (1990) *Efficiency in US Manufacturing Industries* (Cambridge, Mass.: MIT Press).

Central Statistical Office (various issues) *Quarterly Digest of Statistics* (Harare: CSO).

Chen, T. and D. Tan (1987) 'Comparing Technical Efficiency Between Foreign Firms in a Developing Economy', *Journal of Development Economics*, vol. 26, pp. 277–88.

Chenery, H. B. and T. N. Srinivasan (eds) (1991) *Handbook of Development Economics*, vols I, II (Amsterdam: North-Holland).
Chenery, H. B., S. Robinson and M. Syrquin (1986) *Industrialization and Growth* (Oxford: Oxford University Press).
Cohen, W. M. and D. A. Levinthal (1989) 'Innovation and Learning: The Two Faces of R&D', *Economic Journal*, vol. 99, pp. 569–96.
Dahlman, C. J., B. Ross-Larson and L. E. Westphal (1987) 'Managing Technological Development: Lessons from Newly Industrializing Countries', *World Development*, vol. 15, pp. 759–75.
Dasgupta, P. and P. Stoneman, (eds) (1987) *Economic Policy and Technological Development* (Cambridge: Cambridge University Press).
Deraniyagala, S. (1995) 'Technical Change and Efficiency in Sri Lanka's Manufacturing Sector', unpublished DPhil thesis, University of Oxford.
Dosi, G., C. Freeman, R. R. Nelson, G. Silverberg and L. Soete (eds) (1988) *Technical Change and Economic Theory* (London: Printer).
Dosi, G., K. Pavitt and L. Soete (1990) *The Economics of Technical Change and International Trade* (Hemel Hempstead: Harvester Wheatsheaf).
Dunn & Bradstreet (1995) *Country Report: Kenya* (London: Dunn & Bradstreet).
Economist Intelligence Unit (various issues), *Country Report: Zimbabwe* (London: EIU).
Edwards, S. (1991) 'Trade Orientation, Distortions and Growth in Developing Countries', Fourth Inter-American Seminar on Economics, Santiago (mimeo).
Egan, M. L. and A. Mody (1992) 'Buyer–Seller Links in Export Development', *World Development*, vol. 20, pp. 321–24.
Enos, J. L. (1992) *The Creation of Technological Capability in Developing Countries* (London: Printer).
Enos, J. L. (1995) *The Pursuit of Science and Technology in Sub-Saharan Africa Under Structural Adjustment* (London: Routledge).
Evenson, R. E. and L. E. Westphal (1995) 'Technological Change and Technology Strategy', in J. Behrman and T. N. Srinivasan (eds), *Handbook of Development Economics*, vol. IIIb, (Amsterdam, North-Holland).
Federation of Kenyan Employers (1991) *FKE Study on the Impact of Trade Liberalisation in Kenya* (Nairobi: Federation of Kenya Employers).
Fishlow, A., C. Gwin, S. Haggard, D. Rodrik and R. Wade (1994) *Miracle or Design? Lessons from the East Asian Experience* (Washington, DC: Overseas Development Council).
Gonsen, R. R. (1995) 'Technological Capability in Developing Countries: A Case Study of Industrial Biotechnology in Mexico', doctoral thesis, University of Oxford.
Gray, J. (1995) *Enlightenment's Wake* (London: Routledge).
Greenwald, B. C. and J. E. Stiglitz (1986) 'Externalities in Economies with Imperfect Information and Incomplete Markets', *Quarterly Journal of Economics*, vol. 101, 229–64.
Guerrieri, P. (1994) 'International Trade Patterns, Structural Change and Technology in Major Latin American Countries', *Giornale degli Economisti e Annali di Economia*, April–June, pp. 287–314.
Guerrieri, P. (1995) 'Changes and Trends in the World Trade in High Technology Products', *Cambridge Journal of Economics*, vol. 19, pp. 225–42.

Gunning, J. W. and C. Mumbengegwi (eds) (1995) *The Manufacturing Sector in Zimbabwe: Industrial Change under Structural Adjustment*, RPED Survey (Amsterdam: Free University).

Hahn, F. (1991) 'The Welfare Economics of Market Economies', in D. Vines and A. Stevenson, *Information, Strategy, and Public Policy* (Oxford: Blackwell).

Havrylyshyn, O. (1990) 'Trade and Productivity Gains in Developing Countries: A Survey of the Literature', *World Bank Research Observer*, vol. 5, pp. 1–24.

Helleiner, G. (ed.) (1992) *Trade Policy, Industrialization, and Development* (Oxford: Clarendon Press).

Helleiner, G. (1995) *Trade, Trade Policy and Industrialization Reconsidered*, UN Univeristy, World Institute of Development Economics Research, Helsinki, World Development Studies 6.

Helpman, E. and P. Krugman (1985) *Market Structure and Foreign Trade* (Hemel Hempstead: Harvester Wheatsheaf).

Himbara, D. (1994) *Kenyan Capitalists, the State and Development* (Nairobi: East African Educational Publishers).

Hodgson, G. M. (1988) *Economics and Institutions* (Cambridge: Polity).

Husain, I. (1994) 'Structural Adjustment and the Long-Term Development of Sub-Saharan Africa', in R. van der Hoeven and F. van der Kraaij (eds), *Structural Adjustment and Beyond in Sub-Saharan Africa* (London: Curry).

Ikiara, G. K. (1988) 'The Role of Government Institutions in Kenya's Industrialisation', in P. Coughlin and G. K. Ikiara (eds), *Industrialization in Kenya: In Search of a Strategy* (Nairobi: Heinemann Kenya).

Imani Consultants (1994) 'Study of Environmental Factors Impacting on the Zimtrade Support Programme', mimeo (Harare: Imani Consultants).

Jansen, D. (1983) 'Zimbabwe: Government Policy and the Manufacturing Sector', mimeo, study for the Ministry of Industry and Energy Development, Larkspur, California.

Kaplinsky, R. (1994) *Easternization: The Spread of Japanese Management Techniques to Developing Countries* (Ilford: Frank Cass).

Katz, J. (1984) 'Domestic Technological Innovation and Dynamic Comparative Advantage: Further Reflections on a Comparative Case Study Program', *Journal of Development Economics*, vol. 16, pp. 13–38.

Katz, J. (1987) 'Domestic Technology Generation in LDCs', in J. Katz (ed.), *Technology Generation in Latin American Manufacturing Industries* (London: Macmillan).

Keesing, D. and S. Lall (1992) 'Marketing Manufactured Exports from Developing Countries', in G. K. Helleiner (ed.), *Trade Policy, Industrialisation and Development* (Oxford: Clarendon Press).

Keyfitz, W. and N. Wanjala (1991) 'Optimal Tariff Reform for Kenya', Ministry of Planning and National Development Technical Paper 91–05 (Nairobi: Ministry of Planning and National Development).

King, K. (1996) *Jua Kali Kenya: Change and Development in An Informal Economy 1970–95* (London: James Curry).

Knight, J. (1995) *Labour Market Policies and Outcomes in Zimbabwe*, mimeo (Oxford University Institute of Economics and Statistics).

Kosacoff, B. (1996) 'Business Strategies and Industrial Adjustments: The Case of Argentina', Buenos Aires: Economic Commission for Latin America and the Caribbean, Working Paper no. 67, LC/BUE/L.150.

Krueger, A. O. (1978) 'Alternative Trade Strategies and Employment in LDCs', *American Economic Review*, vol. 68, no. 2, pp. 270–74.

Krugman, P. (1979) 'A Model of Innovation, Technology Transfer, and the World Distribution of Income', *Journal of Political Economy*, vol. 87, pp. 253–66.

Krugman, P. (1984) 'Import Protection as Export Promotion', in H. Kierzkowski (ed.), *Monopolistic Competition in International Trade* (Oxford: Oxford University Press).

Krugman, P. (1987) 'Is Free Trade Passé?', *Journal of Economic Perspectives*, vol. 1, pp. 131–44.

Krugman, P. (1989) 'New Trade Theory and the Less Developed Countries', in G. Calvo, R. Findley, P. Kouri and G. Braga de Macedo (eds), *Debt, Stabilisation and Development* (Oxford: Blackwell).

Krugman, P. (1991) 'History versus Expectations', *Quarterly Journal of Economics*, vol. 106, pp. 651–67.

Krugman, P. (1995) 'Technological Change in International Trade', in P. Stoneman (ed.), *Handbook of the Economics of Innovation and Technological Change* (Oxford: Blackwell).

Kumar, N. and N. S. Siddharthan (1993) 'Technology, Firm Size and Export Behaviour in Developing Countries: The Case of Indian Enterprises,' UNUINTECH Working Paper no. 9 (United Nations University, Institute for New Technologies, Maastricht).

Kwon, J. (1994) 'The East Asian Challenge to Neoclassical Orthodoxy', *World Development*, vol. 22, pp. 635–44.

Lal, D. and S. Rajapatirana (1987) 'Foreign Trade Regimes and Growth in Developing Countries', *World Bank Research Observer*, vol. 2, pp. 189–217.

Lall, S. (1987) *Learning to Industrialize* (London: Macmillan).

Lall, S. (1990) *Building Industrial Competitiveness in Developing Countries* (Paris: OECD Development Centre).

Lall, S. (1991) *Kenya–South Africa Trade and Investment Study: Modules on Trade, Competitiveness and Foreign Investment in Manufacturing Industry*, study for The Government of Kenya (Institute of Economics and Statistics, Oxford University).

Lall, S. (1992a) 'Structural Problems of African Industry', in F. Stewart, S. Lall and S. Wangwe (eds), *Alternative Development Strategies in Sub Saharan Africa* (London: Macmillan).

Lall, S. (1992b) 'Technological Capabilities and Industrialization', *World Development*, vol. 20, pp. 165–86.

Lall, S. (1993) 'Understanding Technology Development', *Development and Change*, vol. 24, pp. 719–53.

Lall, S. (1994) ' "The East Asian Miracle" Study: Does the Bell Toll for Industrial Strategy?', *World Development*, vol. 22, pp. 645–54.

Lall, S. (1995) 'Structural Adjustment and African Industry', *World Development*, vol. 23, pp. 2019–31.

Lall, S. (1996) *Learning from the Asian Tigers: Technology and Industrial Policy* (London: Macmillan).

Lall S., G. Barba-Navaretti, S. Teitel and G. Wignaraja (1994) *Technology and Enterprise Development: Ghana Under Structural Adjustment* (London: Macmillan).

Lall, S., A. Khanna and I. Alikhani (1987) 'Determinants of Manufactured Exports in Low-income Africa: Kenya and Tanzania', *World Development*, vol. 15, pp. 1219–24.

Lall, S. and K. Rao (1996) 'Indonesia: Sustaining Manufactured Export Growth', report prepared for the Asian Development Bank, Manila.

Lall, S. and G. Wignaraja (1994) 'Foreign Involvement by European Firms and Garment Exports by Developing Countries', *Asia-Pacific Development Journal*, vol. 1, pp. 21–48.

Lall, S. and G. Wignaraja (1996) 'Skills and Capabilities in Ghana's Competitiveness', in S. Lall, *Learning from the Asian Tigers: Studies in Technology and Industrial Policy* (London: Macmillan).

Lerner, A. P. (1953) *Essays in Economic Analysis* (London: Macmillan).

Levy, B. (1993) 'Obstacles to Developing Indigenous Small and Medium Enterprises: An Empirical Assessment', *World Bank Economic Review*, vol. 7, pp. 65–83.

Little, I. M. D., T. Scitovsky and M. Fg. Scott (1970) *Industry and Trade in Some Developing Countries* (Oxford: Oxford University Press).

Lucas, R. E., Jr (1988) 'On the Mechanics of Economic Development', *Journal of Monetary Economics*, vol. 22, pp. 3–42.

Mankiew, G. and D. Romer (1991) *New Keynesian Economics* (Cambridge, Mass.: MIT Press).

Mans, D. (1994) 'Tanzania: Resolute Action', in I. Husain and R. Faruqee (eds), *Adjustment in Africa: Lessons from Country Studies* (Washington, DC: World Bank).

McMahon, W. W. (1987) 'Education and Industrialisation', draft, background paper for *World Development Report 1987* (Washington, DC: World Bank).

McPherson, M. A. (1991) *Micro- and Small-Scale Enterprises in Zimbabwe: Results of a Country-Wide Survey*, (Bethesda: GEMINI).

Mead, D. C. and P. Kunjeku (1993) *Business Linkages and Enterprise Development in Zimbabwe* (Harare: Confederation of Zimbabwe Industries).

MEIDA (1992) 'Report on the Metal Industry in Tanzania', mimeo (Dar Es Salaam).

Meier, G. (ed.) (1992) *Politics and Policy Making in Less Developed Countries* (San Francisco: ICS Press).

Metcalfe, J. S. (1995) 'Technology Systems and Technology Policy in an Evolutionary Framework', *Cambridge Journal of Economics*, vol. 19, no. 1, pp. 25–46.

Michaely, M., D. Papageorgiou and A. M. Choksi (1991) *Liberalising Foreign Trade: Lessons of Experience in the Developing World* (Cambridge: Blackwell).

Michalopoulos, C. (1987) 'World Bank Lending for Structural Adjustment', *Finance and Development*, vol. 24, pp. 7–16.

Middleton, J. and T. Demsky (1989) 'Vocational Education and Training', World Bank Discussion Papers no. 51 (Washington, DC: World Bank).

Mosley, P., J. Harrigan and J. Toye (1991) *Aid and Power: The World Bank and Policy-Based Lending* (London: Routledge).

Mosley, P., T. Subasat and J. Weeks (1995) 'Assessing Adjustment in Africa', *World Development*, vol. 23, pp. 1459–74.

Mosley, P. and Weeks, J. (1993) 'Has Recovery Begun? "Africa's Adjustment in the 1980s" Revisited', *World Development*, vol. 21, pp. 1583–606.

Muzulu, J. (1996) 'The Structural Adjustment Implications of Real Exchange Rate Depreciation on the Manufacturing Sector in Zimbabwe', in C. Harvey (ed.), *Constraints on the Success of Structural Adjustment Programmes in Africa* (Basingstoke: Macmillan).

Mwamadzingo, M. (1994) 'Industrial Research Institutions and Their Interactions With the Productive Sector: Global Myth and Their Empirical Evidence From kenya', draft, (Department of Economics, University of Nairobi).

Mwega, F. M. (1995) 'Trade Liberalization, Credibility and Impacts: A Case Study of Kenya', final report, AERC Collaborative Project on Trade Liberalisation and Regional Integration in SubSaharan Africa (University of Nairobi).

Najmabadi, F. and S. Lall (1995) *Developing Industrial Technology: Lessons for Policy and Practice* (World Bank: Operations Evaluation Department Study).

Ndulu, B. and N. Lipumba (1991) 'International Trade and Economic Development in Tanzania', in J. Frimpong-Ansah, S. R. Kanbur and P. Svedberg (eds), *Trade and Development in Sub-Saharan Africa* (Manchester: Manchester University Press).

Ndulu, B. and H. Semboja (1994) 'Trade and Industrialization in Tanzania: A Review of Experience and Issues', in G. K. Helleiner (ed.), *Trade Policy and Industrialization in Turbulent Times* (London: Routledge).

Nelson, R. R. (ed.) (1993) *National Innovation Systems: A Comparative Analysis* (Oxford: Oxford University Press).

Nelson, R. R. and S. J. Winter (1982) *An Evolutionary Theory of Economic Change* (Cambridge, Mass.: Belknap Press).

N'geno, N. K. (1991) 'Kenya's Export Performance', in J. Frimpong-Ansah, S. R. Kanbur and P. Svedberg (eds), *Trade and Development in Sub-Saharan Africa* (Manchester: Manchester University Press).

Pack, H. (1992), 'Learning and Productivity Change in Developing Countries', in G. K. Helleiner (ed.), *Trade Policy, Industrialization and Development* (Oxford: Clarendon Press).

Pack, H. and L. E. Westphal (1986) 'Industrial Strategy and Technological Change: Theory versus Reality', *Journal of Development Economics*, vol. 22, pp. 87–128.

Parker, R. F., R. Riopelle and W. F. Steel (1995) 'Small Enterprises Adjusting to Liberalization in Five African Countries', World Bank Discussion Papers Africa Technical Department Series, no. 271 (Washington, DC: World Bank).

Pietrobelli, C. (1997) *Industry, Competitiveness and Technological Capabilities in Chile: A New Tiger from Latin America?* (London: Macmillan).

Ratnayake, R. (1994) *Effective Protection of Manufacturing Industries in Zimbabwe* (Harare: Centre for International Economics/MIU).

Reinikka, R. S. (1993) 'Credibility, Speculation and the Speed of Trade Liberalization with an Application to Kenya', DPhil thesis Oxford University.

Republic of Kenya (1995) *Importer Information Tables 1995* (Nairobi: Government of Kenya).

Reserve Bank of Zimbabwe (1995) *Annual Report 1994* (Harare: RBZ).
Riddell, R. C. (ed.) (1990) *Manufacturing Africa: Performance and Prospects of Seven Countries in Sub-Saharan Africa*, (London: Curry).
Robinson, P. (1993), 'Will Zimbabwean Industry Survive ESAP?', mimeo (Harare).
Rodrik, D. (1992a) 'Closing the Productivity Gap: Does Trade Liberalisation Really Help?', in G. K. Helleiner (ed.), *Trade Policy, Industrialisation, and Development* (Oxford: Clarendon Press).
Rodrik, D. (1992b) 'The Limits of Trade Policy Reform in Developing Countries', *Journal of Economic Perspectives*, vol. 6, pp. 87–105.
Rodrik, D. (1994) 'King Kong Meets Godzilla: The World Bank and *The East Asian Miracle*', in A. Fishlow, C. Givin, S. Haggard, D. Rodrik and R. Wade, *Miracle or Design? Lessons from the East Asian Experience* (Washington, DC: Overseas Development Council).
Rodrik, D. (1995a) 'Getting Interventions Right: How South Korea and Taiwan Grew Rich', *Economic Policy*, vol. 20 (April) pp. 55–107.
Rodrik, D. (1995b) 'Trade and Industrial Policy Reform', in J. Behrman and T. N. Srinivasan (eds), *Handbook of Development Economics*, vol. IIIb (Amsterdam: North-Holland).
Rodrik, D. (1996) 'Coordination Failures and Government Policy: A Model with Applications to East Asia and Eastern Europe', *Journal of International Economics*, vol. 40, no. 1/2, pp. 1–22.
Romijn, H. (1996) *Acquisition of Technological Capability by Small Firms in Developing Countries* (Tilburg: Centre for Economic Research).
Ryan, T. C. I. (forthcoming) 'Kenya/World Bank Interface', Nairobi: paper for World Bank study.
Sharpley, J. and S. R. Lewis (1990) 'Kenya: the Manufacturing Sector to the Mid-1980s', in R. C. Riddell (ed.), *Manufacturing Africa: Performance and Prospects of Seven Countries in Sub-Saharan Africa* (London: James Curry).
Skålnes, T. (1995) *The Politics of Economic Reform in Zimbabwe: Continuity and Change in Development* (London: Macmillan).
SRI International (1992) *Industrial Restructuring of the Electronics Sector in Indonesia* (Singapore: SRI International).
Stein, H. (1992) 'Deindustrialization, Adjustment, the World Bank and the IMF in Africa', *World Development*, vol. 20, no. 1, 83–95.
Stein, H. (1994) 'The World Bank and the Application of Asian Industrial Policy to Africa: Theoretical Considerations', *Journal of International Development*, vol. 5, no. 1, pp. 1–19.
Stein, H. (ed.) (1995) *Asian Industrialization and Africa: Studies in Policy Alternatives to Adjustment* (London: Macmillan).
Stewart, F., S. Lall and S. Wangwe (eds) (1992) *Alternative Development Strategies in Sub-Saharan Africa* (London: Macmillan).
Stiglitz, J. E. (1987) 'Learning to Learn, Localized Learning and Technological Progress', in P. Dasgupta and P. Stoneman (eds), *Economic Policy and Technological Development* (Cambridge: Cambridge University Press).
Stiglitz, J. E. (1991) 'The Invisible Hand and Modern Welfare Economics', in D. Vines and A. Stevenson (eds), *Information, Strategy, and Public Policy*, (Oxford: Blackwell).
Stiglitz, J. E. (1994) *Whither Socialism?* (Cambridge, Mass.: MIT Press).

Stiglitz, J. E. (1996a) 'Some Lessons from the East Asian Miracle', *The World Bank Research Observer*, vol. 11, no. 2, pp. 151–77.

Stiglitz, J. E. (1996b) 'International Economic Justice and National Responsibility', *Oxford Development Studies*, vol. 24, no. 2, pp. 101–9.

Stoneman, P. (1983) *The Economic Analysis of Technological Change* (Oxford: Oxford University Press).

Streeten, P. (1989) 'A Survey of the Issues and Options', in S. Commander (ed.), *Structural Adjustment in Agriculture* (London: Overseas Development Institute).

Swamy, G. (1994) 'Kenya: Patchy, Intermittent Commitment', in I. Husain and R. Faruqee (eds), *Adjustment in Africa: Lessons from Country Studies* (Washington, DC: World Bank).

Taylor, L. (1993) 'Review of World Development Report 1991', *Economic Development and Cultural Change*, vol. 44, no. 2, pp. 265–88.

Teitel, S. (1993) 'Technology Acquisition, Operation and Development in Selected Kenyan Manufacturing Establishments' (Washington, DC: World Bank Regional Program on Enterprise Development).

Thomas, V. and J. Nash (1991a) 'Reform of Trade Policy: Recent Evidence from Theory and Practice', *World Bank Research Observer*, vol. 6, pp. 219–40.

Thomas, V. and J. Nash (1991b) *Best Practices in Trade Policy Reform* (Washington DC: World Bank).

Toye, J. (1995) *Structural Adjustment and Employment Policy: Issues and Experience* (Geneva: International Labour Office).

UN (various years) *International Trade Statistics Yearbook* (New York: UN).

UNCTAD (1995) *Foreign Investment in Africa* (New York: UN).

UNIDO (1995) *Industrial Development: Global Report 1995* (Vienna: UN).

University of Gothenburg Department of Economics, and University of Nairobi, Department of Economics (1994) 'Limitations and Rewards in Kenya's Manufacturing Sector: A Study of Enterprise Development', mimeo (Gothenburg).

Wade, R. (1990) *Governing the Market: Economic Theory and the Role of Government in East Asian Industrialization* (Princeton, NJ: Princeton University Press).

Wangwe, S. (ed.) (1995) *Exporting Africa: Technology, Trade and Industrialization in Sub-Saharan Africa* (London: Routledge).

Weinstein, W., Y. W. Rhee, K. Katterbach, T. Belot and C. Soulier (1992) 'Building a Competitive Edge in Sub-Saharan African Countries', World Bank Industry and Energy Department Working Paper no. 57 (Washington, DC: World Bank).

Westphal, L. E., K. Krityakirana, H. Sutabutr and Y. Yuthavong (1990) 'The Development of Technological Capability in Manufacturing: A Macroscopic Approach to Policy Research', in R. E. Evenson and G. Ranis (eds), *Science and Technology: Lessons for Policy Development* (London: Intermediate Technology publications).

Wignaraja, G. (1996) 'After Adjustment: Foreign Investment Dynamics in Kenya', *International Capital Markets*, vol. 16, no. 1, pp. 19–22.

Wignaraja, G. (forthcoming) *Trade Policy, Technology and Export Performance: Sri Lanka's Liberalization Experience* (Basingstoke, Macmillan).

Wilmore, L. (1992) 'Transnationals and Foreign Trade: Evidence from Brazil', *Journal of Development Studies*, vol. 28, pp. 312–35.
World Bank (1986) *Kenya: Policies and Prospects for Restoring Sustained Growth of Per Capita Income* (Washington DC: World Bank).
World Bank (1987a) *World Development Report 1987* (Washington, DC: World Bank).
World Bank (1987b) *Kenya: Industrial Sector Policies for Investment and Export Growth*, (Washington, DC: World Bank).
World Bank (1987c) *Zimbabwe: An Industrial Sector Memorandum* (Washington, DC: World Bank).
World Bank (1988) *Education in Sub-Saharan Africa: Policies for Adjustment, Revitalization, and Expansion*, World Bank policy study (Washington, DC: World Bank).
World Bank (1989) *Zimbabwe: The Capital Goods Sector, Investment and Industrial Issues* (Washington, DC: World Bank).
World Bank (1991) *World Development Report 1991* (Washington, DC: World Bank).
World Bank (1993a) *The East Asian Miracle: Economic Growth and Public Policy* (Oxford: Oxford University Press).
World Bank (1993b) *Kenya: Employment Growth for Poverty Alleviation* (Washington, DC: World Bank).
World Bank (1994) *Adjustment in Africa: Reforms, Results and the Road Ahead* (Oxford: Oxford University Press).
World Bank (1995) *World Development Report* (New York: Oxford University Press).
Zimconsult (1993) 'Industrial Sub-Sector Studies', mimeo (Harare: Zimconsult).
Zimconsult (1995) 'Cotton Industry Study', mimeo (Harare: Zimconsult).

Index

Note: page numbers in **bold** type refer to illustrative figures or tables.